Of Wars and Worship

The extraordinary story

of

Gertrude and Alvin Blum

To my three beautiful daughters,
Natasha, Riswan and Monique

Keep the flame burning . . .

Of Wars and Worship

The extraordinary story

of

Gertrude and Alvin Blum

by

Keithie Saunders

with the assistance of Prue Rushton

George Ronald, Publisher
Oxford

George Ronald, Publisher
Oxford
www.grbooks.com

Reprinted 2013

A catalogue record for this book is available
from the British Library

ISBN 978–0–85398–563-1

Cover design: Steiner Graphics

Contents

Acknowledgements

Today, people are curious about the 'early beginnings' of Honiara, as the capital city of the Solomons. Through telling the story of my parents, glimpses of the country and its lurching development into nationhood and ultimately independence are hopefully relayed to the reader. I have tried to tell the story with the best of my childhood memories; please excuse any small inaccuracies that may have become blurred over time.

I am indebted to:

Prue Rushton who assisted me and wrote the story through hours of discussion, tapes and research of written records

Dr Graham Hassall, who continually encouraged me into writing down the 'Blum' legacy for generations to come

to the New Zealand and Australian Bahá'í Archives

to Doug Wall, in New Zealand for valuable archival information

to Rodney Hancock for laboriously translating Gertrude's tapes onto computer discs to Gail Morrison and the United States National Bahá'í Archives Department, Wilmette

to Cecilia Edwards for recording further interviews with Gertrude Blum

John and Ruhi Mills for their generosity in sharing with me the memories of their lives in the Solomon Islands

On Alvin's side: Elsa Sobo, who despite being in her 90s and protestations of poor memory offered a clear insight into the young Alvin; Jesse Shapiro, another cousin of Alvin's, who also coloured in some details of Alvin's youth and provided information on the activities of Alvin's grandparents who played such an important role in supporting Jewish immigrants and establishing the Lower East Side in New York; also, Richard Cohn, Rose Sharlat, Elias Savado

On Gertrude's side: Rob Roy, the son of Gertrude's sister Rose, who was very generous in providing information from his research into the Gewertz family history

and not least to my wonderfully supportive family and my special, special Bruce, for their love and encouragement.

Keithie Saunders (Blum)

Prologue

Honiara, 2012

To Alvin and Gertrude,

So much has happened since you left this world. Father, it's been more than forty years; mother, more than fifteen. It's been even longer, almost my entire life, since you threw everything against caution and let the winds of your faith and fate carry you away from the shores of your American homeland halfway across the world. They blew you first to New Zealand and then to this war-torn town with an exotic name.

You were post-World War Two pioneers bearing a revolutionary plan for a new world order where all nations and all peoples would come together in peace without poverty. In trying to change the course of history, you became part of it; both the history of the Bahá'í Faith and of the Solomon Islands. Now, I want to tell your grandchildren and great-grandchildren your story.

I searched for where to begin and realized I had to go back before you two were born. Both of you had Jewish parents or grandparents who escaped from a hostile Russian regime and pogroms, seeking a freer life in the United States. They too knew something of giving up everything. Only they were fleeing a difficult life situation, whereas you actively ran towards it, becoming outsiders in an undeveloped country still bruised and bleeding from recent conflicts waged on its shores.

Father, so many people have wondered why you were the only American Serviceman to return to Guadalcanal. You moved so quickly through life, so busy, you barely thought of writing anything down. There are your speeches, some press clippings and a few letters. I am grateful for the photo scrapbook you kept when you were a United States Army Medic based in the Pacific. The pictures of you holding hands with Maoris and of Blacks in the American Army have given me extra insight into the importance of equality to you. In the letters from my mother you stuck to the pages I see the sweet tenderness of your early romance and the trials of being apart.

In the few years that I got to live with you, you were always so sure, so pragmatic and direct in your impact within your businesses and your community. You'd see a need, then find a way of doing something about it. As with anything being done for the first time, the hurdles were often enormous and difficult. But I was curious about what set things in motion. I wanted to know about the young Alvin you talked so little about. Some of your relatives, particularly your cousins still alive, have been able to colour in part of your early background.

Mother, we had more time together, and you were a faithful letter writer. There are again more press clippings. You were such a loving, gentle presence; it often belied the brave and epic sweep of your own journey through life. At a glance, it is hard to imagine how a shy young woman could emerge from her poor, Orthodox Jewish upbringing and the 'Depression' in New York to head into America's Deep South, alone and intent on helping blacks and whites come together. I am glad we thought to get your story down in interviews. I wish we had done so sooner before time and your health made the memories more distant.

My own recollections are often filtered through youthful perceptions. Small facts give way to interpretation. This is both an account of poignant memory and discovery of the people you were. Through it I hope to give a glimpse into your lives that were informed by such a grand conviction. I want to pass on some insight into your bold, determined approach as well as the simple response of your spirit. That, as much as what you achieved on record, is the reward.

1

Flight to Freedom

And Moses called unto Joshua, and said unto him in the sight of all Israel, Be strong and of a good courage: for thou must go with this people unto the land which the LORD hath sworn unto their fathers to give them; and thou shalt cause them to inherit it.

Deut. 31: 7

Kiev, Russia, 1904

Kiva Gewertz is steering his horse and cart through the centre of town. In the far corner of the square, Cossacks have surrounded a group of men. They keep their hands on their swords. Instinctively, Kiva averts his gaze from the deadly lengths of shining silver and hunches against the icy wind.

He doesn't slow down to see if he recognizes the faces of the men standing huddled before the soldiers. Since the shock attack of the Imperial Japanese Army on Russia's naval fleet in Port Arthur on 8 February, Cossacks have been rounding up Jewish men for conscription. It is surely only a matter of time before Kiva too will be branded into the army of his oppressors.

The cart's wheels spin faster as he flicks the reins. He is no longer aware of the wind that bites at the outer edges of his face. Kiva is thinking about his family and what they and his fellow Jews have suffered for generations in this land.

The blame for the killing of Tsar Alexander II of Russia in 1881, the year after Kiva was born, was laid squarely on Jews. In the years that followed, the men, women and children of Moses were persecuted as 'killers of Christ'. The Tsar-sanctioned, anti-Jewish riots became known as pogroms. Kiva remembers how the Cossacks swept into his village and slaughtered his two uncles. A small shiver runs through him.

Kiva's thoughts turn now to his wife's father. He is a scribe of the Torah. The Jewish people of the village come to him with their problems and their fears. They consider him a wise and learned man with a greater connection to God than their own.

In the last year, the pogroms have returned, more bloody and vicious than before. The Government looks away while Catholic priests march through streets shouting, 'Kill the Jews'. Ordinary gentiles and Cossacks are stirred into a rampage of murder and rape and the looting of what little the Jews have been allowed to accumulate under this regime.

A pressure builds in the centre of Kiva's chest. He knows that the prominence of his father-in-law within the village *shtetl*, just outside Kiev, makes his family a particular and easy target. He shuts his eyes tightly.

Stepping down from his cart Kiva moves to the back of the tray. His hands dig deep into the rough fur of fresh pelts he has bought. He will treat them, taming the wild hairs into soft fabric for the coats and hats necessary for existence in this cold corner of the world. As furriers, Kiva and his father have been more fortunate than most other Jews, building up a trade with gentiles. But it does nothing to take away from the daily horror of being in a place where you are persecuted.

Under his breath, Kiva is singing.

Our hope is not yet lost,
The ancient hope,
To return to the land of our fathers.

He is singing a song of Zion. It is a song of freedom and of home. Kiva pulls again at the pelts; then he studies them slowly, feeling the hairs rise up between the apexes of his fingers and flatten as his hands rub against their natural fall. He knows now that they will be his last.

* * *

The pungent note of beetroot stewing on the stove permeates the air. Kiva comes through the kitchen door and his wife jumps. In Chase's eyes he sees all her fear. Warm bile rises up from somewhere deep inside him and burns his throat. Kiva is angry. Angry that his family cannot feel safe inside their own home. Angry that the same government that has encouraged this rein of terror now wants him to defend it.

'Papa!' a small voice cries out to him. Kiva swings around and sees his son Benjamin, almost two, toddling towards him. He gathers up the wriggly child and inhales his sweet warmth. The snuffled breathing of his youngest son, burrowed into the folds of his clothes against his chest, is a peaceful sound. It calms Kiva and he begins to think of a new life in a new land.

Stories about America have been filtering through the *shtetl.* He hears all the promises of freedom, of being allowed to participate in elections, of being welcome. In his life he has never experienced these kinds of human rights.

Kiva is transfixed by the light of candlesticks on the dining table. He stares up at the eight-pronged candelabra above the fireplace – an ancient beacon against the forces of bigotry and persecution. Chase's face now smiles quietly at Kiva as she serves up soup. He half-smiles back. Already he is planning how he will soon leave for America. It will be under the cover of night and he will head overland to the inland port of Bremen in Germany.

Chase picks up his plate off the table. Kiva reaches across and takes her hand, turning her towards him. He places his hand on her belly and looks up into her eyes. His eyes are wet as he thinks about the young life newly forming inside her. Kiva knows he has to get out of this country quickly. It has been decided that he will go ahead to New York and set up a life for his family to come and join him in.

He wonders how his young family will survive the war and the horrors of this godless regime without him. Kiva turns his head away from Chase. He doesn't want her to see the fear that is also growing in his eyes.

2

Strangers in a New Land

Give me your tired, your poor,
Your huddled masses yearning to breathe free,
The wretched refuse of your teeming shore,
Send these, the homeless, tempest-tost to me,
I lift my lamp beside the golden door!

Emma Lazarus, from *New Colossus*, 1883
Engraved inside the base of the Statue of Liberty, New York

Baltimore, United States of America, 1904

The salt air that Kiva has breathed for almost two weeks goes deep into his lungs. The ship, the *S. S. Breslau*, chugs into Chesapeake Bay. It is the Lady with the Lamp, in the upper reaches of New York Bay a few hours north, with her promise of a new beginning that has truly brought him here, but Baltimore is an easier entry point to this foreign land.

In the year that Kiva arrives, 77,544 Jewish immigrants are processed here, making up more than half the total number of arrivals. Mostly, they arrive from Bremen, Germany as part of a trade arrangement with America. Bremen ships transport humans to service the new country. For the return trip they fill their holds with a trade of tobacco and flour.

Bremen has become renowned for the quality of humanity that it sends. Any emigrant that is rejected entry to America must be returned at the ship's expense. They carry out rigorous health inspections with sharpened German efficiency. Wash and toilet conditions are regularly scrutinized and a doctor is on board every ship. It helps to smooth the processing of immigrants in Baltimore.

Kiva sees a team of American physicians board the *Breslau*. He bristles at the sight of them, clinical and spare, and wonders what they will do to him. He remembers back to the emigration centre at Bremen. He remembers the man with the limp ahead of him and how the medical physician with the keen eye spotted his lurching gait and pulled him out from the long line of queued men. Even though he has always been tall and strong, he remembers testing his weight on both feet – just to make sure.

He remembers the eyelids of men being hooked upwards as physicians peered into eyes. His height allowed him to see what lay ahead: other men and boys standing half-naked as anonymous men of medicine poked and prodded in their search for diseases like tuberculosis or a chronic bad heart. The indignity of the procedure seemed oddly familiar to Kiva. Now, he remembers why. He remembers the lines of frightened animals back in Kiev being inspected for their pelts.

He watches as the American physicians make their way towards him. Silently, he says a prayer to God to keep him safe and healthy for his family, for his new life. He has made sure he has washed his body the best he can, but even in the sea air the peculiar odour of disinfectant mixed with sweat and fear swirls around the deck.

Kiva passes through the corridor of medical eyes into a final line. He feels a little of the tension that's been building inside his muscles for years begin to dissipate. Inside the immigration centre the sounds of foreign tongues and the crying of small children, mothers shushing, echo up noisily to the ceiling.

A man comes up to him and starts speaking in Yiddish. Hearing his native tongue is a sudden, simple comfort to Kiva. He stands now before an inspector who will officially note his passage into this new land. The man speaking Yiddish, a volunteer Jewish social worker, is translating fast for Kiva.

Kiva says another small prayer, this time of thanks. On one side of the hall an enormous sign spells the word 'Money'. Beneath it, Kiva exchanges the few roubles he has for dollars. It is his final severing with Russia.

* * *

Harlem, New York City

He is standing on East 99th Street on the south-east side of Harlem. Kiva looks up at the tenement apartments. The building's face is scribbled with spindly ladders forming stairs. A couple walk past. They chatter happily in Yiddish to each other. Kiva looks back up at the apartments and decides that this will be his family's new home.

In Harlem a delay in the extension of the subway has created a glut in new housing. New immigrants – mainly Jews and Italians and Irish – are quick to take advantage of the falling prices. They settle into separate pockets of Harlem, absorbing the comforts that come with feeling enveloped by their own kind.

Kiva walks around the surrounding streets of his new home. The familiar smells of sausages and pickles coming out of windows and through shop doors make him smile. Already, the Jewish immigrants have begun to organize themselves into '*Landsmanschaften*', benevolent societies, according to the villages they originally came from. They offer mutual aid, insurance, credit, healthcare and social opportunities. Many of these institutions use Yiddish as their official language, as do synagogues, theatres and newspapers.

Not all of Harlem is happy with the inpouring of Jews. '*Kein Juden und keine Hunde*', No Jews, No Dogs, reads one rental sign.

It is almost two years before Kiva's wife Chase arrives in New York with their two small boys aboard the *S. S. Cymric* that has sailed from Liverpool to Boston. They are sitting around the dining table Kiva has bought to create a feeling of home in this unfamiliar land. He looks at the small shining face of his new dark-haired son whom he left behind before he was born. He is now sixteen months old and his wife has called him Abraham.

The candlesticks that have been carried on this long journey are alight on the table. They are an outward symbol of the Orthodox convictions Kiva carries deep inside. He breaks off pieces of the freshly baked twists of bread and hands them to his small sons. Tomorrow morning they will go to the synagogue and celebrate the Sabbath. The next morning after that, Kiva will collect his horse and wagon and go to the markets to pick up the fruit and vegetables he will sell to grocery stores. It is a new profession for a new country: instead of fur his cart is now filled with fruit.

On one of these mornings, Chase is bidding farewell to her husband as he goes out of the door to begin his workday. She watches through a window as he walks up the road. How much has happened to her family in this past year since they arrived. She sighs heavily, thinking about it.

The window has oxidized with a thin film of salt air coming off the Harlem River. It makes it difficult to see things clearly through its misty grime. Chase goes into the kitchen to collect a bucket of soapy water and some rags. She places them on a chair and opens the windows that rise almost to the ceiling. The outside panes are difficult to reach and she stretches up on her toes and leans out over the ledge. She grasps for somewhere to clutch hold of the outer building with her fingers, but she finds nothing. Later, Chase is found, her back broken, on the footpath four floors below. She is only thirty years old.

When Kiva is told the news of Chase his face doesn't change. In accord with his religion, during the following week of mourning he will show no outward display of emotion. Kiva stares into the small faces of his young boys and worries about who will care for them. He looks across at Chase's younger sister Rebecca, who came to New York months earlier than himself. 'Help me,' he says.

Rebecca Bloom was twenty-two when she arrived in New York on board the *S. S. Umbria* from Liverpool on 2 January 1904 with the equivalent of twelve dollars in her pocket. The ship's records state she was a dressmaker and that she went to live with her uncle on the corner of Thompson and 2nd Street in Raritan. Not much more than these few facts will ever be known about Rebecca because she will choose to pass through life speaking little about herself, even with her own children.

Her maiden name is a derivative of Blume, the German word for flower. It suggests the possible origins of her family. Rebecca doesn't speak German or any other foreign language and shows no desire to do so. She has come to America. She will soon agree to be a wife to Kiva without any official record of their union. But Rebecca will cling to the languages of her childhood – Russian and Yiddish – for the rest of her life, never learning English.

* * *

417 E. 100th Street, January 1909

The little girl gasps for air. It re-emerges as a small, raspy burst. Her tiny five-months-old body convulses with the effort. Kiva and Becky, as he now calls her, watch helplessly. The doctors have told them their daughter has flu, it will pass. But the little girl they've called Rose after Becky's mother is fighting something far stronger that has burrowed its way deep into her respiratory system. The doctors miss all the signs of pneumonia that are affecting her heart. All life goes out of her in a final spasm.

They keep the light low in their apartment where their little girl is laid out. Even in death Rose is still beautiful, all dark curls and tiny features. She looks as though she could just be sleeping. Kiva and Becky remain silent and erect as they watch over her for the last time.

Around a year later, Becky's belly begins to swell. On 9 December 1909 another little dark-haired girl is born. She is named Gertrude Gewertz, but Kiva and Becky will call her Gertie. As she grows, her friends will nickname her Gertie Gewertie, making her smile.

3

Searching for Light

What do you suppose creation is?
What do you suppose will satisfy the soul . . .?
Walt Whitman, from *Laws for Creations*

Harlem, 1917

Gertrude is walking down the front steps of the apartment block where her family lives. Spikes of icy rain hit her cheeks and forehead. She pulls her hat a little further forward and heads off towards her schoolfriend's house.

'Gertie, can I come too?' a small, high voice sings out from behind.

Gertrude turns around and sees her little sister. 'No, Dora,' she answers. 'We're going to be studying. I've promised. Go back home.'

'Oh please, Gertie?'

'No, you'll get in the way,' says Gertrude, more forcefully. 'Now you get back inside. It's raining.' The little girl sucks in her bottom lip and her eyes, two black sapphires, turn cloudy. Something twinges inside Gertrude's heart. She knows how her little sister adores her.

Dora is five; two years younger than Gertrude who returns her little sister's love with an openness that makes it hard for her to turn her away now. Dora is very sweet.

Her good nature shines out from her beautiful little face; all high-coloured cheeks surrounded by springy black curls. But Gertrude has made a promise to her friend that they will go over the lessons together properly. It is important to keep your promise, she thinks.

Gertrude moves quickly now, to make the parting easier. She doesn't look back. First Avenue is wide and busy with cars and horses and buggies. To Gertrude they seem to be moving fast and higgledy-piggledy. She takes a deep breath to concentrate. The wet rain makes it splashy and hard to see as she picks her way carefully between the moving masses.

Safely across the other side she begins to think of the fun she will have with her friend as they study. The sickening screeches of wheels suddenly break her play thoughts. Gertrude swings around and sees cars and horses pulled up at strange angles. A group of drivers and passengers are gathered around a small spot. Some clutch their hands to their head as they stare down; others reach for their heart.

Gertrude senses something uncomfortable stirring in her own heart. It beats faster as she walks hesitantly back across the avenue, now deathly still, towards the assembled crowd.

Some men are holding down another man in the front seat of his buggy. He is trying to say things but his words make no sense. They make a sloshing sound in his mouth. Gertrude has walked past a saloon and heard men like this before.

She moves around to the back of the buggy where most of the people are gathered. She follows their eyes downwards. Dora is lying on the road. Her little body is contorted where the wheels of the buggy have run over it. She looks like a delicate rag doll, but her beautiful face is all broken. Gertrude's heart is thumping hard now. She feels like she can no longer breathe. Then she hears herself begin to howl.

* * *

Dora is being laid out in the darkened living room of her family's apartment. Gertrude watches her Mama, almost bent in two, weeping and weeping over the body of her precious, lost, little girl. Her father sits stonily beside her mother as people arrive to pay their respects.

Kiva's silence troubles Gertrude. She remembers her father's eyes after he heard of Dora's death. They looked directly at her, not with comfort but with anger. Papa hasn't spoken to her since. Her seven-year-old self feels his blame acutely. It forms part of the tight lump of pain that is mounting rapidly in the centre of her chest. It is also made up of her own guilt and grief over the deep loss of her adored sister.

All of Gertrude's heartache comes down on her like a cage. She clings tightly to a pillow, burying her head in its softness and muffling the sounds of her sobbing. Her youngest sister Rose pops her head around the bedroom door and dances across to pull the pillow away. She is not yet four and doesn't understand why Gertie won't stop crying and play with her.

Gertrude cries for days, then weeks. Finally, she wakes

up one morning and there are no more tears left to shed. Something has shifted inside Gertrude. Her heartache is starting to be replaced by a yearning. For what, she is not yet entirely sure. Questions start forming in her young mind: about Judaism, about God, about life.

She gets up and sees her father preparing for his morning prayer. He places his little black box on his forehead and begins to wrap the long black ribbons around his head.

'Papa, what's that little black box?' she asks. 'Is there anything in it?'

'Yes, the Ten Commandments are in this little black box,' her father replies piously. 'And in the Old Testament it says that we must make it as a frontispiece before our eyes.'

Kiva is a very upright, disciplined man. He appears proud of being an Orthodox Jew and of his knowledge of the faith he has struggled and suffered so much for. On every Holy Day her father likes to relate its significance to his family. Gertrude listens and has many questions for her father. Kiva takes his young daughter's incessant curiosity as an affront to his authority. 'We can't ask the reason why,' he roars. 'We have to take everything on faith.'

Gertrude jumps when her father speaks to her like this. His anger slices through her, attacking the most sensitive parts of her nature. It is very painful and makes her feel anxious. But Gertrude can't stop asking questions. It is as if something beyond her is driving them and her father's answers do nothing to satisfy the urge. It is the same with the Hebrew teacher her mother employs to come into the home each week and train her children in the old ways of her faith.

When the holidays are imminent, Gertrude still gets overcome with excitement. On these days she gets to meet up with cousins from her Mama's family or go to celebrations organized by one of Papa's Jewish friendly societies. There are now more than two thousand of these *Landsmanschaften* across New York, representing more than nine hundred European towns and around 150,000 Jews in Harlem alone. They organize balls and parties or have big picnics on Long Island.

Gertrude also enjoys it when her family goes to see a play at the Yiddish Theatre. It is in the downtown area and it takes a long time to travel there. Usually, there are four acts.

It is just after Act 2 of a play and Gertrude and her family are clapping. A man leaps up on stage. Loud and impassioned, he starts to call out for people to give money for the Fatherland, to rebuild Israel. She looks across at her Papa and sees something unusual in his eyes. They seem filled with some soft, distant sadness.

When they get home, Gertrude has a question. 'Papa, why do people want to return to the Fatherland?'

Something more familiar returns to her father's eyes. The pupils go very small as they fix themselves directly on their target. Gertrude can feel them boring into her and she wishes she could have stopped herself asking Papa such a question.

Papa's big hands slam down on the table. His body starts to shake and he looks as though he is about to erupt. 'Gertie!' he shouts. Gertrude is terrified and rigid with fear of what might happen next. Kiva takes his gaze off his trembling daughter and transfers it to his wife. He starts screaming something at Becky in Russian.

Gertrude hates the way her Mama and Papa speak to each other in this language she cannot understand. It seems to heighten the growing gap between her and her parents as well as her instinctive worry about what is being said. Why can't they speak in Yiddish like they do with the rest of the family?

Her cousin Irving is already in bed. He and his father, who is Becky's brother, have moved into the apartment seeking refuge from his mother's mental illness. She climbs under the bed covers and huddles close to Irving's warmth. She can hear Kiva in the living room, singing now. 'Come back to Israel, your real home, your ancient home,' he wails.

Gertrude looks up at her cousin's kind face. 'Irving, can you read me a story?' she asks quietly.

'Sure, Gertie,' he replies, giving the little girl a hug.

Gertrude lets the sweet calm of Irving's voice float through her. She loves climbing into bed and listening to his stories. They are always fairy stories, full of magic and good deeds. They have happy endings. Slowly, Gertie drifts off into a dreamland where she has pretty pink wings.

* * *

In the same year that her youngest brother Sidney is born, five of Gertrude's school friends die. The 1918 Spanish flu has broken out in Kansas and soon rips through New York. Over the next two years it will sweep its suffocating cloak across the rest of the world, killing almost five per cent of all humankind. It reminds Gertrude of the stories about the plagues and the Angel of Death she's heard from the Books of Moses.

It is only a year since she lost Dora. She misses her little sister desperately and now so many of her friends too are gone. All of Gertrude's losses create even bigger questions in her mind.

'Papa, why is there so much suffering?' she asks.

Her father snaps shut the paper he is reading and eyes her. 'Well, we mustn't question that,' he says sternly. 'You must take those things on faith.' Kiva opens his paper again.

But Gertrude has another question. 'So Papa, what happens to our souls when we die?' Kiva shakes the open newspaper crankily as a reply. Gertrude fidgets with a seam in her skirt. If we speak about the soul, why can't we know about the soul, she wonders.

Gertrude is only eight years old, but everything that has happened in her young life makes her feel much older. On Sundays she works in the Sunshine Biscuit Factory, while much of her mother's time is spent running a busy poultry shop. Kosher chicken is a favourite Jewish staple. Mama has taught her how to cook Russian stews and sweets, and Gertrude shops for the food and prepares family dinners. On Fridays, she and Rose rush home from school to scrub the floors in special preparation for the dinner on Shabbat eve.

'Papa, why do we have to use different dishes and saucepans for meat and milk? And why do we have to wash the floors?' Gertrude asks after one Friday night dinner.

'Well, we have to distinguish ourselves from other people otherwise we'll be assimilated into Christianity,' her father replies. 'These rituals are ingrained in our history and remind us of how God has saved us through all our tribulations.'

Gertrude has already noticed how the Jews and Christians separate themselves. They use different signs on their front doors. Christians have signs of the cross or guardian angels or the phrase, 'Bless this house'. Jews have a simple Star of David.

There are Christian children at Gertrude's school but she is not allowed to go into their homes. 'What they believe in is evil,' says Papa. Gertrude does not understand why Papa says such a thing. She has seen her Christian friends all dressed up nicely and going off to church.

'Could so many people be believing in the wrong thing?' she challenges.

'Well, the Jewish faith is the first faith. There couldn't be anything else and it's lasted long before the Christian faith and it's lasted all these years since.' Kiva exhales loudly, and then adds for final measure, 'It is the true faith.'

Gertrude's big brothers, Ben and Abe, are now sixteen and twelve years old. She is yet to find out that they are her half-brothers who were born to her father's first wife Chase. Ben is absorbingly engaged in the teenage territory of self-exploration. He brings back stories from his new world that has expanded across the borders of Jewish culture.

The stories capture Gertrude in a way that her father's answers to her questions do not. The sense that there is something beyond all the rituals and must-dos and don'ts she has come to know is growing stronger in her.

Kiva hears the stories too. 'You know,' he scoffs crudely, 'Jesus tried to fly.'

* * *

Papa has just told her she can no longer go to school. In the past few months, since finishing public school, her father has been paying for her to continue her studies at a private commercial school.

Gertrude is fourteen years old and she is aware her father believes that only boys require an education. Kiva cannot see the worth in keeping up with the fees. His daughter understands the value of knowledge and pleads her case. 'You've got your own bedroom,' Kiva responds dismissively. 'That is enough!'

Kiva is oblivious of the impact this single action has on his daughter's life. Many years later, Gertrude will say, 'It was the one thing I held against my father.'

In New York, Jews own most of the garment factories. A friend tells Gertrude about a job as a telephone operator in one of them. 'It's not a very big switchboard,' adds her friend, 'and there's a little bit of clerical work.'

Gertrude begins her first job for a men's clothing

manufacturer. She connects incoming and outgoing calls by inserting cords into the correct holes, but her father has not stamped out her quest for knowledge. In New York many schools offer night classes and Gertrude uses part of the money she earns to study typing, shorthand and bookkeeping.

The world is beginning to open up for Gertrude. She is making new friends who encourage her to see herself in different ways. Ethel, a girl she works with at the factory, has noticed how exquisitely melodious Gertrude's voice is as she speaks. A talent company comes to their workplace scouting for people to go on stage. At Ethel's insistence Gertrude tries out and is selected to sing in the chorus.

At sixteen, Gertrude is unaware that she has grown into a tall and graceful young woman with a lovely figure. Her natural beauty has not escaped her friends and Ethel uses her considerable enthusiasm to persuade her to enter a bathing suit competition. One night at the end of their musical performance, Gertrude overcomes her inherent shyness and stands in line with other girls on stage. The curtain is slowly raised until it is in line with their chins. All the audience can see is a row of shapely figures.

A showman points to each figure, one at a time. The amount of clapping the figure attracts will determine which girl is the most beautiful. When the showman arrives at Gertrude's form, the crowd's whoops of applause are deafening.

'I knew you could win,' Ethel shouts up at her gleefully from the audience. Gertrude is awarded a trophy, but she remains unconvinced. 'Ethel, I think you invited a lot of people who were so loud that I got the prize,' she says as she hugs her friend later.

Not long after this, her family's apartment, now on the ground floor in 102nd Street, is razed by a fire. The trophy, along with other precious belongings and photos, is burned to ashes. They are like refugees again. Kiva is uncertain why this has happened but he knows that he no longer feels safe in Harlem. An influx of black people, often financially and emotionally strained, now comprises almost half of this area's inhabitants. But the Jewish community is still firmly established and Gertrude witnesses the effectiveness of her father's many associations. They offer support, both material and spiritual, to the family as they pick up the pieces of their lives and start over.

* * *

She is running her hands over her new velvet and brocade dress. Being stylish comes easily to Gertrude, and almost without vanity. She appreciates the tailoring of fine fabrics and the way they fall on her. The dress is a small indulgence she has allowed herself with what is left over from her work earnings.

Gertrude's hands stop on a large, dark, oily-looking patch that soils the velvet. 'Rose, how could you?' she gasps.

'I didn't mean to damage it,' says her younger sister Rose through tears. 'I only borrowed it because I wanted to look pretty. Gertie, I'm sorry I didn't ask.'

Gertrude snatches up the dress and storms out of the

room. Rose is simultaneously shocked by her sister's upset and bereft for having caused it. Much later, Rose will say it was one of the few times she ever saw Gertrude cross.

Rose doesn't notice how Gertrude's resentment of her father is inflamed when she learns he is allowing her fourteen-year-old sister to continue on with her education. Unlike the ethereal and contemplative Gertrude, Rose is energetic and flighty. Gertrude has watched Kiva's eyes light up whenever her sister dances into the room, but it still seems unfair that Rose, who isn't interested in studying, should be awarded this privilege.

But Gertrude is incapable of remaining cranky with her sister and Rose accompanies her when she is getting a new dress made. Mrs Roy is a wonderful seamstress. She is Jewish but Kiva doesn't like the woman and makes this known to his girls. Perhaps, Gertrude thinks, Mrs Roy has too much of a flamboyant reputation for one whose husband is so often at sea.

Rose enjoys watching Mrs Roy draping rich fabrics over her sister. Even more, she enjoys watching Mrs Roy's son Herman.

Herman wears the finest suits Rose has ever seen. He works on Wall Street as a runner, learning the stockmarket floor, but he is also clever with investments. Soon, Herman will declare himself a Christian to further his climb up the Wall Street money ladder. He has quickly learned that the financial power Jews hold within their associations and unions is unsettling to those trying to operate in the free market.

Kiva is furious when he learns of Rose's infatuation.

He forbids her to see Herman. 'But Papa, I love Herman!' protests Rose. 'You can't stop me.'

* * *

Something has gone out of Kiva's eyes. Rose is no longer living at home to make them come alive. She has eloped with Herman and Kiva has been wretched ever since, but he will not show it. Instead, he holds himself even more upright, making no attempt to contact his youngest daughter, who is still only sixteen.

Gertrude is watching him now playing cards with her mother. They do this every evening after the dishes are washed. It is a show, possibly the only one, of a simple camaraderie that has developed between Kiva and Becky. Often after these card games Kiva explodes. Like a Pavlovian response, Gertrude has begun to brace herself for it at night: her father screaming in Russian. She remains uncertain why he gets so angry with her mother, but Gertrude can see that it has never been a love match.

This thought becomes solidified in her mind when she overhears her mother and her cousin talking. Gertrude is listening-in hard, trying to make sense of what the two women are talking about. Afterwards, it dawns on her that Becky is not the mother of Ben and Abe. She is both their stepmother and their aunt. Their real mother, who was her aunt, died when they were very small. Gertrude never tells her mother that she knows this. For the longest time she keeps it a secret to herself, making her feel even more alone in her family.

Rose and Herman have moved in with his parents. They live in an apartment in Brooklyn and it takes Gertrude a long time to get there, changing trains at several subways. Rose is proud and stubborn, like her father, and refuses to visit her parents. Inadvertently, Gertrude has become a go-between. She finds this difficult, but Rose is the one in her family she feels closest to. It is Gertrude who must announce to Kiva and Becky that Rose is already pregnant.

* * *

Her mother is rocking, back and forth, as she pours over the Torah. It is a High Holy Holiday and Becky has come to the temple for a special reading of the Books of Moses that her father interpreted so well for the villagers back in Kiev. She and Gertrude are on the balcony in a special section set aside for women. Becky repeats the words over and over. Their rhythmic sound is sometimes broken by her sobs. Gertrude has watched her mother deeply immersed in her readings and weeping many times before. It never fails to move her.

When Becky becomes still Gertrude says, 'Mama, why does it make you so sad?'

Becky looks at her daughter with wet eyes. 'This', she whispers, patting the pages of the Torah, 'is the life of the prophet.'

The simplicity of her answer touches Gertrude. She wonders why being in the synagogue cannot bring her spirit the same satisfaction. Its rituals and rote learning leave an emptiness inside her. She remembers her mother taking her to the Jewish theatre when she was younger. There she saw lyrical plays of tremendous insight that was drawn from the Kabbalah. This mystical part of Judaism spoke directly to Gertrude's soul, but in a way that made her want to know more.

Becky looks at her daughter again. She knows Gertrude is still searching for something: but for what? She does not quite understand herself. Becky is a kind woman and she can see how her daughter, now nineteen, suffers.

She and Kiva have already arranged marriages within the faith for Gertrude's two older half-brothers. Maybe it is time she was married, thinks Becky. When Gertrude hears of her parents' marriage proposal she responds to them with a resolute 'No'.

Gertrude has her own beau. He is a travelling salesman and visits her when he is in town. They go to parties and enjoy each other's company, but one thing Gertrude knows is that a man is not what she is truly looking for.

At New York's Hunter College she has been doing more night courses in history, philosophy and poetry. The poetry teacher asks her students to go to the library and pick out a book. Each must explain why they have chosen that particular poet. Gertrude is drawn to Walt Whitman. She reads his poems aloud, her voice doing gentle arabesques around themes of universal light and the oneness of mankind and religion. These begin to have real meaning for Gertrude.

When she is at the library she also picks out books about Christianity. She realizes that the picture of

Christ painted by her family and other Jews is not accurate. Gertrude still can't make sense of this great divide between the two religions and all the suffering it causes.

She has been let go from her second job where she worked for a cement company that manufactures gravestones. In the early months of 1929 it is becoming harder to find work. Gertrude applies for government positions and is knocked back when she says she is Jewish. The American Government, like Wall Street, is suspicious of Jewish unionism and wants no dealings with it.

This is the first time Gertrude has been made to feel aware of being rejected or discriminated against because of the faith she was born into. It stirs up even more questions and her constant searching for answers is wearing her out from the inside. Gertrude begins to say a prayer in earnest. She is praying for peace of mind.

4

An Uncontrollable Force

The cosmic religious experience is the strongest force and the noblest driving force behind scientific research.
Albert Einstein

Elizabeth, New Jersey, 1927

His eyes scan the white lines marked out with numbers at the edge of the field. He knows exactly how many paces he covers between each long white line that stretches across the green. The number changes depending on what speed he has pitched himself across the ground. Alvin Blum worships this acre of green grass, neatly clipped to an even carpet.

At fifteen years of age, football is his religion. It is the thing that makes most sense in his life and what he does best. He adores everything about it. His cousins yell out his name from the sidelines. He throws back his head and punches the sky with his fist. Milton Shapiro is a year older than Alvin, and Lester Baitler is the same age. They are the sons of his mother's younger brother Meyer Shapiro, and her older sister Annie Baitler, but they are much more than cousins to Alvin.

They are a gang of three. Through their growing years that seem so long in their short lives, they have developed a language of their own. It evolves with every new stage they encounter. Lately, they have begun to discuss girls. Sometimes it doesn't involve words; maybe just a glance, a snicker, they know what it means.

Together they have an aimless bravado, happy and loose, charged with the security that comes with being part of financially fortunate families. It helps to liberate their teenage desires from the carefully observed confines of their Orthodox Jewish background.

When Alvin plays football he finds his greatest release. It is a game that teaches fair play and cooperation, but Alvin also has a talent for running which overrides the coach's strategic moves. When he has the ball under his arm, he already has a vision of what lies ahead and what he must do to get there. The information comes to him fast, feeding directly into his muscles.

His cousins are shouting at him now as they watch him charge down the field. The opposition tries to mount defensive blocks. Alvin curves gracefully around them. 'Go Alvin,' his cousins chant. He doesn't hear them. His heart pumps oxygen and blood around his body. He keeps going hard, but in his mind he has already reached that final white line. Somehow, and he cannot yet fathom how, he always can.

* * *

His mother is talking very loudly again. Pauline Blum's voice rises above and over everyone. 'The Rabbi's daughter is getting married, so of course they will need me to throw a tea party,' she opines. Alvin watches his mother sit a little more upright as she announces her latest social conquest. Inside, he feels hollow.

He glances at his cousins. Lester rolls his eyes and Milton's twinkle naughtily. They make Alvin snort as he chews another mouthful of stew. His father's eyes track the noise of his youngest son. 'Alvin,' Oscar murmurs sternly.

It is Friday night Shabbat. This week it is being held at the Blum household. The families of his two cousins have driven across from Manhattan to the two-storey house in Elizabeth, New Jersey. Now, they all sit around a long oval dining table. Alvin's family always dine formally, never in the kitchen. That is the domain of the hired live-in help. There are always good smells coming out of the kitchen and Alvin often slips inside to watch the pickling and the wine being made.

His Aunt Annie Baitler interjects into his mother's stream of conversation. Aunt Annie is even more upright than his mother and just as direct. Milton's mother, Aunt Anna, is a Suffragette and between them, the three women command the conversation. Even the discussion of the week's menu and what they will be buying is carried out with an air of dignity and importance.

Alvin wants to tell his family something. He wants to tell them how he scored this amazing touchdown, and how his football team won. He can feel the words building in his mouth, ready to explode above his mother's voice. He wants someone, anyone, to listen.

'Alvin! Upstairs!' booms his father. Cousin Lester's

little sister Elsa jumps in her seat. Her silver knife and fork fall from her fingers, landing on the fine china with a noisy clatter. Elsa fails to understand what Alvin has done to make her Uncle Oscar so angry. Uncle Oscar is usually sweet but she knows that when he yells Alvin's name like this, it is serious. She watches her cousin climb the stairs slowly. His broad shoulders are now a narrowed slump.

Elsa wants to run after Alvin and jump up to hug him. 'You'll see, everything will be alright,' she would tell him. Alvin is always so fun and kind to her. She has no idea why her favourite cousin bothers to listen to her as she unloads her eleven-year-old concerns.

Even though Elsa is still young, she can see how Alvin turns to his big sister Lillian for comfort. Lillian is five years older than her brother and has the rare gift of listening without judgement or telling someone what to do. Pauline has never been the sort of mother who would sweep her son in close to her bosom and let him tell her his joys or his fears. Neither is Elsa's mother Annie. Having strong ethics and being respectful is what they preach at arm's length to their children.

Pauline has not noticed that the youngest of her four children is finding all his mothering in his oldest sister. She is always very busy. Her benign charity is flavoured with the excitement of running the main house in the district. Pauline is the instigator of all the key social events and the Blums are well known to the families in Elizabeth. Oscar has made his fortune running a diversified business in coal and timber. It affords Pauline the luxuries in life that make up for the distance between her and her city relatives. She has her own car and driver that can take her wherever, whenever she wants. Having three cars in the garage is one of the things Alvin enjoys most. He loves driving cars, especially with the accelerator pressed hard against the floor.

* * *

1932

Elsa watches Alvin's muscles strain against his shirt as he lifts her school bag and puts it inside his car. Alvin has become so strong, she is thinking. Elsa thinks a lot these days, and often it is about boys. She goes to an all-girls high school and has become preoccupied with how to get boyfriends.

'Alvin?' she asks.

'Uh-huh?' he replies.

Elsa shuffles sideways in the front seat so she can face her older cousin. 'Alvin, do you think you and Lester and Milton would take three of my girlfriends to our graduation dance?'

Alvin looks away from the road to her and chuckles in one gasp. 'Sure, Elsa, sounds like fun.'

Elsa claps her hands, pleased. Her girlfriends are going to love Alvin. He's always so popular and knows just the right thing to say.

After going to the graduation dance, it is as if Alvin has realized that she is growing up. He has begun to talk to her in a new way. Sometimes when he comes to stay with her family in Manhattan, he takes her out to get a bite to eat or they go for long drives where she can tell him about what is going on in her life. She giggles when Alvin tells her about all his girlfriends. She likes hearing his sexy talk; it dilutes the anxiety she feels about what is happening to her family.

The family has gone down in the Great Depression. Elsa's father manufactures knitted goods and it is one of the first industries to be affected. The mothers in their families make a great show of covering up the financial difficulties they are now experiencing. There are still the family gatherings for Shabbat and on Sundays. Only the menu has changed and instead of playing cards for cash they play for toothpicks. One day Annie turns to her daughter. 'Don't you ever forget who you are!' she says with a strange look in her eyes. Elsa hasn't a clue what her mother is talking about.

Cousin Milton's family is hit very hard. Sometimes his mother Anna is forced to serve cooked rice with a lot of sugar in it. When she places the bowl in front of her husband Meyer, he takes a huge spoonful. 'You know,' he smiles at her, 'this is the best rice I have ever eaten.'

Anna cannot bear to go to the shop and ask to buy things on credit. Instead, she sends her youngest son Jesse. 'Just one more time,' the shopkeeper always warns him. During summer Jesse is shipped off to stay with Aunt Pauline and Uncle Oscar Blum. He often lies awake in the oversized bedroom his Aunt has allocated him, listening to the shrill horn and the chugging of steam trains, strange and unfamiliar to the boy from Manhattan. A soft breeze comes through the window, carrying the oddly fresh smells of turf and manure into the room.

He jumps out of bed to wake Alvin. 'Let's get to the truck, fill it up at the oil depot and start making deliveries,' he shouts to his favourite cousin.

'Jesse,' Alvin groans, turning his head away, 'what time is it? It's still dark outside.'

Jesse giggles and shakes his cousin some more. Alvin always makes a fuss, but Jesse knows he'll get up.

Alvin has taken an interest in his twelve-year-old cousin. The young boy likes to read. Alvin does too, but he doesn't think much of the books in the public library. He takes Jesse to a private library. 'Choose whatever you want,' Alvin says to him.

Jesse has developed a habit of tearing off the edges of the pages he is reading and chewing them. He does this unconsciously and uncontrollably. When Alvin takes him back to the private library, Jesse places the pile of mutilated books on the counter. 'I can't give these books out to anyone,' the owner says crossly. Alvin glares down at Jesse. The young boy feels his disappointment and waits for his kind, big cousin to get angry with him. But Alvin never says anything; he just fixes things up with the librarian.

* * *

An idea has come to Alvin. It could help create a new opportunity for his father's coal and timber business, he reckons to himself. 'Brother,' Alvin calls across the yard.

His older brother, also called Lester, is stabbing hard at a piece of paper on a clipboard with a pencil as he talks to an employee. The employee stares at the ground in front of him, a cigarette droops dejectedly from his mouth.

'Brother,' Alvin calls again. Lester reaches around behind his back and waves his younger brother away with short, jerking gestures. Alvin is used to being dismissed by his brother. Lester is only four years older than him but he walks heavily in the world. Everyone, including his parents, calls him Brother. It adds to his gravitas.

Brother has just had a baby girl, Carole, with his wife Fannie. He takes his new status very seriously. He has become responsible as a family man at a time when his world is falling apart. Oscar has already imparted a certain power over business decisions in the failing business to his elder son. Brother wields it over Alvin in a way that leaves him feeling frustrated and defeated.

Alvin has already worked out a few things about himself. He knows he's not interested in pulling people down. He knows that the way business is conducted has to change. Decisions have to be fair and work for everyone, not just a few. He knows he cannot abide material greed and that this, more than anything, has brought turmoil crashing down upon his country.

All these thoughts swirl around inside Alvin in such a way that he doesn't know what to do about them. He doesn't yet appreciate that it was experiences of victimization that forced his grandparents out of their home in a Lithuanian *shtetl* called Keidan. He doesn't fully understand how the promise of fair treatment lured them to this land. And he certainly doesn't know that his grandfather Yechial Shapiro, who died when Alvin was five, and his grandmother Rasha, his 'Bubby' who always needs to be picked up and shepherded around to various family events where she sits slowly losing herself to senility, are regarded as two of the great pioneers of Jewry in the Lower East Side.

* * *

Alvin's grandparents, Yechial and Rasha Shapiro, arrived in New York by boat from Holland, some time around 1885, with five of their six children – Louis, Jacob, Annie, Pauline and Meyer – already born. Unlike most Russian immigrants, Yechiel had money that allowed him to establish himself quickly as a saloon keeper in the Lower East Side. Yechial would become known as Joe and Rasha as Rachel, but neither of them forgot what brought them here, nor their religion.

It didn't take them long to realize that New York was not the Promised Land, yet they had been blessed more than most of their fellow Jews. New immigrants coming in off the boats would arrive in a desperate state: friendless, penniless and without English. Joe and Rachel began going down to the docks and meeting them. The worst of them, the ones who they knew were too damaged from what they had escaped to find their own foothold in this strange, big city, they took home.

On the floor above the saloon they had created a dormitory. It provided free shelter for immigrants while they reorganized themselves into someone who could survive. Joe and Rachel would give them interest-free loans and a few pennies, often including pushcarts to start a business selling vegetables. Gradually their friendship, the rudiments of English they taught, and their introduction to American culture would help new arrivals begin to shift their attention away from the cocoon of the dormitory and out into the streets of New York.

From these beginnings, they established many institutions that would continue to help fellow Jews. Joe became a leader in the community as president of Beth Hamedrash Hagadol, the synagogue on Norfolk Street. Its Rabbi, Jacob Joseph, was the first and only Chief of New York Rabbis. He was also Joe's mentor. Later, Joe would have his headstone modelled on that of the controversial Rabbi's, who died early, unable to bring his old ideals with him into the new world. With a congregation of five hundred at the synagogue, Joe's clout began to extend into politics. A scholar by nature, he wrote about all of his encounters and private thoughts in a daily journal that began with their arrival in New York and ended in his death at the age of sixty-eight.

* * *

Alvin has never read his grandfather's diary. It is written in Hebrew, a language he has never learnt and now does not want to. There are questions that keep swelling inside him and he cannot find the answers to them in the way that he has been brought up. When he looks around, especially at spiritual and political leaders, he sees hearts gone rotten with materialism.

He goes to the synagogue with energy and a heart that is desperately searching for something he can commit to. All Alvin is fed there are stories about things that took place thousands of years ago. 'If there is a God why isn't he taking care of his people like he did back then?' he keeps asking, sometimes hurling the question angrily at people who he knows have no answer. 'Are we lost souls?' he asks in frustration.

5

The Will to Believe

I know that life is given us so that we may grow in love.
And I believe that God is in me as the sun is in the colour
And fragrance of the flower, the light in my darkness,
The voice in my silence.

Helen Keller, from *Light in My Darkness*

Manhattan, 1929

Turn around this corner. Go through that door. Gertrude knows this place, but how? She hesitates a moment, then moves forward to the receptionist's desk. Her eyes scan an office layout through the glass pane in a wooden door, the way the morning sun refracts harshly off the chrome of chairs. It makes them squint. Somewhere, in some other time, she has seen all this before.

The employment agency has sent Gertrude to this office to apply for a position as a telephone operator and typist. Gertrude has never been to this part of the city. 'Why does it feel so familiar?' she asks herself.

A woman is questioning her about what speed she can type. Has she ever operated a telephone system like this one? Gertrude forces herself to focus on her answers. For many weeks she has been putting on her best frock and trudging through town along pavements littered with stagnant crowds of people. Finding work has begun to get hard for everyone. She wriggles her toes as she formulates how she will respond to the woman. Gertrude can feel the small burn marks that are growing bigger beneath the balls of her feet. With every knock-back of work, the soles of her shoes, like her confidence, are wearing thinner and thinner.

She answers the woman with a buoyancy that belies what she is feeling. Her voice, wonderfully warm and round, wins over the woman. Gertrude has a new job. As she expresses thanks, her voice begins to warm her up on the inside. She smiles, easily now, and turns to reach for the door handle, then something makes her snap her hand away. The same niggling knowing creeps back into her mind. She watches the door handle carefully as she slowly turns it. A dream she had a few weeks earlier comes clearly into her consciousness. Then she remembers. The door handle, the woman, the office – they all occupy her waking memory and now her future. 'But why?' she still wonders.

* * *

A well-dressed woman with leaflets over one arm comes through the office doorway. Gertrude is answering the telephone and smiles a silent hello in recognition. She has been working here for three weeks now and there is something different about this woman from the other people who normally walk in. Not too long after, Gertrude will link this singular event to her dream and come to regard it as a prophecy of how her life was about to be reborn.

'I want to tell you about a series of ten lectures by a wonderful woman called Orcella Rexford,' announces the woman, handing Gertrude a leaflet.

The leaflet lists topics that include diet and food combinations, mental telepathy, numerology and how to bring out your creativity. As Gertrude reads through the leaflet an excitement begins to take hold of her body. There is a cost listed at the bottom of the page. She calculates in her head whether she can put aside money for such an activity. In her heart she has already decided it is well worth her savings, even in such difficult times.

* * *

Inside the Astor Hotel, Orcella Rexford is conducting a lecture about colour harmony. Orcella is a noted writer and professional lecturer on subjects that are emerging from the Freethinkers movement. All of Gertrude's senses are concentrated on the new ideas that she is hearing.

At the end of the lecture a woman in the audience speaks to her about Rosicrucianism. Gertrude has never heard of this, but, she thinks, maybe it will help quiet all these questions that keep tumbling around inside her.

The woman, a widow, is kindly and Gertrude agrees to go to meetings at her home to find out more. On some nights she listens as the woman speaks about love, compassion, selflessness and finding your inner truth. On other nights the woman takes her along to listen to lectures by a Hindu Swami. He has pushed himself through many different thoughts and philosophies and speaks about 'mind over matter'. Rabbi Stephen Samuel Wise, co-founder in 1914 of the National Association for the Advancement of Colored People, is another influence the woman wants Gertrude to hear. He argues passionately for equal rights, regardless of race, religion or national ancestry.

One night, inside her living room, the woman becomes oddly distant and distracted. She says that she must contact spirits for guidance and begins to chant in a slow rumble. The room fills with the rhythmic burble of foreign words. The woman's eyes roll upwards and her body bends backwards, dangerously low. Prickles of adrenalin accelerate through Gertrude and she can feel the pulse of her breath making sharp shallow puffs. Suddenly, all life seems to go out of the woman's limbs and Gertrude watches her slump hard to the floor. She rushes towards the woman.

'Don't move her!' A gentleman friend of the woman stretches an arm out to block Gertrude. 'I'll just gently bring her back,' his voice softens. Gertrude's cheeks are burning with fear. The woman's eyes flutter and her body braces and ripples as the man holds her. Gertrude shivers. I don't want to get into that state, she thinks to herself.

Gertrude's investigations keep leading her back to the smart hotel room where Orcella Rexford conducts her weekly lectures. Tonight is the final lecture and Gertrude looks around at the crowd that has gathered. It is much smaller now, maybe only one hundred and fifty people, down from the audience of one thousand that packed the room to the outer corners at that first lecture six weeks ago. Her eyes catch the nicely dressed Italian boy smiling at her. She blushes self-consciously.

Mercifully, the moment is foreshortened when Orcella Rexford flamboyantly swoops into the room. She is fabulous, dressed in an Oriental headdress and wildly-coloured silk robes. 'This', she announces, 'will be the best lecture of them all.'

Gertrude shifts a little more forward in her chair. Slides of the Holy Land, golden and exotic, parade before her as Orcella tells them about the Bahá'í Faith. Orcella is pacing the floor, expressive hands fluttering as she speaks about how in Baghdad, Iraq, in 1863, Bahá'u'lláh announced that he was a messenger from God, part of a long line of prophets that includes Abraham, Moses, Buddha, Zoroaster, Jesus and Muhammad, all sent by God through the ages to teach about spirituality. And how Bahá'u'lláh is the latest prophet who has been sent for this day and age, and with him has come a blueprint to usher in a new era called 'The Most Great Peace'.

The idea of 'oneness' captivates Gertrude. The oneness of God. The oneness of all religions. The oneness of mankind. The essence of these Bahá'í principles that Orcella is outlining resonates with things she has instinctively cherished since childhood.

'After this,' finishes Orcella Rexford, 'I am going to another city and I will leave you. But for those who are interested, there's a group of ten free lectures that will be given at this hotel by a very outstanding woman.' Her name is Keith Ransom-Kehler.

* * *

She doesn't understand much of what Keith Ransom-Kehler is saying. A lot of the words sound strange. Often there is a soft hissing sound in place of a hard consonant. Gertrude doesn't know that this is common in Oriental languages, but she is transfixed. She wants these talks about the oneness and equality of all people and religions to go on and on.

Keith Ransom-Kehler is a travelling Bahá'í speaker who also lectures on child psychology – a subject she has a Bachelor's Degree in from New York's Vassar College – as well as interior design, the role of women in modern society and comparative religion. Well-educated, well-travelled and independent, she is a lover of beauty and different cultures. With her silver-blonde hair swooped into delicate waves and her collection of Chanel ensembles, she is a magnetic presence, but it is the sight of Keith Ransom-Kehler's high spiritual evolution that will stay with Gertrude until the end of her days.

Keith Ransom-Kehler first met 'Abdu'l-Bahá – Bahá'u'lláh's son who became the 'Centre of His Covenant' and the exemplar of the Bahá'í Faith – in London in 1911, and after becoming a Bahá'í in 1921 she quickly became a prolific writer and deeply moving teacher. When she speaks about the Báb, known as 'the Gate', the martyred forerunner of Bahá'u'lláh, Gertrude sees tears in her eyes.

Instead of becoming dimmer, the gentleness of her face becomes more translucent in a way that seems to infuse her words with a sincerity of heart.

At the end of the ten weeks, Keith Ransom-Kehler stands up and stretches open her hands. 'Bahá'ís are building a New World Order,' she says, looking around at her students. 'Who would like to be part of this and become associated with the Bahá'í Faith?'

In life, things come down to one moment. You can peer into the past and tally up experiences to be dissected and analysed and weighed for their contribution, but all are building to a singular point of change.

The question instantly darts its way deep inside Gertrude. She does not hear it so much feel it. The noise in her mind dies. The searching and endless questioning that has held her waking moments hostage for so many years ceases. It is as if all that has happened in her short life has been leading her to this one decision.

Gertrude shoots up her hand. She makes a tiny gasp, a little surprised by her own sudden forthrightness. Slowly, she looks around the room. There are empty seats scattered between the fifty or so people who have turned up for this last lecture. She watches as nine other hands emerge above the horizon of heads. In a back corner, the smart Italian boy is smiling at her again. This time she doesn't turn away.

* * *

She angles the peaked front of her jaunty hat a little to

the side and looks in the mirror. Her winter coat falls gracefully over her figure, darts nipping at her waist. A new coat is something she can ill afford. At least this one, a few seasons old, is well made, she thinks. She pins a marcasite brooch through the thick wool fabric covering her left breast. It shimmers gently, lifting the coat from monochromatic obscurity. Gertrude smiles.

Her mother Becky is in the kitchen, preparing a chicken soup for dinner.

'Bye, Mama,' says Gertrude, 'I'll be back in a few hours.'

'Where are you going?' asks Mama. 'Don't you want any soup?'

'No, Mama. I'm just going out to meet some friends,' she sings out as she closes the front door behind her.

Gertrude hasn't told her mother about the nice Italian boy she has met at the Bahá'í lectures. Nicholas is an exquisitely fine tailor, and darkly handsome. Although he is now a Bahá'í, he was brought up as a Catholic. Gertrude knows her parents would never consent to a Christian liaison.

Nicholas is waiting for her outside the Bahá'í Youth Centre at 119 West 57th Street. He has invited her along for a Nineteen Day Feast. It is the centrepiece of Bahá'í calendar. Each Bahá'í month has nineteen days and the Feast is celebrated on the first day of the month, consisting of three segments – devotional, administrative and social interaction.

The delicate creases Nicholas's smile makes in his face when he sees her are becoming deliciously familiar. Little wings make fluttery movements in her belly. She covers it with one hand and presses in strongly, trying to squash the emotion. Gertrude has already decided that she and Nicholas will only be good Bahá'í friends.

His lips brush her cheek. 'Bella,' he whispers as he escorts her inside. She feels herself pulling away a little. Gertrude has never been to a Nineteen Day Feast and the anticipation of it makes her step up the stairs a little quicker. A room is filled with people of such apparently disparate persuasions, a medley of skin tones and accents, laughing and mingling.

A black man introduces himself and his girlfriend to Gertrude. She studies them both: the man in a neat suit and tie, the woman in a fashionably cut navy wool dress. For a moment no words come to Gertrude's mind. Images of drunken, brawling black men in clothes, filthy and wretched, are occupying it. Those men are casualties of the vast unemployment and lethal race relations that are overrunning Harlem. They travel in compact hordes, ready to steal or drink enough alcohol to fuel themselves into becoming potent forces able to unleash their anger and their fists, to leave their mark on the world.

Her father and mother have told her to cross the road when she sees 'blacks'; to stay away, they're bad people. 'Where is their self-respect?' growls Kiva. Often Gertrude lies in bed, listening to their screams or howls, full of anguish and pain, snaking up through the tight grid of tenement buildings into the night sky. They are frightful sounds.

A black hand with fine fingers and neatly cut nails stretches out to meet hers. Gertrude stares up into the man's eyes. They are shining brown ponds surrounded by clear white. She clasps his hand, feeling its warmth. Her breath skips a beat as she tries to re-order her mind. The discovery that she has dismissed blacks as somehow lesser shoots a small, sharp stab through her heart. 'How could I have been so prejudiced?' she chastises herself.

On more nights like this at the Bahá'í Centre, she lets Nicholas guide her through the meeting of people from all kinds of backgrounds and race. She begins to experience for herself how this religion is all-embracing. On 1 January 1930, Gertrude will declare herself a Bahá'í. She is twenty years old.

* * *

Kiva is watching his daughter as she flits from the bathroom to her bedroom. This is the third night in a row she will be skipping family dinner. He looks across the table at his wife and cocks his eyebrows in question. Becky heaves an exhausted shrug in reply.

'Gertie, come here,' Kiva commands. 'Where are you going?'

Gertrude arrives by the table. The awkwardness of telling her family about her new faith is suddenly surpassed by a bubbling desire for them to understand it. She talks about the 'oneness' of all religions, and how Bahá'u'lláh has provided a blueprint for organizing the world into a global commonwealth of nations in which the extremes of poverty and wealth are eradicated, where there is no room for prejudice of any kind, where there is universal education, no war, and real equality for men and women. Her face is flushed with excitement as she watches for her father's reaction.

Kiva glares at Gertrude over the top of his glasses. She looks into his eyes and sees that she has given her father yet another reason to dismiss her. 'Bah,' he finally exhales in disgust. 'You don't know what you're talking about.' Kiva brings his hand down hard on the table then wipes the air above his head with it. 'You're up in the clouds,' he growls, then returns to his dinner.

'If it is God's will,' her mother mutters softly into the room in Yiddish.

Her half-brother Abe has come with his wife Molly for dinner. Gertrude goes searching for empathy in his eyes but he rolls them heavenwards and shakes his head dramatically as he too digs his spoon into his soup. An invisible barrier is arising between them. Abe has always been someone Gertrude could get a kind word from when life seemed hard. But Abe is now a married man and upholds the Jewish orthodoxy of his father. It is as if the demands of being a husband have combined with the numerical focus of being an accountant to produce a hardline detachment.

Gertrude visits her sister to tell her about her faith. Rose stretches back in her chair trying to shift her stomach, swollen with her first baby. 'Oh, there is no God,' she snaps at her sister, who is mid-sentence.

The words act like an electric shock to Gertrude's ears and she grabs hold of them. 'Rose, how could you say a thing like that?'

Gertrude leaves the Brooklyn apartment where her sister is living, still estranged from the family. A ball of confusion is turning inside her. 'Why should I, out of my whole family, have accepted the Bahá'í Faith?' she is wondering. Quickly, she arrives at her own conclusion. Much later in her life she will explain, 'I almost felt that my little sister Dora [who died] was helpful in guiding me. She was such a beautiful child.'

* * *

The thought of how God and science could be inextricably linked has never occurred to Gertrude. Her mind, filled with the gentle, fluid rhythm of poetry, doesn't easily bend to rationalist, didactic methodology. She has heard how 'Abdu'l-Bahá has said: 'Religion and science are the two wings upon which man's intelligence can soar into the heights, with which the human soul can progress. It is not possible to fly with one wing alone!' The words paint expressive images that are easily absorbed by Gertrude's innermost being.

Now, the man standing out front in the auditorium with his woolly greying hair and moustache has her full attention as he speaks. Albert Einstein is equally lyrical in his expression. 'The cosmic religious experience is the strongest force and noblest driving force behind scientific research,' is his New York message.

Einstein is speaking at the New History Society. It is a group that gathers in some of New York's best hotels, ostensibly to promote Bahá'í teachings, and attracting many of the leading world thinkers of the day. On another occasion Gertrude listens to Helen Keller, whose own message of gender and social equality finds new inspiration in the Bahá'í theme of universal peace.

New thoughts are rapidly reshaping and expanding Gertrude's world view. Sometimes she finds it hard to contain all this information. However, a small darkness is lurking.

She watches as Ahmad Sohrab, the head of the New History Society, paces the room with exaggerated purpose, calling on divine inspiration. Something inside Gertrude flinches. She has been told Sohrab was secretary and interpreter to 'Abdu'l-Bahá from 1912 to 1919, but her instincts tell her that something is not sincere about the man. Julie Chanler, a gentle, wealthy woman, seems devoted to this man. She and her prominent New York politician and lawyer husband, Lewis Stuyvesant Chanler, have turned their home over to his cause. It is Julie Chanler's millions that are funding Sohrab's expensive speaking engagements and writings that seem more designed for his own promotion than that of the Bahá'í Faith.

Gertrude decides to stop going to the New History Society meetings. Her intuition is proved correct when, later, Sohrab and Mrs Chanler are found to be opponents to the Bahá'í institutions, thus attempting to split the unity of the Bahá'í Faith.

Even amongst the young people who have become Bahá'í believers, there are many who come from wealthy and prominent backgrounds. Gertrude goes quiet in their presence, letting them take the lead. Her new Bahá'í friend, Mildred Mottahedeh, is only a year older than her but she is forceful and confident. Gertrude likes to hear the story of how a seven-year-old Mildred marched her friends over to President Woodrow Wilson's holiday house and demanded to see him to discuss something that was worrying her.

Mildred is an interior decorator and has a clientele of New York high society. But Gertrude also admires Mildred's imaginative selflessness. Mildred is already married to a Persian Bahá'í, Rafi Mottahedeh, and they live in a Greenwich Village apartment. Once a month they rent a double-decker bus and fill it with deprived children, then drive to candy and clothing wholesalers to treat and dress the children before taking them to the Bahá'í Centre where they make sure they get a decent meal.

* * *

She doesn't worry about food. Her parents, through the making of their own livelihoods selling vegetables and chicken, always manage to put meals on the table. But the daily effort to find new work since her receptionist position was lost to the economy's continuing downturn sits like a dull, heavy weight in her stomach.

One of Gertrude's young friends at the Bahá'í Centre has noticed that her smile is becoming stretched. He persuades her to tell him what's wrong. 'Well,' he says, 'come

Pauline Blum with her children, 1916.
Right to left: Lester, Ruth, Alvin and Lillian

The Gewertz family, 1926 or 1927:
Rose, Kiva, Sid, Rebecca and Gertrude

Alvin in New Jersey, 1930s

Alvin in Army uniform, 1943 . . .

. . . and in New Zealand with Maoris

Alvin and Gertrude's wedding,
The Cabin, Teaneck, New Jersey, 1945

down to the factory where I am a foreman. I think I can get you a job assembling Midget radios.'

The soldering gun feels oddly comfortable in her hands as she begins her new job. Gertrude welds the wires and metal together in the tiny box shape and a half-smile crosses her face. What would Papa and her brothers say? In her head she hears their scoffing: 'Wafty, too dreamy Gertie.' Now, here she is part of a production line that makes the world's smallest radios.

Gertrude herself is a little surprised. Her brain physically aches from the required concentration for the mechanics of her new job. She inhales a quick burst of air when she hears her mind complaining and picks up the gun again.

Really, she is grateful to find any work. Benjamin Abrams, a Romanian Jewish immigrant who now owns Emerson Radio and Phonograph Corporation, has had the vision to develop the 'Midget' radio. Since its launch in December 1932, more than 200,000 Emerson Model 25s have been sold in only six months. Saks Fifth Avenue is even offering an edition with a pigskin carrying-case for an additional ten dollars. Gertrude wonders who all these people are to be buying so many radios.

When she finishes her work, she goes out into the streets. A grubby child grabs hold of its mother's skirt; her hands are hidden in piles of garbage as she forages around for food scraps. Sullen young men hang about on footpaths, their backs curved inwards, old before their time. The Great Depression is aptly named.

She can hear shouting coming from the kitchen as she

closes the front door of her family apartment. Her father is roaring at her mother again. Gertrude braces herself and scurries down the short hallway into her bedroom. It offers a small bulwark against the barrage of noise.

Her father's rants have become an almost nightly accompaniment to the economic desolation the majority of New Yorkers find themselves in. He cannot abide his wife's generosity. The queue outside her mother Becky's poultry shop grows incrementally with the desperation that is overtaking lives. Men line up, broken, hungry and humiliated. How can she refuse them a bowl of free soup?

Gertrude is not sorry she cannot decipher the Russian words her father is hurtling against her mother. She already knows the arguments are about finances. Always money.

* * *

The young man strides across the hall at the Bahá'í Centre and introduces himself. 'Hello, my name is Irving.' A girlfriend of Gertrude's nudges her. She looks up and around the faces of her female friends to see that the young man is in fact introducing himself to her. 'Oh,' she gasps, but the young man doesn't shift his focus. She tries to hide her embarrassment by asking him questions. He tells her he has come tonight with his sister who is in the same youth group. Gertrude keeps on with talk of Bahá'í activities. He doesn't move from her side.

The next morning when she wakes up her mind is still trying to unravel why Irving, a pharmacist, has chosen to notice her amongst the more confident and outspoken girls in the group. It makes her feel that somehow Irving has a greater understanding of what is going on inside her. It makes her affection for him grow. Within a year she agrees to marry Irving.

One night, she accompanies Irving out to dinner. 'So Gertrude, is your Messiah going to save New York?' sneers one of Irving's young Jewish friends to the rest of the table. 'Will he make us all rich again?' another asks, digging deeper.

Gertrude turns to her fiancé, hoping he will offer support. The coarseness of his Jewish friends reminds her of the scoffing she endures from Papa and her brothers. She looks into his clear green eyes that spread out from his aquiline nose and remembers how softly intelligent Irving seemed in those early days of courtship.

She is beginning to believe that accompanying her to Bahá'í meetings was just his way of getting close to her. Over the past couple of years that they have been together, Irving has become increasingly less tolerant of the amount of time she spends on Bahá'í projects.

He turns and looks at her. Not with love, she thinks, but with condescension. She has turned down attending a Bahá'í meeting to be with Irving tonight. Now, he raises his eyebrows and shrugs away any apology for the behaviour of his friends. Then he pats her knee. Gertrude turns away and bites her lip hard. Tears begin to sting her eyes. 'How could I be so stupid?' she asks herself. As she moves up the stairs to the family apartment she can hear her father's rage. This time something is different.

Her mother, usually such a silent figure, bent and accepting amid Kiva's torrents, is howling. Gertrude moves very slowly towards the kitchen. She notices her parents' playing cards, scattered like litter on the floor. Her father's back is to her. She watches her mother's hands nervously stroking the air in front of his face, not daring to touch it. It looks like she is pleading for calm. Her father pulls away. A growl, primal, erupts from his mouth.

Becky hears Gertrude's muffled scream. She sees her daughter standing with both her hands clasped tight over her mouth and signals hurriedly for her to go away. All Gertrude's fears fall into her feet, turning them into a single cement block. She is an immovable statue in this pantomime of pain.

The brusque shove of her father's shoulders nearly topples Gertrude as he staggers past her. Becky looks back at her daughter. There are no words that can be said between them. Later, Gertrude will find out that her father has taken to threatening her mother with committing suicide.

No comfort is found lying in bed. Digging her head into pillows, Gertrude cannot shut out the sound of Kiva. His intermittent wails are strung with the sorrowful longing of his Homeland songs, girdled with thousands of years of accumulated pain. He is a man locked out of life by his grief and self-pity, and his wife has no key.

* * *

She is laid off the production line of Midget Radio. The rush of enthusiasm for this cheap form of family entertainment has died, suddenly but not unexpectedly. Finally, after months of searching, it is Franklin D. Roosevelt's 'New Deal' program that gives Gertrude an opening at Mount Sinai Hospital typing diet menus. Not long after, she is back again in an office doing typing and switchboard. A light switches on now and she plugs the hole beneath it.

'So are you coming with me tonight?' a voice asks without saying hello.

Gertrude feels herself bristling. 'No,' she says without mentally processing the word. 'No, Irving,' she says more resolute. 'I am going to the Nineteen Day Feast. It is important to me.'

'Why do you always put your faith before me?'

She has heard his question before.

'You should make a decision. I'll call back.'

The light goes out on the switchboard. A corner of Gertrude's heart grows dim. She cannot bear any more quarrelling in her life. Irving keeps calling back. In between his calls Gertrude realizes something else. Her faith really is first in her life.

A light switches on again. Gertrude takes the call.

'Gertrude, I'm a very busy man,' says Irving. 'Don't keep me waiting.'

'Irving, I don't think you should call again,' she hears herself say. 'I don't think it will work out.'

She quickly pulls the plug out of the switchboard and the engagement ring from her finger. She will give it back to Irving.

'Gertie, what do you think you are doing?' gasps

Mama when she hears that her daughter has broken off her engagement. 'Irving is a pharmacist.'

In her mother's small statement, Gertrude knows so much is implied. Her mother's own marital state has corrupted her sense of what makes a happy marriage. Becky is convinced that as a pharmacist Irving can provide Gertie with a financially secure future. 'Gertie, you are twenty-five years old now, what will you do?' she frets. But she is unable to dissuade her daughter from her decision. Becky goes silent, taking the event on board as another of her personal failures.

* * *

Gertrude does not grieve for the loss of yesterday's future. The broken relationship brings no tears. She has cried enough during it and the decision to say goodbye to Irving is propelled by a deeper sense of what she can do in this world.

Her friend Mildred Mottahedeh keeps her busy five or six nights a week as they work on projects together: race relations, the poor, the sick and the homeless. The Depression years leave no shortage of needs. On other nights she learns how to stand up and speak about what she believes in. Having a sense of higher purpose gives Gertrude a new freedom with her words.

She mixes with the giants of the early American Bahá'ís. Among them are Juliet Thompson, an artist who painted a portrait of 'Abdu'l-Bahá, as well as of President Woodrow Wilson and Presidential wives and is a friend of the writer Kahlil Gibran; Louis Gregory, a prominent black lawyer who had one of the first interracial marriages; William Sears, a former sports commentator and television producer who would become one of the great Bahá'í teachers and authors; Horace Holley, one of the first members of the National Spiritual Assembly of the United States and Canada; Martha Root, a journalist, public speaker and the foremost Bahá'í travelling teacher; May Maxwell, the 'beloved disciple' of 'Abdu'l-Bahá who established the first Bahá'í community in France and became the wife of William Sutherland Maxwell, one of Canada's most distinguished architects and a devoted Bahá'í.

In 1931, May Maxwell decides to organize a Bahá'í national youth group in conjunction with the completion of the superstructure of the first Bahá'í House of Worship in the West, at Wilmette in Illinois. She offers to pay the way for any of the youth who can get to the National Convention in Wilmette.

Gertrude has never travelled so far away from home. The journey is over one thousand miles and takes four days. The parameters of her movements, held so tight by her rigid childhood and the Great Depression, begin to expand rapidly. Activities are arranged with other youth groups in Washington DC, New Jersey, Pennsylvania and Connecticut.

May has a way of making Gertrude feel special. 'Who is this child?' she asks when they first meet. Eight years later, in 1939, when May hears Gertrude reading at the memorial for Martha Root, she will turn to her niece

Jeanne Bolles with softened eyes. 'As she reads I see her soul,' she will say. Only just over a year after this, Philip Sprague, a wealthy businessman and respected Bahá'í teacher and administrator, will ask Gertrude to read at May's own memorial meeting in New York.

Gertrude now has two weeks holiday each year. One of them is spent at the Bahá'í summer school at Green Acre in Maine taking her knowledge to new levels. 'I really grew up in the National Youth Committee and the Nineteen Day Feasts,' Gertrude will later say. 'A whole new world opened up to me.'

* * *

Green Acre, Maine, 1931

The pasture beneath her stretches out smooth like rich emerald green fabric rolling gently over curves. She flops back against its softness and stares up into the sky. Gertrude has never experienced such a stillness and space as she finds here at Green Acre. She hears a squeal, and rotates her head backwards in its direction. Mary Maxwell is scurrying up a pine tree. Wild, warm, wonderful Mary. A smile spreads across Gertrude's face.

Mary Maxwell is only a year younger than Gertrude, but she is the freest spirit Gertrude has ever encountered, untamed and untainted. Gertrude loves to hear the story of how Mary came to be in this world.

She is told that Mary's mother May Maxwell was frail and unable to have children. When the Maxwells were in Haifa on pilgrimage in early 1909, 'Abdu'l-Bahá saw May holding one of his infant grandchildren and asked her if she wanted her own child. She answered, 'Yes, if it is God's wish.' 'Abdu'l-Bahá said he would pray for her. Back in Canada some months later May became pregnant. She viewed Mary as the answer to 'Abdu'l-Bahá's prayer. After Mary was born, 'Abdu'l-Bahá took a great interest in her upbringing, guiding May on the child's physical and spiritual education.

Mary jumps down out of the tree and runs over to Gertrude. She stretches her arms out and twirls, her eyes staring straight up into the sun. Her giggles reach Gertrude's ears. It makes her think of just how different their childhoods have been. Mary's so guided and financially secure. Her mother, so committed to her child's artistic and spiritual development that she introduced the first Montessori school into Canada.

Gertrude watches Mary now without joining in. There is still something that holds Gertrude back, making her retreat into the quieter parts of life. She admires how Mary can let herself go, say what she thinks, so unafraid of her effect on others.

6

The Meeting

What is that mystery underlying human life which gives to events and to persons their power of mutation, of transformation?. . .Or who can understand the reason why a chance perusal of a book, the presence of a friend or the meeting with a stranger often alters a determined course of action, profoundly affects our attitude toward life, and, not seldom, so nearly reaches the roots of being and the springs of action that never after is life quite the same?

Howard Colby Ives, from *Portals to Freedom*

Evergreen Cabin, Teaneck, New Jersey, 1936

His friend is flagging him down from the side of the road. 'Hey Blum! Alvin! Stop!' His arms make the urgent flapping movements of a large pelican about to take flight. 'Hey there, what do you want?' asks Alvin.

His friend goes to say something, then he stops. He is thinking about how to tell Alvin that he is going to a meeting of the Bahá'í Faith. He knows 'Bahá'í' is such a strange word, he'll have to explain it. And he knows if he mentions the word religion, Alvin will step on the gas and he won't get his ride. Alvin has been getting really difficult about religion lately. His friend has even heard Alvin, when he was feeling really pushed, declare himself 'agnostic'. A thought comes to him. He knows how fresh ideas work on Alvin like oil, softening up any cranky parts and getting him going.

'I'm going to a meeting of "Freethinkers"', wanna come?'

Alvin frowns at him, then shrugs. 'Sure, hop in.'

Inside Evergreen Cabin, Alvin sees clearly wealthy people sitting next to poorly dressed blacks. A small surge of adrenalin courses through him. He begins to imagine what his mother might say if she saw this. Then he becomes occupied by what is being said. They have begun to speak about the kinds of things he's wanted to hear for such a long time. In simple statements he hears how God has not deserted the world and how he has again sent a new teacher, a new messenger, who is giving answers for this day and age.

He listens hard as a range of women and men talk about how this religion can provide answers for so many of the problems people are facing. How a plan has been given to run modern business, not just in America but also around the world. How there is a way to eliminate poverty and inequality for good. And how ordinary people, even Alvin Blum, have a part to play in shaping a better world. Pins and needles stream down his arms from his heart. His eyes are shining.

* * *

West 57th Street, New York City

First, Gertrude smells the spice-edged smoke. It curls around her nostrils, making them flare in sudden, excited movements like tiny insect wings. Her eyes trace the arc of its path. The wooden legs of a chair scrape heavily on the floor as its occupant pushes back against it too quickly to get up. Gertrude hasn't met the handsome young man who now stands with straight, broad shoulders, puffing, confidently she thinks, on his big fat cigar.

Inside the New York Bahá'í Center, the voices of young Bahá'ís echo across the thoughtfully cleaned surfaces and upwards to soaring ceilings. Even the muffled burbling of the anxious and self-doubting can be heard as they practise how to give talks on Bahá'í principles and their purpose.

The handsome young man exhales a small cloud. Gertrude's ears twitch ready to hear what he says. 'My name is Alvin Blum,' his voice booms, 'and this happens to be my fifth Bahá'í meeting this week.' His mouth pulls sideways in a wry smile. 'And when I know more of the Faith, I'll give a longer talk!'

The room chuckles lightly with him. Gertrude smiles.

She slips across the room to introduce herself. She takes Alvin's hand and shakes it with the assuredness of being one of the senior youth members; not as shy Gertrude Gewertz who thinks the handsome young man is rather interesting. She admires the ability to speak one's mind, to not sculpt words to please the requirements of others. She already recognizes this in Alvin. His directness highlights her hesitation.

Alvin cocks an eyebrow as he meets the green gaze of the beautiful young woman in the well-fitted frock. 'Pleased to meet you, Gertrude,' he breezes. He is all politeness, but Alvin's mind isn't focused on meeting new women. His spirit has been woken up from its dozing, dulled by the three-thousand-year-old promises he has heard all his life. He has a hunger, voracious and unstoppable, for the new ideas he is hearing. He takes great greedy gulps of the knowledge emanating from men he respects instantly – prominent Bahá'ís like William de Forge, Philip Marangella, Horace Holley and Roy Wilhelm.

It is a week now since he first heard about Bahá'u'lláh, and it is not enough. He wants more. The parties, the social events in his life have been cancelled. 'Alvin, you'll get spiritual indigestion if you attend meetings every night,' Billie de Forge jokes with him. Each time he leaves a meeting he feels more passion, a little better armed to face the barrage of opposition he knows his parents will put up when he begins to tell them about the ideas that are filling his head.

* * *

New Jersey

His mother's disappointment in him is voiced loudly. It rises above his father's dismay and, usually, across the long, mahogany platform of the dining table that has become a private family battleground. Alvin wishes he could express the gentle uniting force of the words he has been hearing in a way that would help his parents understand. But he still feels young and raw in his faith, and the air in this house is heated with hurt and humiliation.

Pauline hates having to explain and excuse her son's new behaviour to her family and friends. She is affronted by his absence at Shabbat and other gatherings because he is off at some Bahá'í meeting. But above all she cannot abide that he now accepts that ridiculous impostor Jesus Christ as a prophet of God.

'If you want a philosophy of life like the Bahá'í Faith, that's ok, we're not interested in this new kind of thought,' Pauline tells her son. 'We don't know who this Bahá'u'lláh person is. But, the fact that you've accepted Christ . . . She turns her head away. She has no more will to finish the sentence and leaves it to hang as an admonishment.

Alvin searches out his sister. He hopes for one kind word. Lovely Lillian, who looks like her mother but has a heart that's always so sweet and non-judgemental. She has two boys of her own now, Martin who is eight and Richard who is five, but she still has time for Alvin. She brushes the back of her hand down his cheek. Her eyes smile softly, then she wraps her arms around him. 'This is OK, Alvin,' she croons in her gentle voice, 'you're not hurting anyone.'

Alvin has been quickly and deeply impressed by the number of people willing to work together towards a new world. The practical application of Bahá'u'lláh's blueprint for a fairer, more equal society resonates so clearly with all the things he has been trying to express to his brother and father that he is beginning to feel truly heard, even understood, for the first time.

Three weeks after first hearing of the Bahá'í Faith, Alvin declares his belief in Bahá'u'lláh.

Pauline can feel her son slipping away from the way of life her parents worked so hard and faithfully to bring about for the Jewish immigrants of New York. While he is living under their roof she demands that he observe Judaism. Alvin knows that he must leave, but to go where?

Through January 1937 the Ohio River floods, creating an epic natural disaster that leaves 385 people dead and a million homeless. There is non-stop news coverage. Lacking any other widespread technology, radio is used to carry messages to be relayed to rescue crews. It brings an intimacy to the scale and horror of what is happening, as it plays out live in the living rooms of ordinary households.

Alvin listens to the radio. He hears how in Cincinnati a whole house was swept down the river with five people hanging out of its windows screaming. Louisville in Kentucky is hardest hit. Citizens stand on the streets in its east as they watch its west sink under a yellow torrent. Three-quarters of the city has now become a water world stewing with disease.

For thirty days and thirty nights, rain, snow and sleet pummel into the Ohio River, maintaining its rage and nearly matching Noah's record. The biblical proportions are not lost on Alvin, but he isn't looking back thousands of years for answers. He senses the urgency of help that is needed. In his mind, he has already left home and is in Kentucky. He is thinking about what he can do.

* * *

Memphis, Tennessee, 1937

On most weekends Alvin drives to the home of Howard Colby Ives and his wife Mabel. It takes him a few hours to get to Memphis from where he is now living in Nashville, Tennessee. Since meeting 'Abdu'l-Bahá in New York in 1912, Howard has given up his position as a Unitarian Minister to be of service to the Bahá'í Faith. It has cost him his marriage and a life with his baby daughter, as well as any sense of regular income. As dedicated pioneers to the southern states of America, he and his second wife Mabel Ives eke out an existence through selling books and giving lectures, often free, that centre on principles of the Faith.

Mabel, dainty and dressed in the second-hand outfits she has remodelled, is a powerhouse. Howard, in his shiny grey suit with his neat moustache and kind eyes, has a strong, calm, centred warmth. They make fun times out of a life marked by mini-crises, thinking little of their age and difficult circumstances.

Alvin has been given a car as part of his job as a travelling salesman for a shirt company named Wings. His father also gave him a car when he announced he was leaving home and going south to see how he could help after the Great Flood in Kentucky. The car engine caught fire the very next day, like a symbolic severance from his family. Alvin shakes his head.

Since leaving home he is discovering so many things about himself. In his job he has found an outlet for the dominant aspects of his personality: his love of dealing with people, his knack for listening and learning what people need, and something new and developing – a sense of service.

Howard has been teaching him a lot about this. His new friend has recently completed writing a book about his encounter with 'Abdu'l-Bahá, which lasted for the eight months of 'Abdu'l-Bahá's travels in North America. In it he describes the son of Bahá'u'lláh – the Centre of the Covenant of the Bahá'í Faith – with great lyrical beauty, capturing the transforming effect of his supreme humility, servitude and love.

'Abdu'l-Bahá was sixty-eight years of age when Howard met him. He had spent twelve of those years in exile and another forty in a Turkish prison fortress in 'Akká near Mount Carmel in what is now known as Israel. Howard finds the presence of 'Abdu'l-Bahá immense and unfathomable and writes of his erect, majestic figure with its white hair and beard moved by the breeze, and his eyes all-knowing and full of love.

Alvin listens as Howard tells him a story where 'Abdu'l-Bahá was seen pacing outside an inn where he was staying during his visit. He was busy dictating to his secretary when an old man, wretched and filthy, walked by. 'Abdu'l Bahá called the man back and smiled at him, talking gently. He soon began fumbling under his

Persian overshirt. 'Abdu'l-Bahá, a man acknowledged and welcomed as a dignitary by leaders around the world, dropped his trousers and handed them to the man, then continued his dictation as if nothing had happened.

Alvin smiles back into the eyes of his friend. Howard is unaware that he is changing the way Alvin sees being a man. Just being in the same room as Howard makes him feel different. Howard has called his book *Portals to Freedom*. None of these portals have anything to do with what can be found in the outside world.

Maybe Howard is a spiritual mentor, or a father, or a brother to Alvin. Maybe he is all three. Alvin just knows he loves the man, and Mabel. When he leaves their house he feels strong in his faith and sure of what he is doing. There is a particular description of 'Abdu'l-Bahá in Howard's book that lines up with his ideals: 'He treads the mystical way with practical feet.'

The weekdays in Nashville are long and busy, but often lonely. Alvin, so far away from his old life in New Jersey, is lonely for company: friends, family, a woman. His colleagues at the Wings shirt company know about Howard and Mabel. 'Off to see the old folks again this weekend,' they chide. Alvin loves women and during visits to his many clients he meets a beautiful girl. She is a petite blonde of Jewish background, and the way she looks up at him when he's telling stories quickly melts his heart. Her name is Lucy, but he calls her Sugar and they soon are married.

* * *

New Jersey, 1938

Alvin has brought Sugar back home to meet his family. He watches as his mother, Pauline, takes his young bride off upstairs. He knows what his mother is doing. She is trying to dress Sugar up in a way that she considers appropriate to meet the family. Fashionably smart, of course. Alvin starts pacing around the living room. He nearly bumps into the baby grand piano that sits on show. In a small corner of his mind a regret is beginning to breed.

Pauline has organized an event to introduce Sugar to her family and friends. Alvin looks across at his young wife now. He has never seen her look so small and quiet, lost amid his family's quick wit and loudly voiced ambitions. Maybe it has been a mistake to bring Sugar here. Maybe it has been a mistake to marry her.

They are on the brink of divorcing when Howard and Mabel ask them to follow the Bahá'í principle of first separating for a year. Sugar has been attending Howard and Mabel's lectures and has decided to become a member of the Faith. She chooses New York as her place of membership. Alvin thinks this is odd, as he has no intention of returning there.

In the year that they are separated, Alvin embeds himself more deeply in the teachings and work that Howard and Mabel are doing in the South to bring the black and white communities together, offering his help whenever he can. He has already asked Wings for a transfer in his work base to Memphis and Mabel is supporting him by asking the National Spiritual Assembly for a transfer of his Bahá'í membership too. At the end of their year of separation Alvin and Lucy quietly divorce.

Not long after he arrives in Memphis, Alvin meets another beautiful young Bahá'í woman called Virginia Taylor. He is impressed by the way she handles herself. Her ability to voice her opinions is matched with a great willingness to have fun. He is newly divorced, but already he is falling in love. Howard and Mabel watch their romance unfolding. They were very fond of Sugar, but they can see that Virginia is the one. Alvin can see his future life. When he feels something so strongly, Alvin has never held back. Only now, something is blocking his way.

He begins to write a letter to his parents to tell them he wants to marry Virginia. He wracks his brain for a way to explain that she has a Christian background. Virginia is a Bahá'í and that's all that matters to him, but he knows that his own feelings won't be strong enough to override the prejudice of his parents. He screws up another piece of paper and throws it across the room into the wastebasket. He doesn't miss.

One of the few personal laws in the Bahá'í Faith is the need for parental consent from all living parents before a Bahá'í marriage can take place. This is to preserve the unity within the family. Without his parent's approval he cannot have a Bahá'í marriage. He knows how his family feel about him marrying out of the Jewish Faith. Even though Virginia is a Bahá'í, to them she is a Christian. Alvin feels something cold beginning to clamp down on his heart. It is as if something precious to him is already lost.

7

Forging South

To be alive in such an age!
To live to it!
To give to it!
Rise, soul, from thy despairing knees.
What if thy lips have drunk the lees?
The passion of a larger claim
Will put thy puny grief to shame.
Fling forth thy sorrow to the wind
And link thy hope with humankind . . .

Angela Morgan, from *To-day* (1914)

New York, 1939

Words have never felt like this for Gertrude. They reach out to her from the page, compelling and powerful. She feels like she is reading about the beginning of a new era – not just for Bahá'ís, or for America, but for herself.

America, young and unencumbered, has always been regarded as a special place where faith and the belief in a better world could prosper. Now, she holds in her hands the outline of a seven-year plan of how ordinary American Bahá'ís can play a role in bringing peace to the world. *The Advent of Divine Justice* – the plan – penned by Shoghi Effendi, 'Abdu'l-Bahá's grandson and appointed Guardian of the Bahá'í Faith, calls for one Spiritual Assembly to be formed in every state of the Union, in every province of Canada and every country in Central and South America. Latin America gains special mention.

Gertrude rests the pages in her lap, her hands still holding tightly to both sides. 'Well, why can't I go?' she asks herself. From this moment Gertrude becomes consumed by the need to uproot herself from her New York cocoon and head for South America.

She walks over to her dresser and picks out a piece of paper to write to the leading Bahá'í administrative institution in the country, the National Spiritual Assembly of the United States and Canada, and ask if she can become a pioneer. Later, Leroy Ioas will tell her she was the first person to volunteer for Central or South America. A few weeks pass and Gertrude arrives home to find an envelope addressed to her. It is postmarked Haifa in Palestine. She clutches the small crinkled rectangle to her heart, knowing that it contains the future course of her life. In the small privacy of her bedroom, her eyes read and reread the Guardian's reply. It tells her to go to South America, to look for a way to earn a living but to not let it stand in her way if she cannot.

President Roosevelt is still trying to nursemaid the United States out of its Great Depression. The Works Progress Administration has been installed since 1935, providing millions of people with new opportunities for work and study. Gertrude enrols in a course in Spanish. At the Bahá'í Center in New York she begins promoting pan-American culture. Each month, a group of women from different areas in South America display their dances and songs and food. Gertrude wonders how she can possibly make herself financially independent when she is there. After a few weeks an idea arrives. She takes a course on sweet making and confectionery so that she will be able to open a small store in whichever country she ends up in.

Kiva barely registers Gertrude's presence anymore. The silence between them is noisy, full of the palpable disgust he feels about his daughter's decision. It is Mama's aloofness that troubles her. Mama's shaking head and heavy sigh greet her when she walks into the room. She wishes she could find a way to help Mama understand. Then, one day, she sees it.

Lidia Zamenhof, a Bahá'í, has arrived in New York to teach Esperanto, the language originated by her father Dr Ludwig Zamenhof who was born a Russian Jew. Dr Zamenhof's aim to create a global language that allows all people to communicate fits easily with her new Bahá'í beliefs. Gertrude hears that the Zamenhof story will be appearing in an edition of the Jewish daily paper. For the first time her mother will be able to read about Gertrude's faith in her own language.

A warm sense of expectation is building inside Gertrude as she watches her mother read the Zamenhof article. When Becky finishes reading, she puts the paper down on the table, smooths it with her hands and sighs.

'Mama, what do you think?'

'Well,' her mother starts slowly, 'this won't come in my lifetime. Not in your lifetime. Not even in your children's lifetime. It will only come when the Messiah comes.'

'But Mama, the Messiah *has* come. And he's given us the teachings for building the Kingdom on Earth like it says in the Old Testament.'

'Agh!' Becky's face contorts in a desert of wrinkles, her mouth turning down at its corners. 'Why do we still have wars? Why are the Jews being persecuted?'

Her mother's long list of the world's ills erupt from a heart that has hardened through years of living with unanswered prayers. She uses them as proof. For Gertrude the answer seems so clear and simple. 'Well, Mama, that's why He came here, to do away with this.'

'No,' her mother shoots back. 'When the Messiah comes it will happen overnight. There will be no more wars and the dead will rise out of their graves.' Becky wipes her hands over her closed eyes and face. She begins to rock gently and her hushed whispers in Hebrew close off the conversation.

* * *

New Jersey, 1939

On the last Sunday in June, Gertrude convinces her mother to accompany her to a picnic at Evergreen Cabin in New Jersey that sits on the expansive property of a coffee importer and prominent Bahá'í, Roy Wilhelm. They catch the ferry from Manhattan. Gertrude watches the sea breeze play with the loose strands from her mother's tight bun.

There are well-dressed Persians, Europeans and blacks

chatting in clusters on the green rolling hills when they arrive at the property. A group of musicians play gently in the background. Gertrude looks for a reaction in her mother's eyes. She doubts that her mother has ever seen such a diverse collection of people interacting so unaffectedly. They have gathered together from across the country for the annual Unity Feast that celebrates a speech given here by 'Abdu'l-Bahá in 1912.

Gertrude quickly searches out a Bahá'í woman who is also of Jewish background. They eat together and the woman begins a conversation in Yiddish with Becky. Gertrude watches her mother relaxing a little. Finally, she decides, her mother can see that she isn't just going off to all these different kinds of meetings with funny kinds of people. The reading of 'Abdu'l-Bahá's speech begins. Becky watches intently, hearing, but not understanding the English words.

After attending the feast her mother stops questioning. She gives up on her fears of what will become of her unmarried daughter, now determined to head off to wild unknown places in South America. 'If it is God's will,' she says, quietly surrendering.

* * *

Manhattan, 1939

She is retyping a letter that has been given to her by the National Spiritual Assembly. It contains assurances for obtaining a visa that Gertrude will be under their auspices in South America and has their support. It is getting late and the keys resonate a rhythmic tap dance across the empty workplace. When she finishes she flips over her double-duty desktop to hide the typewriter inside it. Once again it is a smooth workbench and in her mind's eye she sees the letter resting on it.

The next morning she waits patiently at her desk for the man from the State Department to interview her. When he arrives she looks up at him with huge hope in her heart. The man stares back at her with eyes made vacuous by officialdom.

The dark force that is shadowing Europe has begun to spread into Latin America. By 1939 there are numerous United States operatives across South America trying to gain intelligence on the influx of Nazis into the region. Gertrude is no longer sure of whether she is viewed as someone in danger or as someone who is going to cause it.

'Now, Miss Gewertz, this shouldn't be too hard,' says the man, unconvincingly. 'Why do you think we should grant you a visa?'

'Well,' Gertrude starts, 'I have a letter of support I can show you.'

She reaches across to where she remembers she left the envelope but only feels the desktop beneath her fingers. She stands up quickly and flips the desktop over feeling her way around the body of the typewriter.

'It's here. I had it here last night,' she says, her voice rising.

The man starts to evenly tap the end of his pen on his clipboard. The sound of it acts on Gertrude like an alarm.

She pulls open her handbag and rifles around inside of it. She dips under the desk scanning the floor for the white envelope. She upturns the trashcan. The small pile of crunched paper doesn't hold the object of her search.

The man watches Gertrude in silence. His eyes are beginning to fill up as more minutes go by. Gertrude straightens up and stares across at them. They seem stony with suspicion. Her heart surges with fear.

'I can't find the letter,' she blurts out.

'Now, Miss Gewertz,' the man says again. 'I'm a busy man. I think we can say that there is no letter. I think we can say that we don't want to be responsible for a young Jewish woman going into these parts alone. I think, Miss Gewertz, that we, the State Department, can say we will not grant you a visa.'

Gertrude watches the man's eyes narrow. Something dies in the centre of her chest. She has no words. The man gets up packing his neat clipboard into his briefcase.

'Good day, Miss Gewertz,' he says, turning quickly.

When Gertrude goes home she walks straight to her bedroom. She shuts the door and slowly lowers herself onto the edge of the bed. Great sobs engulf her, holding her rigid with wrenching bursts. In the coming months she sheds many tears as she watches pioneer after pioneer head off to South America.

She is called up to Green Acre to discuss with the National Spiritual Assembly where she might go. They ask Gertrude whether she would consider becoming another part of the Plan that is focused on North America and Canada.

'Yes, I would,' replies Gertrude.

It is decided that she will go to Brattleboro in Vermont. Gertrude tries to cover her disappointment. Instead of going a long way south, she is to head a short way north. When Gertrude arrives she finds a town that is bustling about like a newly walking toddler. It is teeming with people trying to find jobs and she pounds the muddy unpaved streets, unable to find any work. She decides to retreat to Rutland, seventy miles away.

Rutland is more established and Gertrude is able to set up a model display of the temple in Chicago and begin speaking to families. When Nisa Bissel, the assigned pioneer for Rutland, returns from a meeting in Green Acre she is furious to find Gertrude. Nisa considered Rutland her territory and the policy at the time was that there should be only one pioneer in each town. Many years later, Gertrude will quietly muse that Nisa Bissel was a First World War nurse who believed in numerology and her number added up to One.

A telephone call has come through for Gertrude. It is the Secretary of the National Spiritual Assembly. 'Gertrude, what are you doing in Rutland?' she hears Horace Holley call down the line.

'Well Horace, I couldn't even get a place to stay in that war-boom town you sent me to,' she replies.

'I'll tell you what. You'd better come back to Green Acre, Gertrude. Nisa Bissel's been banging our ears.'

Back in Green Acre Gertrude is asked, 'How about Alaska?'

Her friend Amelia Collins, also on the National

Spiritual Assembly, sees the light go out of her face. 'Don't send Gertrude to Alaska!' she pipes, 'It's so cold there! How about sending her to Alabama?' A small eagerness begins to ignite Gertrude again. She thinks about all the experience she has gained in being part of the Bahá'í Race Relations Committee, trying to build a connection between whites and blacks in upper Harlem. She knows this is important to the Plan as well. Shoghi Effendi has described the deeply difficult issue of race relations as the cancer of America. Gertrude agrees to go. Maybe she can play a part in its cure.

* * *

Birmingham, 1940

New York is days behind her. Gertrude rests her head against the car window and looks up through the rows of tall, silent trees. They are vertical towers, made by nature. Their leaves form a dense filter that the sun finds its way through to softly trace its light on the road. Terah Smith, a Southern Bahá'í friend, has offered to drive her towards her new home and they have now been travelling together for two days. They reach the mountains in Virginia. 'I have never been so far south before,' Gertrude is thinking.

The sound of the engine has eased to become an even background clatter. But now as they climb through the curves of mountains something breaks its rhythm. Sharp popping bursts erupt into the green and golden stillness.

Terah pulls up to look at the engine. 'We'll have to try and make it to a garage,' she concludes.

Terah is explaining the engine problem to a mechanic. Gertrude listens to his answer. It sounds like a high sing-song gobble cut intermittently by a slow 'We-ell'. It is the only word her ears can decipher. A thought grips her mind and she panics. 'Goodness!' she exclaims to herself. "I can't understand a word they're saying. I may as well be going to a foreign country.' And then a more desperate thought intrudes. 'How am I going to take dictation?' This is a real question for Gertrude. As a pioneer you are meant to find your own work and support yourself. Much of how you share your beliefs should come from how you go about your daily life.

They arrive in Atlanta, Georgia, where Terah will be staying on. In the week Gertrude gives herself there she tries to train her ear to the new strange sounds that will form everyday conversation. She is also making the most of Terah's company. Once she leaves Atlanta she will be on her own.

Gertrude looks up at the window of the train she is about to board for Birmingham, Alabama. Painted on it is the outline of a hand pointing forward with the word 'Whites' written above. It catches her gaze and makes her gasp. She reluctantly follows the direction of the pointing white finger.

When the train sets off Gertrude is still thinking about the sign and all the other signs of segregation she is beginning to see. Her brow furrows trying to make sense of this. 'Oh my,' she breathes softly to herself. Outside, the train passes towering furnaces billowing ominous puffs of steam from the steel mills. They creep through cracks and open doorways and windows into the train. When Gertrude arrives at Birmingham station her white blouse has turned a sooty black.

There is no one to greet her at the station and she knows no one in this city. In the excited lead-up to the journey Gertrude has never accounted for how she might feel about arriving like this. She sucks in the coal-soiled air and heads off for the only place she thinks she might find a bed to stay. At the YWCA she is told she is allowed to stay for two weeks before she must find her own accommodation. When she wakes up in the morning she does not know how to begin her day. Old feelings of being lost, both in spirit and place, begin to gather inside her mind. She wanders the streets whispering small prayers for reassurance. Some days she feels so lonely she cannot eat.

Food has always been a source of comfort, but the food here is as foreign as the voices. Beans are fried until they turn a dark muddy brown – in pork fat. With her Jewish upbringing, Gertrude has never tasted pork fat before. Without a job, she has little money for food anyway.

* * *

The woman who manages the YWCA watches Gertrude come slowly through the door. 'Gertrude,' she calls out, 'there is a lady who wants to share a flat with somebody. How about you get in touch?'

Gertrude knocks on the front door of an apartment and a woman in her late forties answers. Bonnie is virtuous and neat. She fusses over cushions as she shows Gertrude around the single-bedroom apartment.

'Where am I going to sleep?' Gertrude asks in a small voice.

'Well, here!' answers Bonnie. She opens two big doors in the living room and pulls out a Murphy wall bed. Gertrude swallows any sign of disappointment. She knows her options are few.

Gertrude has learned from an early age to make concessions for the people she lives with and a routine is quickly established. Gertrude rises early to put the bed away and use the bathroom so that she doesn't disturb Bonnie's movements. Bonnie is a strict Baptist and before breakfast she reads prayers from a book. 'You know, we have some beautiful prayers in the Bahá'í Faith. Do you mind?' Gertrude asks one morning when she finds the courage. A new routine is established where they alternate prayers each day. Bonnie's boyfriend, a homespun farmer, is the only visitor to the home. Beneath his Sunday suit he is a tall, sinewy and silent presence with a large Adam's apple that pops out atop his shirt collar.

She finds work as a stenographer with the American Plumbing Company. The manager is also from the North and it becomes a mutual bond. The rest of her colleagues are from the South and keep their distance. They cannot understand why a single woman from the North would come here, nor are they interested enough to find out. But she feels them watching her, waiting for her to slip up.

One day, Gertrude's wastebasket is full. She sees the janitor, a black man, and calls him over. 'Mr Washington, would you mind coming here?' She feels something suddenly change in the room. She looks around. All her colleagues' eyes are on her. Only, this time they are burning. 'We don't call any nigger Mister,' yells an angry voice.

'Well,' she blurts out, 'he's an older man and I was brought up to respect older people.' The eyes glare harder. Her lips are pursed with the effort of trying to hold back any hurt. 'I don't know him,' she tries to explain further, 'so I couldn't call him by his first name.'

In this single action, Gertrude has sealed in her colleagues' minds what they always suspected. She is the nigger-lovin' enemy from the North. Her work life becomes one of daily harassment and exile. Much of it is spent in tears. Eventually, she will go to the manager and say she thinks she can no longer stay there.

She walks back home along the street. Her bones feel as if they have gone soft with exhaustion. The intensity of feeling between whites and blacks is like a tsunami. She begins to think about what dramatic events would have to happen in the world, and what spiritual heights would need to be reached to even begin to turn the tide.

Soon after, Gertrude receives news that Mabel Ives, the itinerant Bahá'í teacher, will be arriving to give lectures and classes in Birmingham. She looks upon this as an answer to her fervent prayers. For the four months that she has been in Birmingham, Gertrude has been searching for people who might be interested in helping to bring about change. She finds possible names she can include through places such as the Theosophists Society and the Women's Civic Clubs.

Downtown, Gertrude smiles across at a young black boy shuffling a ball along the road with a stick. It is unusual to see a child outside of what is called 'nigger town'. He eyes her carefully and retreats, uncertain of what to do with this nicely dressed white woman's attention. Already, he understands that if they are caught speaking together they could both be arrested. Gertrude takes in air quickly and it re-emerges as a deep expression of weariness.

All around her is evidence of disunity. Ordinary citizens are continuously divided by the words 'colored' and 'white' that are stamped on toilets, on buses, on water coolers, on diners, on hotels, and even on churches. How could it have come about that someone's inner worth would be so judged by their skin, she wonders. An urgency quickens her steps and breathing as she walks around the streets with no particular destination. She begins a prayer to feel some calm.

She prays for a sign of help. And then she notices something. Attached to a brownstone house she sees a sign with the name Dr Juanita Johnson. It is unusual to find a woman doctor in these parts; especially one who is an osteopath and diet specialist. Gertrude knocks on the door.

A well-dressed lady opens the door. 'Hello, Dr Johnson?' Gertrude asks.

'No,' the lady says, watching Gertrude carefully, 'Dr Johnson is my sister. She's in Atlanta giving a course.

You're from the North, aren't you?' she asks, noticing Gertrude's accent. 'What are you doing here?'

'Well, really, my main purpose for being here is to help promote the Bahá'í Faith.'

'Oh. Well, what's that?' she asks. Gertrude tells her about bringing all people together, regardless of race or religion. 'You know, I think that my sister is going to be interested in that. She's interested in all kinds of funny things.' Gertrude smiles quietly back. Dr Juanita Johnson sounds interesting herself, she decides, and makes a mental note to visit her when Mabel Ives arrives.

She is only just beginning to understand how difficult and delicate it is to organize meetings for blacks and whites to attend. Only within the limits of the business district can this happen. The threat of lynchings looms over Gertrude's arrangements and she tries hard to shove it to the back of her mind. Mabel Ives works quickly to firm up invitations when she arrives. A hotel in the business district is booked for introductory lectures.

Gertrude's hunch proves correct and Dr Juanita Johnson is in the audience. At the last lecture Mabel asks who is interested in more discussions. A number of people put up their hands. Dr Johnson is one of them. Later, Gertrude is talking with her over coffee. She is worrying about finding a place where they will be able to meet. They can no longer afford to book the hotel.

Commercial places, stores and doctors' offices within the business district are the only places where black and white people are able to come together. 'Well, you can meet at my home,' offers Dr Johnson. Gertrude's coffee spills over the sides of the cup. It is not just the offer that has touched her, it is a powerful sense that there is something much bigger than her at work, helping to turn what seem to be insurmountable mountains into molehills. This feeling that she is always being guided will stay with Gertrude for the rest of her life.

* * *

She is reading for insight through some of Bahá'u'lláh's teachings. The ringing phone jolts her back into clock time. She looks up and sees it is 8.30 p.m. It is a friend calling to tell her that Louis Gregory will be in town to give a lecture at the University. Louis Gregory, a prominent member of the National Spiritual Assembly, is regarded as an intellectual and spiritual giant. Born to freed black slaves in 1874, he was a rising star lawyer in Washington DC where he worked alongside other civil rights leaders such as W. E. B. DuBois before giving his career away to devote his energy to teaching racial unity. Gertrude hangs up the phone, and decides to telegraph Leroy Ioas at the National Teaching Committee in the morning. She wants to ask if Louis can do some speaking engagements in the black community while he is here.

When Louis Gregory arrives she goes to collect him from Birmingham station. Gertrude's heart seizes when she sees him emerge from one of the Jim Crow cars reserved for colored people. His wiry grey hair and suit are sooted. Louis shrugs it off. He doesn't react to the indignities in his life. Years earlier, his grandmother watched her husband murdered in a lynching and barely survived herself. Her conscious decision not to hate greatly influenced the young Louis.

Gertrude and Louis walk together through the town. A white mother grabs her little girl and crosses the street to the other footpath. Her steely glance reaches angrily across the gap she has created between them. Two businessmen approach. One forces his elbow into Louis' side as he passes. Louis lets out a small moan as he unbalances sideways. Gertrude's breath catches in the back of her throat, startled. They move forward together in silence.

'Louis,' Gertrude starts, 'I was surprised to hear that you were coming so close to Birmingham without letting me know.'

'Actually Gertrude, I had no intention of being anywhere near Birmingham. Where did you get that idea?'

'Well, your lecture was advertised in the paper and that is why I wrote to Leroy Ioas.'

'Oh no,' Louis shakes his head and chuckles quietly, 'that's another Louis Gregory. We're always getting each other's mail.'

Gertrude looks across into Louis's eyes. They are liquid brown pools with a gentle stillness that has somehow remained undisturbed by the sacrifices he has made in his life.

A friend of Gertrude's has found a black couple who have opened their home to Louis as none of the hotels will accommodate colored people. When they arrive, she notices the woman immediately serves him a cup of tea. It is the first place he has been able to get a cup of tea since starting his journey. A stinging wetness fills Gertrude's eyes.

She has met Louis in both New York and Green Acre where he is both revered and treated as an equal. Such an elegant man. He is married to a British white woman, also a Bahá'í, called Louisa Mathew. It was one of the earliest interracial marriages, Gertrude is only now beginning to imagine what they must endure when they travel south in these parts.

The editor of the local black newspaper has heard of Louis's lectures and turns up with around thirty other black people at the YWCA to hear him. Gertrude isn't there to hear Louis speak. The lectures are being held in 'nigger town', and her presence alone could stir up trouble. After Louis leaves, they are able to form a Local Spiritual Assembly consisting of five black people and four white people.

There are no priests in the Bahá'í Faith. When a group of nine people or more are in a community, a Local Spiritual Assembly is able to be formed. Each year on 21 April by secret ballot – no canvassing is permitted – an election is held to select nine persons who will serve as administrators of the community for the next twelve months. At this time, the fledging Spiritual Assembly is the only organization in Birmingham that is practising racial integration.

* * *

Route 65, Birmingham to Chicago, 1941

Alvin is captured by Gertrude's voice, the way she talks of her faith. He can tell when she's excited; her even, melodious purr suddenly speeds up, becoming faster and higher. A short, honey-rich giggle punctuates her spoken thoughts. He takes his eyes off the road to look across at her. She catches him looking and diverts her eyes down into her lap. He wishes she wouldn't do that. He can't understand this sort of shyness when in her eyes he sees a clarity of belief.

It is two days since Alvin picked up Gertrude and they set out from Birmingham with a car full of friends to drive to the National Bahá'í Convention in Chicago. Alvin likes to hear Gertrude's stories about the Bahá'ís she has already encountered: May Maxwell, Juliet Thompson, Leroy Ioas, Martha Root. He appreciates her understanding of the words of the Bahá'í teachings she can recite so well. He also likes the way she listens to him; not just as if she is lending a courteous ear, but as if she is processing what he has to say in her innermost parts before she will give a reply.

After Convention, it is another several days' drive back to Birmingham. They are buoyant, full of future promise and courage. Gertrude and Alvin know they each share a lifetime of what it is to be Jewish, but they speak little of it. Alvin thinks of himself as a Bahá'í now, his Jewishness is something in his past. Gertrude watches him. His energetic vision of the Faith and the future acts on her like a magnet.

Alvin looks back across at Gertrude. Her beauty catches

his breath and he chuckles awkwardly. He shakes his head, confused at what he is feeling. Gertrude has been a surprise. Mabel Ives had spoken highly of her to him, but when he first started coming down to Birmingham to see Gertrude a few months ago it was simply as a Bahá'í acquaintance from New York. He has been amazed by her depth of faith and her courage to come down here alone and keep working in this strange and difficult place so far from her home and anything she has known.

Alvin smirks at himself and rubs a hand across his mouth. It feels too soon after Virginia, the Bahá'í he had wanted to marry, for such feelings to be opened up again. He presses harder on the accelerator pedal.

* * *

Birmingham, 1941

Gertrude sits on the edge of her bed, hearing the movements of her flatmate in the kitchen as she clangs the nightly dishes together. In her hands she holds a letter from John Sterns, who has pioneered to Ecuador. He has invited her to come down and help him in his candy factory there. He knows she has studied the art.

She fiddles with a button on her blouse. Gertrude can't believe this invitation has come. Just recently, the original letter of commendation for her visa was found, fallen beneath the cracks in her old work desk back in New York. And now, at last, she is thinking, her opportunity to go to South America has arrived. But her mind has already become preoccupied with Alvin. She pushes the button inward hard into her chest. So strange, she and Alvin.

She remembers all those years ago, sitting on the edge of her bed, just like this, in her parents' apartment in Harlem. She remembers praying hard about what to do about her pharmacist fiancé, Irving. All those hours spent trying to decipher the next move for her future. Mostly, she remembers a voice that came so clearly through the stillness, telling her she would marry Alvin.

Gertrude barely knew Alvin at the time and she shook it off. Only recently had she dared to believe that maybe this has been Bahá'u'lláh once again guiding her.

She gets up and inserts some paper into her typewriter. She writes a letter to Alvin telling him about John's invitation and that she is seriously considering going to Ecuador. She writes another to the Guardian asking for his advice on going south. A few days later she receives a letter from Alvin asking her not to make any decision until he sees her.

When Alvin arrives his decision has already been made. He asks her to marry him. She answers him quickly with a kiss. Together, they feel that there are many paths that lie before them. There are so many places in the world that are in need of help.

They decide that they will get married in February 1942. Each writes a letter to their family to tell them of their news and ask for their written consent. Both with Jewish backgrounds, neither foresees any objection.

* * *

8 December 1941

He puts his arm around her shoulder and holds her tight. She turns her head and buries it into the warmth of his chest. They are listening to President Roosevelt relay the events of the Japanese attack on Pearl Harbour.

His statement of finality comes through the radio: 'I ask that the Congress declare that since the unprovoked and dastardly attack by Japan on Sunday, December 7th, 1941, a state of war has existed between the United States and the Japanese Empire.'

Against her face, she can feel Alvin's heart beating faster beneath his shirt. She shuts her eyes tight and they cling to each other in silence.

'Well,' Alvin exhales finally. She pulls away from him to look up into his eyes. Through a soft, sad mist they smile back at her. Her fingers reach up to cover his lips gently. She doesn't want to hear him say the words. Already, she knows what he feels he must do.

8

Peace in the Battle

There's a land they call 'Down Under'
In the South Pacific Sea,
And what can be the worth of it
Sure beats the like of me.
They call you 'Yank' or 'joker'.
Frankly, I don't get the jest,
And if you act American
You're a 'queer bloke' at the best.

Unknown US soldier, from *Down Under*

Memphis, Tennessee, February 1942

He has known this moment is coming. The letter is as he imagined, cold and perfunctory. How else do you ask a human being to become a number, a machine that will kill? He already knows what he has to do. In the months since his country declared war he has been constructing the words he will use to explain himself.

As a Bahá'í Alvin understands he must be loyal to his government and obey the law of the land implicitly. It is a basic tenet of their commitment to peace and unity. As he fills out his Draft papers he states these beliefs as clearly as he can. He will agree to become a number for his country, but he requests non-combatant duties.

He is called before the Draft Board to explain himself in person. Inside an administration room, a large American flag is tagged to the wall. Beneath it a group of officials wear expressions and uniforms the colour of beige.

'Sit down, Mr Blum,' says one.

Another is reading through papers. Alvin watches the creases between his brow grow deeper. 'What part of the Jewish Faith is Bahá'í?' he asks.

Alvin smiles back at the beige men. This is his kind of question. He uses it as an opportunity to explain what it is about his faith that can unite this troubled world.

On 2 April 1942 Alvin is sworn in to the United States Army and placed in the Medical Corps. 'Well, there it is,' he shrugs, staring at the paper informant in his hands. 'I'm glad they haven't given me a semi-conscientious objector's rating,' he tells Gertrude later. She reaches across, holding his face in both hands, and smiles her answer. She is so proud of the way the man she is going to marry has handled this situation.

Alvin is sent first to North Carolina, then to Chatanooga, Tennessee, where he receives training in bandages, splinted fractures, treating wounds, medication and injections. Just before he is due to be sent to the West Coast, Gertrude goes to visit him.

* * *

Chattanooga, Tennessee

He flexes the freshly-tuned muscles in his arms to help steady Gertrude as they climb up a hill. Lookout Mountain was made famous as a Civil War battleground that became romanticized as 'The Battle above the Clouds'. Gertrude is silent as they look back down across the rocks and the river that snakes through the plain like a squiggle drawn in the dirt. She squeezes Alvin's hand a little tighter, determined not to cry. Alvin's profile looks strong and handsome. Sometimes she thinks he looks like a movie star. She needs his strength. The force of this Faith that runs through both of them, she is sure that it will keep him safe. She begins to pray aloud. Alvin turns towards her, watching, then he joins her. Together they pray for racial unity in the south and for Alvin's protection.

Their parting is softened by their decision that Gertrude will come out to San Francisco where Alvin is being stationed, and then they will be married. But war has already begun to transgress any intimacy. It makes pawns of private plans. Within two weeks, Gertrude has lost all contact with Alvin.

* * *

San Francisco, August 1942

In war there are many things that induce horror and fear. Among them is the fear of not knowing. It plays on active and creative minds, swooping them down a whitewater rapid of wild imaginings. Even in the Medical Corps there has been so much secrecy surrounding their future movements. They are kept in a permanent state of not knowing what's next.

Alvin has come to rely on having a clear vision of the 'Big Picture', of being able to see a course and act on it. Now, that has been taken away from him. They have been told nothing: neither when they are leaving, nor where they are going. Each of his troop mates sense something is up. Whatever it is, it is coming sooner than expected. Alvin sees the terror growing in their eyes.

At night he lies awake listening to their ruffled sounds. A young man beside him wheezes sharply, then exhales in a scattered groan. Alvin watches the shudder of his shadowy outline. He stretches across and pats it. 'Don't worry,' he whispers, 'it will be all right.'

Alvin leans back on his pillow and stares wide-eyed at the black rectangle of the bunk above. He feels an inward gathering of darker forces. A line starts repeating in his head. 'Nearness to God is heaven and remoteness from Him is hell.' He begins to pray and something inside him starts to shift. He realizes that he has never fully understood the meaning of this statement until now. He makes a conscious decision. It is a true and real surrender to what will be.

Dawn arrives, spreading fingers of light through the mess room. The dusky monochrome of beige and khaki somehow seems brighter to Alvin. He feels untroubled as he leaps out of bed. It is as if the not knowing no longer drains him of power. He moves through whatever the days bring with a grin and a wisecrack. The happiness in him puzzles his troop mates. 'What's gotten into you, Blum?' one fellow jibes him.

* * *

Birmingham, November 1942

The letter looks as if a child has gotten at it with a pair of scissors. It is all cut up and pasted back together. Gertrude holds it close to her eyes, reading and re-reading Alvin's words, trying to decipher any hidden clues between the army-censored lines. Another letter has arrived in the same mail. It is postmarked New Zealand. Gertrude has never heard of this place. She thinks it must be in Africa, something to do with the Zulus. She opens the letter and it is from a Bahá'í lady called Dulcie Burns. 'We've received a wonderful visitor at our Nineteen Day Feast,' she writes. Gertrude puts down the letter, mystified as to why this woman would write to tell her such a thing.

She is on the phone to a friend. 'I've received a letter from Alvin. I don't know where he is, but he's alright and he's met some friends,' she says, excitedly. 'But it's very strange, I've also received a letter from a lady in New Zealand. I don't know why she is . . .' Gertrude pauses, and then it clicks . . .

'Gertrude, are you there? Gertrude?' A small, muffled voice comes through the earpiece she has clasped to her chest.

'Yes, yes,' Gertrude answers back into the phone,

suddenly remembering her friend. 'I've just realized this woman is trying to tell me that Alvin is in New Zealand.'

When she hangs up the phone she rushes to find a map of the world. She looks through Africa and cannot find New Zealand. She uses her finger to slowly trace a journey east, searching through countries she's never thought about. Finally, she comes across two long, skinny islands hanging off the east coast of Australia in the Pacific Ocean. New Zealand, it says alongside them. She looks further east finding Birmingham and then back at all the water that lies between them. 'My precious Alvin,' she says aloud and alone in the room, 'I've never felt closer to you.'

* * *

Auckland, New Zealand, December 1942

'Where are you off to, Blum?' yells a medic.

'Tea!'

'What? You mean dinner. Again?'

'Yeah,' chuckles Alvin, slapping his fellow medic on the shoulder as he passes.

Most Friday nights, through his early contact with Rabbi Astor, the foremost Rabbi in New Zealand, he finds himself at a Jewish home eating a kosher meal. On other nights he gets invitations to tea. Already he is getting used to their strange 'down under' customs. They eat tea instead of dinner and they drink tea instead of coffee.

To the small Bahá'í community of Auckland, Alvin is an answer to their prayers. He is the first international

Bahá'í to pass through these parts since the phenomenal teacher Martha Root visited three years earlier.

New Zealand's confidence has been badly shaken since submarine-launched Japanese float-planes buzzed Wellington and Auckland earlier in the year. Britain is unable to help and America seems the only ray of hope. Just struggling out of their own Depression, the sight of thousands of handsome young men, full of charm and money in their pockets, is very welcome. Already, the Auckland Bahá'í community is captivated by Alvin and can see what a great speaker he will make. They begin to organize places for him to deliver talks.

'Really, I'm just an ordinary man with a simple mind,' Alvin insists when he hears of this. 'I've never given talks to audiences.'

'Look,' says Dulcie Burns, soon to become Mrs Dulcie Dive, 'I can help you write your talks. But Alvin,' she adds, 'you'll be terrific.'

Alvin stretches out his hands and lifts up his shoulders in resignation. Something flickers through his mind that makes him smile. He is thinking of Gertrude and how she said he would be sent to the right place.

The next week brings two letters from Gertrude in the army mailbag. They are the first he's had since arriving here; one-page-only censored mail known as V letters. 'My precious Alvin,' she begins. She is full of praise of him, as always. 'An ambassador of hope,' she calls him. He feels a good warmth begin to pulse around his heart. When he reads the next lines it contracts to a cold thud. Gertrude's father has been killed in an accident. She received the news by telegram. Then came the awkward decision. Does she make the journey for his funeral even though she can't afford it? She has decided not.

Gertrude doesn't tell Alvin about her father's fury. The way his eyes looked when he was angry, as if possessed by something wild and unnatural. Nor does she mention the years she spent living in fear of it. 'He was very unhappy when I left home,' she writes, 'but the cage is broken now, his spirit has taken its immortal flight into the realms of light and his pains and sorrows are behind him. It will be so much easier for him now to see with the eyes of reality and oneness.'

Her father's death was tragic. His skull and ribs were badly crushed by a truck. The horse and cart, his lifeblood, from which he had peddled since arriving in New York, wiped out by the collision. It was a road death not unlike that of his young daughter Dora all those years earlier, only Kiva lived for another five hours, his chest filling with blood as he passed, slowly drowning, into another world.

Alvin has never met his future father-in-law. He feels the loss more for Gertrude. He wants to put his arms around her and pull her close to him. For the first time in months pain creeps into his mind. It takes the form of regret. Regret for all the wasted time; time that he could have spent together with Gertrude. He could have met her father, married her so much sooner. And now, what a mess, all this distance.

* * *

She is staring at the two piles of letters she has created. One is larger, stacked with the rush of letters that have arrived from New York since her father's death. The other pile contains letters written by Alvin's hand.

The letters from New York have further complicated her difficult decision. Many of them urge her to return. 'Your mother needs you,' they plead. A few of them advise her to do what she feels is best for her. Molly, her brother Abe's wife, tells her she had a conversation with her father shortly before his death. 'He was very happy to hear the news of your engagement to Alvin,' she writes. This news provides a small window amid the hours she spends pacing and praying about what she should do. For days Gertrude has felt as though she is being physically wrenched in two – duty to her family or to her faith. Now she decides that she is staying here in Birmingham. 'I felt this is what I had to do,' she writes simply to Alvin.

She winces and rubs a hand across her stomach. Darts of burning pain sear across her middle, doubling her over. Dr Kesler, her physician in Birmingham, has told her it is exhaustion. He wants her to stay in bed and rest. She picks up Alvin's pile of letters and pulls warm covers back across her tired body. Her fingers unfold the thin, crackling paper to read one again.

Eight little words stand out on the page. 'Except I wish I was home with you.' She drinks them up, reading and re-reading them, allowing them to float around filling every aching inch of her with joy. She is so glad that Alvin has written them.

Hearing about all the new people Alvin is meeting,

feeling his excitement, has been tough for Gertrude. She is caught in an uneasy dance between her happiness for him and her yearning to be with him. She has tried to make it right in her head, writing to him: 'I wouldn't feel a bit jealous of anything you did, for jealousy vitiates the very essence of love.'

Gertrude's home situation has become unstable. Her Bahá'í flatmate Virginia has been moved on to a new city and Gertrude cannot afford the rent by herself. She has been put on a factory line, like so many other women right across the South, assembling B29 bomber planes. It takes an inordinate amount of her concentration to coordinate her hands into using the foreign tools, and the pay is small.

In many ways it would be easier to go back to New York, but she doesn't. She has news that another Bahá'í girl, Nina Howard – 'All the way from Hollywood', she writes Alvin – will soon be arriving. They will get an apartment together, this time within the city limits where there are more black people they can befriend.

In the meantime, she is staying with Mr and Mrs Inglis. Mr Inglis is manager of a department store and has become interested in the work Gertrude is doing in Birmingham to bring white and colored people together. Mrs Inglis is also very fond of her, she tells Alvin in a letter. This is the first time Gertrude has been able to observe a marriage up close, outside of the turmoil of her parents' union. She is beginning to learn what makes a marriage happy.

Words on a page no longer feel big enough to describe

their love. 'You will only feel it in your heart,' she writes to Alvin. Gertrude searches a hundred times for a way to express the fullness of what she is feeling. She doesn't want Alvin to be burdened by any thoughts of what might have been. 'Darling do not for a minute regret one thing that happened in the past . . . it was all in the plan, every bit of it, every lesson, every heartache. I am confident He wanted us to know a very beautiful love and so one has to be trained and moulded for such a love.'

Gertrude looks for small ways to rein in distance and time. She buys Alvin a watch, paying several dollars more for it than she can afford. 'So this will be our watch,' she writes, 'think of me when you look at it.'

In another letter she concentrates her focus on plans for their life ahead: 'We will leave it all in His hands, for we can hardly imagine what the future conditions will be like, but we will have each other.' When she writes this, Gertrude does not realize how prophetic this statement will become.

* * *

Princes Wharf, January 1942

He moves swiftly through the bodies that are sprawled around him on stretchers. Broken, bloodied and blackened, he has learned how to quickly assess which ones need to be sent off to hospital immediately, those who can wait and those for whom help has arrived too late.

Stationed in the dispensary at Princes Wharf, the

troop ships bring in the wounded from Pacific battles with increasing regularity. The dispensary becomes filled with the fetid odours and haunting groans of men trapped in a twilight of pain and horror. Many have gone mad with malaria. Sometimes they have to be held down. Alvin never writes about the moments spent repairing their damaged bodies. All he will say to Gertrude is that he prayed many a young boy into the Abhá Kingdom.

When the rush is over he goes and showers, removing clothes that are stained with his own sweat and the blood and fluids of strangers. He feels the water, barely warm, run over the top of his head and trickle down his body. It helps to wash what he can do no more about out of his mind.

'Come on Blum. Let's go for a drink at the pub. Just a beer,' taunts one of his army mates.

'Yeah, come on. What will it hurt?' eggs on another. 'What's the matter with you?'

Alvin pulls the buckle of his belt a little tighter and tries to grin back at them. 'Nah, I'm fine.' He doesn't want them to feel that he thinks any less of them. He understands why they drink. At first it seemed like they were having fun. It was a new country. There were pretty girls. Great efforts have been made for their entertainment. There are dances and jazz clubs that host travelling artists such as clarinettist Artie Shaw. But as the months have worn on something has altered. They are no longer drinking to get happy, they are drinking to become numb, both to what they have seen and the unspoken fear of what might become of them.

He knows they are beginning to think he is odd: Alvin with his weird religion, the way he won't drink or play with the girls. The worse things get, the more determined he becomes to give more talks. He hates what this war is doing to the men. He wants it over too. But he sees the situation differently. He is more convinced than ever that he is witnessing the birth pangs of a new cycle of human power which will lead to a great peace and unification of the whole world. He believes in the possibility of how this can happen sooner if more people act together, if they replace lip service with deeds, if they put service before self.

Talking before an audience now comes easily to Alvin. He doesn't see this as something he is doing so much as something greater that is moving through him. He speaks with an engaging mix of practical 'can do' and passion. Each talk must be presented ahead of time to a censor and then a security agent sits observing him in each audience to ensure that he doesn't stray from the submitted script with subversive ideas.

The Bahá'í community organizes speaking engagements for Alvin in Auckland and surrounding towns, sometimes two or more a week. They place ads in newspapers. Often they are accompanied by endorsements from internationally prominent persons such as Members of Parliament, or one from former President Eduard Beneš of Czechoslovakia who says, 'The Bahá'í Faith is one of the great moral and social forces in all the world today. I am more convinced than ever, with the increasing moral and political crises in the world, we must have greater international co-ordination. Such a movement as the Bahá'í Cause which paves the way for universal organization of peace is necessary.'

Alvin uses his furloughs and service railway pass to travel to other cities such as Wellington and tiny Whangerai in the north. In Napier, where there are no Bahá'ís, he gives a series of talks on subjects that include 'A blue-print for an enduring world's government'. In a country of just 1.6 million people, there are many who are hungry for modern thoughts and ideas of a new future. Many of Alvin's speeches are reported and printed up in newspapers the next day. When he speaks to the Travel Club in Auckland there are four hundred people in the audience.

He spends time considering his different audiences and thinks about what might be interesting to them. His subjects are wide-ranging, from the importance of child education to practical plans for a future world economy that operates without the extremes of wealth and poverty. Rather than viewing New Zealand as a tiny backwater, he encourages them to see their country as a contributing force in the world. 'A million and a half people united, presenting unity and an intelligent approach to a problem, can accomplish more than five hundred million people who are pulling against each other,' he reasons. 'The world does not hesitate to call upon you for an army, food and financial assistance, so why shouldn't they think enough of you to listen to your voice on matters concerning your welfare.'

He reaches out to other men, leaders in their religions, to

join with him in encouraging people to see themselves in a new and powerful way. Reverend Chandler is an Anglican Minister who lives in Cambridge, New Zealand, and has a regular newspaper column. Alvin is attracted to his liberal views and contacts him. They meet and become fast friends, with Reverend Chandler inviting Alvin to speak to his Parish audience. 'It is imperative that we should be stirred and moved out of our complacencies,' the Reverend says when introducing Corporal Blum for a talk.

In a letter to Rabbi Astor after an early introduction, Alvin finds himself explaining how it could be that a man brought up as Jewish Orthodox could take on this new religion. The pair soon become friends and Alvin often joins Rabbi Astor and his family for Shabbat dinners on Friday nights.

New contacts also begin to come through his everyday world. He walks into a print shop to order a new sign for the dispensary. Three young boys are behind the counter. They introduce themselves as Hod Vale, Doug Wall and Bruce McComb. They are young and eager and hopeful for a better world. They ask Alvin to tell them about himself. Instead, he talks about what he really believes needs to happen in the world and how they can play a great part in its future. He speaks about an international governing body with an international police force to back up its decisions and a central authority to regulate a world currency and a system of world education for even the poorest of nations.

Alvin seems to answer something that they already know within themselves. Soon after this, Doug writes to Alvin: 'I have had numerous conversations with the fellows here on the subject of Politics and World Affairs and the ones that have given any thought to it, all agree that radical changes are necessary to bring unity and harmony to this bloody torn up world . . . When you are an old man and haven't any hair to part you can look back and see the avalanche you started in a sign shop out here and the wonderful friendships you brought about.'

For months he has noticed how the carpenter who works near the dispensary keeps an eye on him. Alvin passes by the man. 'Good morning, sir,' he says breezily. The man breaks the rhythm of his hammer, turning to stare at him. He follows Alvin into the dispensary.

'Blum?'

'Yes, that's me.'

'Blum, I've been told to stay away from you.'

Alvin looks up from the pile of bandages he is sorting and chuckles. 'Really?'

'Yes.' The man puts his hammer down on the counter. 'Now, why would that be?'

'Well,' grins Alvin. 'What's your name?'

'Harnish.'

'Alright, Mr Harnish, I happen to be a member of the Bahá'í World Faith.' Alvin keeps the description of his faith clear and to the point. The expression on Mr Harnish's face begins to reshape itself into one of interest. When Alvin finishes, Mr Harnish picks up his hammer again. He points its knobbly head at Alvin and it gently bobs forward in his hand as if providing a rhythm for the words he is thinking.

'Blum,' he finally says aloud. 'I think that sounds like something my wife might be interested in. How would you like to come to tea at our place?'

Alvin finds firm friends in his new acquaintances. Margaret Harnish and her daughter Beryl begin to meet with other New Zealand Bahá'ís. They soon discover there is something undeniable about what they are hearing and they want to be part of it.

* * *

News arrives in the compact, contracted form that the V letter standard demands. Gertrude's words tell him that Mabel Ives is dead. A lump forms, tight and hard, in his throat. He rolls over in his camp bed, turning to face the wall. It is hard to gain privacy inside a mess camp.

Howard Colby Ives, full of wisdom and humility, who taught him what it is to be a man, has already left this world. And now Mabel. She has been like a spiritual mother to him, showing him patience, guiding and advising him. She was a rock when he didn't know how to handle his first marriage. She stood by him when he said goodbye to Virginia, and she welcomed Gertrude. 'If you and Virginia could not make a go of it – I can not think of anyone who would be a better choice for you than Gertrude,' she wrote.

Mabel worried about him at war and what his faith might demand of him. When she heard he had been sent away with his troop ship she wrote, 'It has just come to me Alvin dear, that should your hospital unit

– or ambulance in what you are carrying wounded, be attacked by the enemy, according to what 'Abdu'l-Bahá said, you would be justified in protecting your wounded. That is, defence of others is permitted, nay, obligatory, as otherwise you become accessory to the act.'

Alvin flips his body back around quickly and pulls some paper and a pen out of his drawer. He begins to write a letter to Gertrude. He tells her how he wrote a letter to Mabel, just a few weeks ago, expressing his love and appreciation for all her assistance on all levels. He feels Mabel has been living on borrowed time for the last few years. He remembers one time she had a week of lectures lined up in Little Rock, Arkansas. He arrived to find her in a hotel bed ill with laryngitis and fever. He watched her get up out of bed and deliver a perfect talk. 'It was most extraordinary how she could draw on some hidden power to serve her. Mabel set a high standard for us,' he writes to Gertrude. 'We must not let her down.'

Alvin begins to double his efforts. Every fifth night he works late to get extra afternoons off. He meets friends for tea as often as he can and speaks to groups about three times a week. To celebrate the 100th anniversary of the Declaration of the Báb in May 1944 he helps to organize a dinner. On the night, there are close to three hundred guests, including outstanding members of leading organizations and thinkers throughout New Zealand. His friends Rabbi Astor and Reverend Chandler are there, along with Mr Au Chu, a prominent Chinese lawyer, and Mrs Owens who represents Maoris.

Around this time, Gertrude writes that her work in

Birmingham is complete. The Local Spiritual Assembly, which has brought both black and white people together, is strong enough to manage on its own and she will be moving on to Greenville in South Carolina to help the Bahá'ís there. Alvin feels a pride swelling inside his chest as he reads her letter.

* * *

Auckland Harbour, 12 December 1944

He looks up at the sun, squinting in the brightness. He closes his eyes to let its warmth radiate right through him. It smooths out some of the tension gripping his body. When he opens his eyes he looks back from the deck of his medical transport ship, watching all that has been familiar to him for the last twenty-six months grow small in the distance.

The Japanese have been pushed back from the south and central Pacific and the war has moved further east. General MacArthur has been going hard in the Philippines. America has been determined to isolate the Japanese from their occupied countries in south-east Asia, depriving them of oil supplies. After invading the island of Leyte in late October, the United States begins the largest naval battle in history in the Leyte Gulf. The Japanese are vastly outgunned and outmanoeuvred. In desperation they begin to organize the first kamikaze attacks.

Alvin has been informed he is headed for the Philippines. He knows little of the details. He is grateful he has had the opportunity to say goodbye to his friends. The farewell party in the rented hall was his big thank you. There were one hundred and twenty-five people of all different races present who had been part of his life. Maoris sang and danced.

It is only later that he will count up the one hundred and twenty-five public talks he gave during this time. He views it as a miracle that he has been based in New Zealand so long. Why was it that he was not sent to the front lines? Many of his division were sent there and most did not return. Those who did return, after a short furlough, were sent straight back to the front lines.

The last sliver of mainland is disappearing into the horizon. 'God Bless New Zealand!' he says under his breath.

* * *

Alvin's ship passes through the Solomons. Being a hospital ship, it anchors off Guadalcanal for several weeks, but he will never speak nor write about this period.

Lunga Point, a prominent finger of land near Henderson Field on Guadalcanal, is being used as a supply and medical support base for the battles that are still raging against the Japanese to the north in Bougainville. The air and sea battle of Guadalcanal that extended from 1942 to 1943 had been urgent and brutal with heavy losses on both sides. The US troops renamed Sealark Sound, a beautiful body of water that extends out between the islands here, Iron Bottom Sound. Thirty-two American ships, one Australian cruiser and fourteen Japanese ships, the bodies of men still trapped inside, now lie deathly still on its cold sea bed.

On land, it is the Japanese who have been hit hardest. Cut off from food and with no quinine to fight malaria, most have been too weak to dig themselves into trenches in the coral ridges that pervade Guadalcanal. Many of them simply curled up and died to the sound of advancing American troops. Many thousands of Japanese lost their lives on this island alone.

* * *

Manila, Philippines, June 1945

The jeep's wheels make a guttural whir, spitting great globules of deep red mud. Alvin is juggled sideways in his seat as the tyres dip dangerously low, then up high amid the rocks and bombed-out craters that now engulf what once were roads.

'Woah-ho!' he sings happily to the driver, 'that was close.' Since yesterday morning he has been hitchhiking his way up north from Manila to Solano in the mountainous centre of Luzon Island. Since he arrived in the Philippines back in April – first based in Leyte Island, now in Manila – he's been waiting for the moment when he could follow up on the lead he's received from Horace Holley in a letter about the sole group of Bahá'ís in Solano.

When the news came through that the Japanese occupation of the island was over, Alvin applied for a three-day pass so he could make this journey. What he has seen of frontline battles over the last few months is being replaced by a focus on how to get through what has been the last stand for the Japanese in this region. Rail and other communications have been obliterated in these parts and his travel has involved hitchhiking from one jeep to another with the occasional 1920s Greyhound relic.

'So where are you from?' Alvin shouts above the engine noise to his latest driver, a US army Lieutenant.

'I come from Chicago, near Wilmette.'

'By the way, have you ever visited our Bahá'í Temple there?'

'Yeah. I've been by that building a thousand times but I've never gone in. What's it all about?'

Alvin begins a brief explanation. 'Well, we don't talk religion at home,' the Lieutenant says. 'My wife's a Catholic and I'm a Protestant.'

Alvin grins back at him and the Lieutenant drives him on a few miles to the next cross-road. As Alvin steps out of the jeep, the Lieutenant calls across to him. 'Sergeant, are you a minister in the Bahá'í Faith?'

'Lieutenant,' Alvin chortles, shaking his head, 'no, I don't have any authority in the Bahá'í Faith. And I'll tell you something else, Lieutenant. If you went into the Bahá'í Temple in Wilmette and every seat was filled up with people and you told them you knew Alvin Blum, nobody would get up and give you a seat. That,' he slaps his thigh, enjoying his story, 'is how much authority I have in the Bahá'í Faith.'

He leaps from the Greyhound bus into the main street of Solano. As his feet hit the ground, something jams in his back and he grabs at the pain with his left hand, trying to smooth the aches from nearly two days of rough terrain. The centre of town appears like a moonscape before him. Children in rags and skinny dogs pick amid the rubble.

It is a place that has lost all time. What was once here, the buildings that could mark out its history, has been blown away. Alvin treads his way nimbly, balancing on rocks and jumping across ditches, through crooked, crumbling streets. Eventually he sees a wooden sign still wedged in the debris. 'Bahá'í Reading Room. All Welcome', it states. This is all that is left of the small Bahá'í Centre. He starts asking the few village people who remain here, 'Where are the Bahá'ís?'

* * *

He is surprised by the strength in the wiry brown hands that are clutching his forearms. They pull Alvin close into a hug and the man kisses him hard on both cheeks. Alvin looks into the man's eyes and feels the same tears beginning to well in his own. He grabs hold of the man's shoulders, pulling him into another embrace and patting him gently on the back.

The hair on Felix Madella's middle-aged head has been turned white by the war. The bombings have robbed him of his hearing, leaving him stone deaf. Alvin takes in a deep breath. 'What this man has been through,' he is thinking, 'the faith in him.' A few years earlier, this one man happened to come across a brochure on comparative religion that a passing Bahá'í, Loulie Matthews, had left in a library. Felix wrote to the address on the back of the pamphlet, that of the National Spiritual Assembly of the United States and Canada, which followed through by sending him books and information. From that single pamphlet he built up a community of fifty believers.

When they gather the community together on this day there are only twenty left. The rest are either dead or missing. Alvin pushes any of his backslapping awkwardness aside to give each of them an enormous hug and kiss. For Alvin, who has been living for months on GI rations, the feast that they manage to prepare for him, seemingly out of nothing, is overwhelming. He is the first outside Bahá'í they have ever met and Felix stares at him full of hope and gratitude. Alvin has never felt more humbled.

Good as his word, Alvin finds a way to get back up to see this tiny community before his Company is pulled out. He wants to leave them with something. As best he knows how, he helps them organize their first Local Spiritual Assembly. It is the first in the Philippines. He writes urgently to Gertrude asking her to gather as many books and as much food and clothing as she can and send them across to this fledgling Bahá'í community.

* * *

Evergreen Cabin, Teaneck, New Jersey, November 1945

As she stands dressed in her wedding outfit she can feel his eyes tracing over her body. He begins with the peacock plumage that she's placed in her hair, then follows the pleated trail of silky blue fabric. On her arms she wears dark hands-free gloves. Her nails are painted blood red. She looks back into his face and sees Alvin quietly glowing with admiration. He saunters across and pins a white orchid to her breast. 'Ready to be my wife?' he smiles.

Alvin is dressed in his army uniform. The war separated them for more than thirty-eight months and when Alvin finally returned in October, last month, he didn't want to waste any more time. 'Let's get married now,' he said, not wanting to let her out of his arms.

Gertrude's fingers follow the lines of shallow wrinkles that have formed around his eyes, then they brush lightly across the new flecks of grey that strike through his dark hair. The situation has aged them both, she realizes. Then she smiles. In her eyes he looks more handsome than ever.

Alvin and Gertrude marry in the modest Bahá'í Centre, a wooden cabin in Teaneck, New Jersey, where Alvin had attended his first Bahá'í meeting. It is a simple Bahá'í ceremony witnessed by some of their dearest friends and Alvin's sister Lillian and her husband Frank. Not long after, they get married again. This time it is for their families. The Jewish Rabbi from a synagogue in the Bronx where Gertrude's brother Abe lives performs the ceremony. 'What is your religion?' the Rabbi asks. 'Bahá'í,' they both answer.

'No, no, what is your religion?'

Gertrude and Alvin look at each other in silence. They hear an uncomfortable rustle go through their seated guests. 'Well, what religion were you born?' the Rabbi asks, flustered. Alvin rolls his eyes and grins. 'Jewish,' they both answer.

Wings Shirt Company offers Alvin his old job back. 'Blum, we'd like you to locate yourself at the geographical centre of your three-state territory in the South.' After consulting with the Bahá'í National Teaching Committee, Alvin and Gertrude set up home in Little Rock, Arkansas where they're told their help is needed most. Alvin's boss can't work out how he has decided that Little Rock is the epicentre of his business world, but he doesn't stop him. 'Well, alright Blum,' his boss throws up his hands in resignation, 'but make sure you're good at it.'

* * *

St Louis, 1946

He lays the Wings shirts out in the lounge area of the hotel suite, arranging them carefully according to the different sizes, styles and occasions he thinks might appeal most to his customers. With his hands on his hips, he stands back assessing if there is a little extra touch he can add to his temporary store.

Alvin has done this many times before in hotels across the South; in places like Georgia, Louisiana and South Carolina. When he is on the road he sees if there are any Bahá'í speaking engagements he can do.

The phone rings.

'Alvin, where are you?' says the voice on the line.

'Well, I'm here in the hotel, waiting for my customers.'

'But you should be here. Didn't they tell you that the meeting had been changed to this afternoon?'

As Alvin hangs up he is already writing a note to apologize and explain to his customers that he has another appointment. He leaves the note beside his order book then grabs the speech that he has already typed on the Hotel Statler, St Louis letterhead. The question of whether he should attend the meeting or not never enters his mind.

'I am not here this afternoon to try to convert anyone to the Bahá'í Faith,' he says to his audience. 'What I am going to do is to report what the Bahá'ís are doing regarding this great vital subject "Brotherhood".'

In his talk he opens up about what he has experienced in the army and all the disillusionment he still sees.

> In the dictionary we read the definition of brother: 'one closely united by a common interest with another'. In the last four years I have been closely united with my fellow men in a common cause . . . yet I can honestly say that true brotherhood did not exist. Hate, power and greed dominated and it was military law and the thought of repelling the common enemy that held us together . . .

> It did not exist – this brotherhood in the army – because the army carried over the prejudice and hates of the present world . . . There was no force released by the army or any attempt made to bring about love between the Christian and Jew and love between the white and colored man.

He talks about how little international peace pacts or legislation or even war itself have moved the world forward. It seems that there has never been so much talk about unrest and foreboding of some unforeseen calamity. 'Proof of my statement is very obvious,' he argues, 'just listen to the radio, read the newspapers and think of what has happened these last 25 years – two great world wars and talk of more to come. Makes one stop to think. Should make one stop to think.'

It is dark and the hotel suite is empty when he returns. Alvin scans through the order book and is amazed. It is the biggest round of orders he has ever received. He sees a note on the sidetable. 'Who is she?' it asks. Alvin smiles to himself, realizing that one of his customers has decided that his absence must mean he is on a date.

* * *

Little Rock Arkansas, 1946

A baby is already growing inside Gertrude. She marvels at her swollen belly. This is a pregnancy she has hoped for, but at her age of thirty-seven she knows she has to be careful. She rubs her hand across her stomach and smiles. She is thinking of the togetherness of things. So much has happened in their lives that has kept her and Alvin apart. Now, the three of them are to be a family.

'Joy gives us wings.' She loves this phrase of 'Abdu'l-Bahá's. Gertrude feels as though she is flying. Her current state doesn't seem to hold her back. She continues to meet with blacks and whites, not only in Little Rock but also in several other southern cities.

Their home in Little Rock is the centre of many gatherings. Situated in a mixed residential and business area, it provides a rare haven where black and white people can come together without fear of being harassed. In the few moments she has to herself Gertrude likes to get out into the garden, feeling the earth between her fingers.

This is a new pleasure and her joy of gardening is sometimes greater than her knowledge of it. She reaches across to tear at a piece of vine that is growing in an untethered tangle. Her hands begin to flare up almost immediately, causing her blood pressure to rise dramatically. When Gertrude arrives at the hospital she finds out that she has been ripping down poison ivy. For the last two months of her pregnancy she is confined, uncomfortably, to bed rest at the hospital.

Alvin is visiting Gertrude when he hears someone call out to him. 'Hey, Blum! Where have you been?' Alvin looks up quickly, recognizing the voice. One of his former army medic friends is now looking after Gertrude. He slaps both his hands down on the front of his thighs, grinning at this latest coincidence as he gets up from the bedside chair to shake his friend's hand.

When Gertrude goes into labour, Alvin retreats to a friend's house to say some prayers. It will take his army medic friend a couple of hours to find Alvin and tell him that Gertrude has given birth to a little girl.

I am born in Little Rock on 28 September 1946. One month and one hundred miles separates the loci of my birth from that of Bill Clinton. My mother wants to name me after the lady who first brought her into the Faith – Keith Ransom-Kehler. I am called Keith Wilma Blum.

9

A Distant Shore

Your work is to discover your world
and then with all your heart give yourself to it.

Buddha

Little Rock, Arkansas, 1947

Alvin jiggles one leg as he sits in an armchair. His mind has become occupied with an incessant series of questions. Chief amongst them is: where should he be?

There is a mood for change sweeping the globe. After the war, fifty nations came together to complete the Charter of the United Nations. The Bahá'ís presented a submission on the wording of this groundbreaking document, and now the Bahá'í International Community is represented at the United Nations. Gertrude's friend from her early New York days, Mildred Mottahedeh, has been chosen as one of the Bahá'í representatives to attend meetings and conferences. Alvin is inspired by the promise of this involvement and wants to be part of bringing something more, something united, into the world.

The Little Rock Bahá'í community now has its own Local Spiritual Assembly and Alvin feels they are able to leave without upsetting its continued progress.

He writes the questions in his head down in a letter to

Shoghi Effendi, the Guardian of the Bahá'í Faith in Haifa. He wants the Guardian to tell him where he is going to be of most use in this world: should he stay in the American Southern states or go back to New Zealand where he served during the war?

In May he receives his answer. A cable from the Guardian reads: LOVING PRAYERS ACCOMPANYING YOU, URGE CONCENTRATE MULTIPLICATION CENTERS NEW ZEALAND HEARTFELT APPRECIATION SHOGHI.

Energy that has spent months in restless wanderings inside his head is suddenly redirected to the rest of his body in one surge. He feels like shouting the Greatest Name – 'Yá Bahá'u'l-Abhá', O Thou the Glory of Glories, and that is what Alvin feels most directly is the answer to his prayers.

Alvin goes back inside the house. He sees Gertrude sitting in a chair breastfeeding their six-months-old daughter. My tiny fingers are wrapped firmly around my mother's pinkie and her forefinger is stroking my cheek as she hums sweetly to me.

'Gertrude!' His voice breaks the nursery scene. 'The most wonderful thing has happened. I have asked the Guardian where he wants us to be and he has told us to go to New Zealand.'

My mother stops humming suddenly. 'What?' her voice questions tightly. 'Alvin, you can't have. You never consulted with me. What about our plans?' she protests, her voice now rising. 'What about South America?'

Gertrude looks up at Alvin, searching for answers. In his eyes she discovers that their fate is already sealed.

'Oh Al-vin,' she wails. In the heave of her sobs her breast snatches itself away from my mouth. I begin to cry and we join together in making a sad siren sound.

When my mother finally gets me to sleep she reads back through Alvin's letters from New Zealand. She should have seen how attached he was to the place. In almost every letter she finds new praise for their future homeland: the weather, the beautiful gardens, the friends, the food. She stops on one. It is dated 17 August 1943.

'It hardly seems possible that I can go back to my old job and be satisfied with working four states when the whole world is shrinking down to a small ball,' she reads. 'I would like to get the Exporters and Importers Guide Mag as it reports on business of export and import companies. While it may be difficult to break into the international picture after the war, I think it will be worth the try as in a few years the rewards will be that much greater. I feel we will come back this way after the war.'

Slowly Gertrude refolds the letter and ties it back in its box with the others. Her hands fall back heavily into her lap. Something long held and treasured has died for her. In her heart she says a final goodbye to her dream of pioneering to South America.

Once his course is set Alvin works quickly. Everything in their house is sold. All of my parents' possessions have now been shrunk to fit inside two large steel travelling trunks. As they are preparing for the journey he receives two very good job offers that promise a successful career and financial security for our family. One is from La Salle Hat Company, makers of the largest-selling Champ Hat.

They are based in Philadelphia. Another is a partnership in a fast-growing manufacturing company. In Alvin's mind they are never a consideration.

The Little Rock Bahá'í community find it hard to bid farewell to our family. In the eighteen months that they have been here they have had a great impact in bringing blacks and whites together and spreading the word on the importance of equality and unity. Gertrude and Alvin are also sad to say goodbye, but my father is already looking ahead to new challenges.

* * *

Nevada Desert, mid-1947

My mother rests against one hub of the Buick, hushing my cries. In the cold box on the back of the car, my father scratches around for the powdered milk. Once a formula to my liking has been made he passes the bottle to my mother. Its rubber teat stops my hungry noise.

Gertrude watches Alvin as he pulls out a blanket for them to sit on and eat sandwiches. He smiles back at her full of the good calm that comes with the certainty of knowing that you are on track with your purpose in life. Gertrude feels her cheeks begin to glow again.

In the weeks leading up to their departure her attention has gradually shifted from what she is leaving behind to the adventure they are beginning. She has no idea what the future holds but she too now is certain His hand is guiding them. Together, she and Alvin will soar.

She leans over, burying her lips in the furry warmth on the top of my head with small smooches. Her fears of travelling with a young baby are also fading. How different this journey is to when she arrived in Birmingham all alone, she thinks. The emptiness of that time creeps back into her bones like a forgotten hunger. She shivers, and then it is gone.

* * *

Marine Phoenix Troop Ship, Pacific Ocean

My mother is carrying a tub of water back to bathe me in the bunkroom that we share with other women. The water sloshes out with each long, sideways lurch of the ship. When she puts me into the tub there is barely enough water to cover my legs. The seas have been very rough since we left San Francisco. There are only four toilets for the women to use, which has made the situation extra tough.

The former troop ship has not been refitted for commercial use by paying passengers. Men and women are still segregated. My mother tries to make things as comfortable as she can for us on this sparse iron barge. She has to beg for a rail that she can put against my bunk so I don't roll out and onto the floor with all the ship's movements.

Alvin lies awake in his bunk somewhere else on board. He knows how difficult this situation is for Gertrude and he prays for calm seas. A tiny moment of doubt enters his mind as to what he is getting his family into. Before it has time to take hold he rolls over and pulls out the cable they received from the Guardian in May. The first few words mean the most to him: 'loving prayers accompanying you'.

* * *

Auckland, July 1947

My mother is wearing an elegant coat with matching felt hat when we disembark on 10 July 1947. She looks regal, more like a movie star than someone who has ventured far from home in a large leap of faith. Even on a shoestring, style has remained a natural point of expression for Gertrude. She stands out against the New Zealand women gathered on the pier to meet the boat. New Zealand has yet to emerge from the long austerity induced by both the Depression and the War. They dress in sober and sombre tones of cloth.

Gertrude is carrying me in her arms. Alvin, in a suit, shepherds her down the gangplank. A picture of us, my parents smiling, is taken to mark the occasion.

An elderly woman with a silver bob and soft, crinkly cheeks moves forward with her daughter to greet us. Alvin darts across, greeting them warmly. He introduces them to Gertrude as Margaret and Beryl Harnish. They are as she has conjured in her imagination from the many times Alvin wrote of them in his letters during the war: very kind, very friendly.

In the Harnish home where we live while my father organizes work, there is a presence missing. Mr Harnish, the good-natured carpenter who 'dared' to approach Alvin at Princes Wharf, has gotten progressively ill in the intervening years and, sadly, has died.

* * *

Alvin strides through the foyer of the immigration building. A slight anxiety pinches his heart. The doors of the lift open and he ushers a well-dressed middle-aged woman inside with a swoop of his arm and 'Good morning, Ma'am.'

'Oh,' she says, taken by his gallantry, 'you're American. What are you doing here?'

'I'm here to speak to immigration about setting up a business,' replies Alvin.

'What is your occupation?'

'Well, I was the Southern Manager for this big American company that manufactured men's shirts.'

'Really,' the woman says, studying him. 'As a matter of fact, I'm trying to sell my own business.' She pauses to weigh Alvin's reaction. 'That is, if you're interested in buying a business.'

Alvin and Gertrude regard this meeting as divine intervention. He becomes the owner of a small clothes manufacturing business. It operates from a shop in a suburb called Kohimarama which is Maori for 'gather light'. The equipment is out of date but Alvin is undaunted. Already the vision of what it could be is big in his mind.

He decides to call his company Wings; he likes the soaring promise of his old employer's name.

Alvin writes to his father in the United States asking him to send new machines. When they arrive they turn out to be the latest in fancy embroidery machines. For a moment he stands shifting his hands from his hips to crossing them in front of his chest. He refuses the disappointment by realizing the market opportunity: producing napery for morning and afternoon tea parties. They are a focal point of the New Zealand housewife's day and every hostess has a tea table ready. Alvin advertises for embroiderers and five Irish women experienced in the trade apply.

They begin to embroider linen and organdie tea settings as well as supplying hem-stitched bed linen and embroidered handkerchiefs. They make pretty and elaborate borders and patterns, the like of which have never before been available to New Zealand women. The business takes off quickly and Alvin is kept on the road, busy with customers and orders. Even with his inbuilt energy, the pace often tires him out. Sometimes when he is on the road he slips into a cinema to have a nap.

My father likes the freedom his work allows him. He again contacts local Bahá'í groups and organizes speaking engagements when he travels to other cities. My mother is also involved with speaking engagements, but being a housewife and mother proves more difficult. The modern conveniences she has grown used to in America, even on a modest income, have not yet reached these parts. I have taken after my father and am full of his active curiosity. Being a non-stop bundle of energy proves a constant and challenging counter to my mother's gentle etherealness.

The Harnish house where we are living is across the road from a lovely swimming beach. Not long after we arrive, my mother hears a knock on the front door. When she opens the door strangers are holding me, dripping wet.

'Oh my goodness!' my mother yelps, clasping her heart, when she sees me.

'We found her crawling into the sea with the waves going over her,' my rescuers say accusingly.

I have bounced my playpen down off the front porch and crawled across the road from the Harnish's home to the beach. Gertrude was in the back yard, singing as she hung out the washing, believing that her small daughter was safely contained in her pen.

When I am three, I wander down the road and two strangers put me inside their car. My mother looks up from the garden when she hears the rubber burn of tyres turning too quickly. She moves faster than she ever has in her life, yelling as loud as she can. Finally, they stop the car and tip me back out saying, 'We were only going to take her for a ride.'

Sometimes my father takes me in the car with him on his working rounds to give my mother a break. Seat belts are as yet unheard of and I stand next to him on the bench seat as he drives, like a small sea captain keeping watch. One day he turns around a corner and the passenger door flings open. I pass through it so quietly that my father is a minute down the road before he realizes his little mate is no longer there.

My father's face has turned the colour of the sheets

we are delivering when I see him again. His breathing is heavy as he grabs me up in his arms and holds on tight. 'I thought I'd lost you,' he says quietly. I am told, very firmly, that I can no longer stand up beside him. I am to sit down and sit very still until we get home. My mother tells me much later she had never seen Alvin so sick with fright.

* * *

Auckland, 1949

The young man does a pirouette in the foyer of the theatre when he sees Alvin and Gertrude descending the staircase after seeing a ballet. Alvin in his suit responds to his friend with an athletic arabesque. Their wives burst into helpless fits of laughter. The two men are always clowning around. They have plenty of opportunities to up the stakes of their repartee as the tall young man, Anthony Voykovic, and his wife Marie are living in our house.

The two couples met soon after we arrived in New Zealand. Alvin and Gertrude were giving a talk at a gathering of the Theosophists Society and Anthony had been asked as a guest to sing, but he was cynical about spirituality, coloured by his childhood experience of the Catholic Church in Croatia. As a boy of ten he served mass for a priest who insisted on continuously predicting the end of the world. The priest would pray to God that the loved ones in the congregation be saved and the rest of the world destroyed. For a very long time after, the young Anthony would kneel before the crucifix in his home and pray: 'Dear Lord, let me see the Second Coming but please don't destroy the world.'

When Anthony hears Alvin saying that the Second Coming has already happened, he cannot believe him. He harangues Alvin with questions that mortify his wife. Alvin has an answer for each of them that is pragmatic yet compelling. Anthony's old fear of the messages inside his head begins to fade. At the end of the night Alvin smiles and shrugs, saying, 'Don't take my word for it, investigate it for yourself.'

Six weeks later Anthony and Marie head inside the Town Hall building one evening and knock on the office door of the Bahá'í Centre. Alvin pulls the door open. 'Well!' he exclaims. 'Of all the people that promised that they would come and investigate, I thought you would be the last ones.'

Anthony is an accomplished actor and singer, but there is not much call for acting, singing and radio work in New Zealand. He struggles to earn money and pay for a rental property. Recognizing the young couple's plight, Alvin and Gertrude invite Anthony and Marie to come to live in our home; they stay two years.

Food and laughter become the cornerstones of our little commune. The comforting smell of frying bacon drifting down the hall to my bedroom on a Sunday morning is my earliest memory. My parents have long ago stopped observing the Jewish food laws of their childhood and Gertrude is a wonderful cook.

Produce is plentiful in New Zealand and Gertrude's natural ease with flavours allows her to develop an impressive range of meals. Marie follows her around in the kitchen asking questions. On Thursday it is Open House for the Bahá'í community, who come for a talk and supper; but there are usually guests for tea every night. Alvin is all-embracing and loves entertaining. People adore him back.

Often the two couples will be sitting down at the dining table and there is a knock on the door. Three people will come in reminding Alvin that he invited them to dinner. 'Sorry, Gertrude, I forgot to tell you,' says Alvin. Gertrude slips quietly away into the kitchen and always manages to stretch the meal. Nobody notices this feat until Alvin, full of bonhomie, asks whether anyone wants seconds. Marie has to stop herself from saying, 'Please Alvin, don't offer them seconds.' She knows how difficult it must be for Gertrude. Somehow, like the five loaves and two fishes, Gertrude always manages to return back to the table bringing more food.

Marie admires my mother's gentleness and grace. She likes listening to the lilting calm of her voice and the way she laughs so sweetly and so often. She records my mother reciting poetry and Gertrude and Anthony begin to sing duets together at events.

People are drawn to both Alvin and Gertrude, but they love them for different reasons. Anthony and Marie have discussed this in the quiet hours, how their friends operate at both ends of the scale. They are deeply loyal and consider Gertrude to be the perfect complement to Alvin's go-getting dynamism.

* * *

Alvin's contacts are expanding. He is a member of various organizations including the World Federalist Movement, the Executive Council of the United Nations Association, the Chamber of Commerce and a businessman's club known as the Optimist Club. He is regularly asked to give talks to them. My father is not one to sit at home and ponder. He prefers to go out and see what he can do about a situation. Often, something spontaneously occurs to him. It has now happened so frequently to him that he knows to follow through on this without questioning.

He is sitting next to Bert Hymer, who is President of the Tip-Top ice cream company at an Optimist Club luncheon. Bert, the Bahá'ís are looking for a place that we can build up for our Summer School.'

'Bert pulls back in his seat to look at Alvin more squarely. 'That's strange that you should talk to me now,' he tells Alvin. 'We bought a piece of property for my daughter when she was getting married, but they'll never make farmers and I'm putting it up for sale today.' Alvin doesn't view this as coincidence. He finishes chewing a piece of lamb. 'Bert,' he smiles, 'that sounds terrific.'

The property is beautiful. Alvin puts his hands on his hips as he surveys twenty-two acres of rich, rain-fed pasture, one curving hill arching into another. A soft, cool breeze comes up through the valley, blowing the long tips of grass. He stares down into it and sees a stream that will be perfect for swimming.

Alvin is excited when he bursts through our front door that evening. 'Gertrude,' he sings out. 'I've seen it! I've seen the property we're going to buy for the Summer School.'

Gertrude wipes her hands on her apron and kisses him. 'Darling, that's wonderful news,' she says, but her enthusiasm is already tempered by another thought. How are they going to get the money to buy it? The property costs more than one thousand pounds. That night she lies in bed and prays about it. She twists the rings on her fingers. Suddenly, it comes to her.

The dawn backlights the thin curtains on their bedroom window. Gertrude gently nudges Alvin awake. 'Alvin, I know how we can get some money.' Alvin peers across at her through half-closed eyes. 'How?' he mumbles sleepily.

'Well, remember the huge diamond ring your mother gave me when we were married? The one we keep in the bank safe. Well, I really can't imagine ever wearing it here in New Zealand. It is quite ostentatious in this society,' she says, wriggling her ring finger. 'And, well, I was thinking that maybe Bert might take it as a downpayment. It must be worth a lot.'

Alvin allows his eyes to fall shut again as he smiles. He likes this selflessness and lack of pretension in his wife. He strokes her arm without opening his eyes again.

Bert Hymer jumps at Alvin's offer of the diamond ring. 'Actually, I would be interested in that,' he says, 'because I've got to go to the States to get new machinery for the icecream business.' In post-war New Zealand you are still not allowed to take large amounts of cash out of the country. The diamond ring provides a solution. Its size of three carats is worth seven hundred pounds. With a large downpayment met, other Bahá'ís, including Hugh

Blundell and Kitty Carpenter, contribute to a collection of smaller amounts to make up the total of the amount required to build the Summer School.

From these early beginnings, the Bahá'í Faith quickly establishes itself. By 1957 the New Zealand Bahá'í community has outgrown its joint National Spiritual Assembly with Australia to form its own. Today, the original Summer School my father found is also the location of the National Bahá'í Centre for New Zealand and there are Local Spiritual Assemblies in all major centres and many smaller towns spread throughout the country.

* * *

Suva, Fiji, September 1951

I giggle as I say the strange new word. 'Na-ma-ste.' I like the way my tongue clicks down hard from the roof of my mouth as I say the first syllable. I repeat the greeting over and over, clapping my hands together, like a prayer, and jumping high in the air to its three measured beats.

'Now, you say "hello",' I command my new friends. They cover their mouths in shy giggles then burst out in a round of 'hello, hello, hello'. We grab hands and form a circle, running around and around yelling each other's native greeting.

It is my fifth birthday and my mother and I are visiting a Bahá'í community in Suva, the capital of Fiji. My playmates are Muslim Indian. They are the darkest children

I have ever seen, but I don't seem to notice the difference between their smooth chocolate colour and my own bony whiteness. Even though we don't speak each other's language we have made up our own code that keeps us amused for hours. I learn how to climb coconut trees and play hide and seek amid the long green spikes in the bush. I am unaware that the hopes of my mother are beginning to unravel.

There has been trouble in the small Bahá'í community. The man who taught them about the Faith has also been borrowing money from Bahá'ís and non-Bahá'ís without paying it back. This is not the first time. Two years earlier Alvin was elected to the National Spiritual Assembly of Australia and New Zealand and asked to go to Suva to see what was going on. The man had disappeared.

Gertrude uses all her gentleness and love to try to explain that this man does not represent the Bahá'í community or what it stands for. She is deeply embarrassed by what has gone on and saddened by the wariness that has now been created about the Faith in some of the local Bahá'ís. Patiently, Gertrude keeps engaging with the community and during this visit there is a remarkable turnaround. A wonderful Muslim lady, Zaynab Khan, and her husband and family decide to become Bahá'ís and act as a catalyst of the early Bahá'í community in Fiji. Gertrude is able to leave Suva feeling that something positive is now building here.

* * *

Sometimes my mother still calls me Keith Wilma, but I have become known as Keithie. Not long after we arrived in New Zealand, it was pointed out that Keith is a man's name. In fact, the Governor-General of New Zealand at the time was Sir Keith Hollioak, making the spelling of my name even more acute.

I am already beginning to understand how the Faith works in my parents' lives. One day when my mother is ill in bed I go in and try to comfort her. 'Shall I say the Greatest Name so you will get better?' I ask. I pray with my parents and in the evening I watch my mother get up out of her sick bed.

My father sometimes travels to Australia both for business and to attend Bahá'í meetings or give talks. As a member of the National Spiritual Assembly of Australia and New Zealand, he is required to attend the bi-monthly meetings. Whether he is there or not, our house is always full of visitors. There are people from Persia and India. The women wear head scarves and saris in shimmering fabrics. We even have a Chinese couple and their child arrive to stay. My parents don't distinguish between the different colours and dress of their guests. All are treated to my father's sense of fun and my mother's warmth.

One time, my father is at a Bahá'í conference in Sydney. He has met up with two of his friends, Frank Khan and Collis Featherstone. Collis is a wonderful Australian-born Bahá'í who will later become a Hand of the Cause. Frank is the first Muslim to become a Bahá'í in Australia, and his son Peter will later become a member of the Universal House of Justice. The three men are unable to afford individual accommodation so they agree to share a room. Unfortunately, it only has one double bed. When my father is tucked up he looks either side of him. 'Well, here we are,' he chuckles. 'A Muslim, a Jew and a Christian all sharing a bed. If that is not the oneness of mankind, what is?'

By 1952, we have become well established in New Zealand. We own our own home and my father has built a factory near where the new Summer School has been built in Henderson. Sometimes we become inadvertently caught in the country's growing pains. Just when New Zealand seems as though it is riding the crest of prosperity, strikes at the waterfront halt its lifeblood of exports and imports, creating a national emergency as troops are brought in to handle the perishing cargo. Nevertheless, my mother views this country as more advanced in many ways than the United States. In her annual round robin letter to friends she writes how social security takes care of the common man and how the indigenous Maori enjoys the privileges of the European. Although, she notes, you can detect that there is a social distinction.

When I am six years old, my parents begin to feel restless. They want to push into new territory where they believe they can be of more use. The south island of New Zealand has no local Bahá'í assemblies and they decide that we will move to Wellington. Gertrude will go ahead to secure a house that can also be used as a centre. My father will stay in Auckland to sell his business and our house.

* * *

Boarding School, Ranui, 1953

The flesh around my toenails is turning purple. I watch the colour deepening, my knees huddled under my chin. I shiver and try to stretch the small thin blanket around my body tighter. I am past the hunger. The sharp arrow of pain in my tummy no longer exists. The feeling of cold has not quite been eliminated. I don't hear Miss Crowe when she comes through the door. I make no sound. My toes now occupy all my senses.

'Keithie, you may join the other children now,' announces Miss Crowe. 'Keithie, did you hear me?' she says, raising her voice when I don't respond. 'I said you may join the other children now.' Her voice filters through my stupor like a distant radio. 'Yes, Miss Crowe,' I murmur.

I am not sure whether Miss Crowe has arrived at her decision to release me because she views my state of being with triumph or with concern. I have been in solitary confinement for a number of days since I was caught stealing vegetables. My initial defiance and howls of protest, I now suspect, have prolonged my ordeal.

My mother has sent me to boarding school while she finds us a new home in Wellington and then, with my father, attends the International Bahá'í Conference in New Delhi, India later in the year. In 1953 there are four major world conferences being held, the conference in Delhi being the last. From there, my parents are planning to go onto Haifa, in Israel, to make a pilgrimage to the Bahá'í Shrines. The boarding school in Ranui is housed in a converted old farmhouse on one hundred and twenty acres of land. The beauty of the land where food for the school is grown mesmerizes my mother when she first goes to inspect it. She is told the animals she sees in abundance are like pets for the children. There is native bush to run around in and beaches nearby.

Most importantly, she and my father feel that the school is unique from a Bahá'í point of view. They are told everything is done through consultation, and co-operation is practised in all things. The children hold courts when someone does something injurious to the whole. 'The object is to free the mind from fear and encourage what talent the child has,' she writes in a letter to friends. And we are to be taught all religions. In a school report back to my mother, she is informed that I am doing well and that I lead the prayer every night in my dormitory. My mother seems satisfied by what she is told and, always believing I am being looked after, does not feel the need to investigate the school further.

In truth, I am not doing well at all. The school is as austere as it is natural. In winter you are only allowed to wear shorts and tops. They only take children to twelve years old, which is appropriate considering the unusual way it is run. In summer you are supposed to wear underpants only and swim naked. Every day, in both summer and winter, you are expected to swim in the river. The one thin blanket we are given does little to protect us in the harsh New Zealand winter.

We must work in the gardens to produce our food. There is never enough to eat and we always need more. I am the youngest and smallest child. One day the bigger children dare me to crawl under the narrow opening in the fence to steal some food from the garden. I am both precocious and hungry enough to agree. When I have picked some vegetables I hold my full hands high above my head, taunting the children who are just out of reach on the other side of the fence.

My celebratory dance is brought to an abrupt end. 'Children!' shrieks Miss Crowe. 'What is going on?' None of the older children come to my defence. Not one dares admit their role. They martyr me with their silence. I am marched off to be put in solitary until my behaviour improves.

This kind of treatment is alien to me. I am used to living in a comfortable environment, the only child of adoring, freethinking, older parents. Restrictions on my movements in life have been few. I respond to this kind of authority not with fear but with insolence and mount a bold, but ill-fated, rebellion.

* * *

Delhi, October 1953

The slogan for the Pioneer Committee in New Delhi is 'Go! Go! Go!'. Alvin has been elected Chairman. He is fired up by the number of people, a cross-section of humanity, who respond to this latest call for pioneering. This is the last of the four conferences that have been held around the world. Over two hundred people

– housewives, businessmen, plumbers, electricians and bakers – have spontaneously volunteered to uproot themselves from their everyday lives. A delegate sitting in the audience watching events unfold makes a simple note in her diary: 'Alvin in fine fettle!'

The Conference has attracted much publicity in New Delhi. Here is a religion that accepts and unites all classes of Indian society and embraces such a diversity of other major religions, races and creeds. Organizers of the Conference, including my father, have been invited early on to meet President Prasad and members of his Cabinet. The President has expressed his admiration of the Bahá'í Faith and its ideals and assured the group of the Indian Government's support in their aims.

Bahá'ís do not have churches as such. In small communities, a meeting house or hall is often used for gatherings. However, in every continent Houses of Worship have been built, and in the future every country and every town and village will have its own House of Worship. Today, there are seven continental Houses of Worship around the world (and an eighth currently under construction in Chile). They all have nine sides; the reason is the association of the number nine with perfection, unity and the word 'Bahá'. In the main halls of the Houses of Worship only the holy verses of the great religions are read or sung. In 1986, a most beautiful House of Worship was erected in New Delhi; it is known in the region as the 'Lotus Temple' because of its petal-like structure. It has won almost every possible international architectural award and is visited by hundreds of thousands of people each year.

Gertrude watches Alvin's enthusiasm spread through the room. He has a light that shines from eyes already able to see the large vision of what they are about to embark on. Through him others are able to envisage it too. This is what first drew her to her husband, and what makes her able to forget, almost, his recent indiscretion. Sometimes she is able to shut down on the hurt that welled up in her when she found out that her husband, yet again, had altered the course of their lives without consulting her. She understands the impulsiveness in him, his need to act as soon as things present themselves. There is nothing gained by trying to stop him, she reasons to herself. Though she has not yet managed to convey to him that, really, she should be consulted first. Equality of husband and wife, and consultation, are centrepieces of Bahá'í marriage.

While Gertrude was away looking for a future home in Wellington, the outline for the Guardian's Ten Year Plan came through. Without hesitating Alvin wrote to ask where they should go next. A cable from Haifa came back with: 'Advise any virgin island Pacific, Love Shoghi.'

The unity of purpose at the conference overcomes any individual doubts about the realities of pioneering. Everyone is uplifted by the possibilities of playing a part in building a new world. News arrives that one pioneer has already had her visa revoked. A report in *The Australian* newspaper on Lilian Wyss's impending pioneering to the Solomon Islands has attracted adverse publicity. Alongside a story that is heavy in its implication that she is off to convert the savages is a strange picture of a snarling Lillian. Burns Philp, the agents for the British High Commission for the Solomons Islands Government, have revoked her contract.

The ease with which intentions can become twisted has a sobering effect. What Alvin remembers of the Solomons is the shelled-out waste from terrifying battles lost and won that litters the land and lies deep and unseen in the sea. He cannot think of a place or a people that need more building up, both in spirit and economy. He looks across at Gertrude and she knows. She knows that Alvin has decided they are to go.

After the conference, there are still three weeks before they are to make their pilgrimage to Haifa. They send a request to the Guardian asking how they can help now. It is met with a simple cable: 'Teach India.' The Bahá'í Faith, with its emphasis on oneness and acceptance of all religions, is seen as being the only religion that has a chance of overcoming the inequalities of the caste system.

Alvin and Gertrude criss-cross nearly four thousand miles of India speaking at schools, lectures and gatherings at the Bahá'í centres that link throughout the country.

Often they turn to each other, holding a hand to their bellies and giving a withering look. Then they shrug. Both Alvin and Gertrude are experiencing the dreaded Bombay Belly, making it a difficult but unforgettable journey.

They travel by train, and usually the friends give them so much food that they decide to give it to the thousands of beggars they see lining the railway stations. When

Members of the Spiritual Assembly of Little Rock Arkansas, 1947 Alvin and Gertrude Blum *in the back row, far left and far right*

Alvin with sister Lilian, Hot Springs, 1946

Gertrude and Keithie arriving in New Zealand, 1948

Bertha Dobbins, Keithie, Alvin and Gertrude, New Zealand 1949

Alvin and Ethel Dawes meeting the President of India, Dr Rajendra Prasad, 1953

Point Cruz in the 1950s

A man-made island in Langa Langa lagoon

Typical Malaitia dress, 1950s, and typical chief's dress

Police recruit, Solomon Islands, 1955

Royal Solomon Island Police officers with Assistant Commissioner Alan Lindley, 1960

Original Police Headquarters, Rove; Quonset huts left by the US troops

Guard House at the old Government House (now the Heritage Hotel)

First Bahá'ís in the Solomon Islands: John Mills, the Blum family, and Bill Gina

Alvin, Gertrude and Keithie, 1955

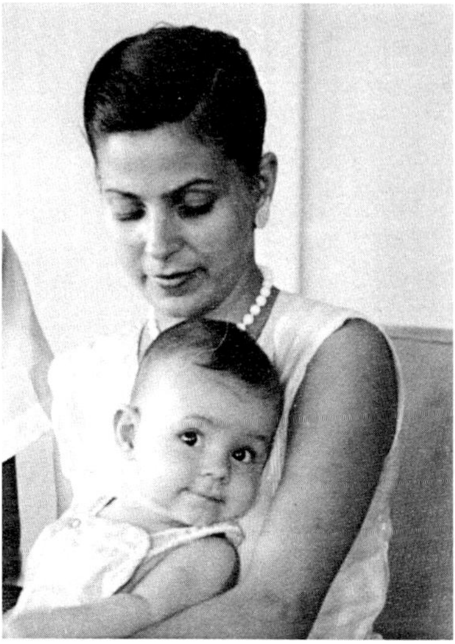

Above: Ruhi with six-month old Leroy

Left: Ruhi Yaganegi, 1955

Keithie and Gertrude with John, Ruhi and Leroy Mills, Honiara, 1957

The first Local Spiritual Assembly of Honiara, 1957. *Back row*: Geoff Dennis, Shebual Mauala, Alvin Blum, Bethuel Bama, John Mills; *front row*: Harry Chandra, Gertrude Blum, George Kwota, Ruhi Mills

they first give the food away, they are mobbed. Gertrude remembers seeing the lines of hungry people during the Depression but never has she seen this need in such overwhelming numbers. She and Alvin search for a way to still give out what they can, deciding to wait and pass out food to people as the train pulls out of the stations.

* * *

Haifa, December 1953

The air is full of salt that has evaporated from the noisy harbour below. Alvin no longer hears the sound of its daily traffic as he takes in the glorious architecture of the newly finished Shrine of the Báb that sits high on Mount Carmel in the centre of Haifa city. The structure is breathtaking in its beauty. Alvin watches how the sun magnifies the luminescence of the Shrine's golden dome. His strides become broader as he propels himself up through the nine elaborate gardens that terrace Mount Carmel's slopes.

Gertrude can hear her breath erupting wheezily as she forces her legs on to catch up with her husband, who is pulling fast ahead. Alvin turns around as if he wants to say something to her. No words arrive. It is as if there is no collection of consonants and vowels that he can attach to what he is seeing and feeling. He exhales in a soft chuckle, marvelling at the inadequacy of words.

Later, the Guardian embraces him. 'Welcome, this is your home.' Alvin can feel a deep aliveness. It begins with a vast peace at his centre that stretches out to become a tingling sensation in his extremities. He realizes that, perhaps for the first time, he does feel at home.

Alvin and Gertrude make the short journey to the Mansion of Bahjí near 'Akká. Bahá'ís consider this place to be one of the holiest on earth. Bahá'u'lláh, the founder of the Bahá'í Faith, is buried here. They are the sole pilgrims and for two days they exist in a state of complete holiness, alone in their prayers at the Shrine of Bahá'u'lláh. Often they pray separately, their timing guided by what they are feeling, rather than the hour of the day or night.

When they return to Haifa, they have dinner with the Guardian, addressing him by his name Shoghi Effendi, and with his wife Rúḥíyyíh Khánum, once, so long ago, the Mary Maxwell Gertrude knew at Green Acre. Rúḥíyyíh Khánum greets Gertrude as her old friend and apologizes for her illness which has kept them apart. Gertrude doesn't go looking for the childhood Mary she was so fond of. Her life is as changed through her marriage to the Guardian as her mother May Maxwell said it would be, years ago in a letter back in New York.

Rúḥíyyíh Khánum takes her through into a red room. It is filled with pieces of furniture from her former life in Canada. They are a poignant reminder of the young Mary Maxwell. Rúḥíyyíh Khánum reaches across and squeezes Gertrude's hand. The pair meet each other's eyes with an understanding that needs no words.

By day, Alvin assists the tour guides for the thousands of visitors to the Shrine of the Báb. 'Oh! Would I love to live and work here,' he later declares to the Guardian.

'Not yet,' the Guardian is reported to reply. For over two thousand years the Jews have been scattered. Now that they finally have their own country, the homeland they have been longing for, the Guardian doesn't feel they can be expected to be interested in the Bahá'í Faith at this time.

'A million Arabs left the country and a million Jews arrive,' he tells them. They are not attached to religion but to race. Materially, the Jewish people will lay a firm foundation and develop the State of Israel. Over time, the Bahá'í institutions at the Bahá'í World Centre will develop. As the Jewish people start to understand the teachings of the Bahá'í Faith and see world leaders acknowledging the Faith, it will become better known and their eyes will be opened. The Guardian sees this as taking a period of time, maybe hundreds of years.

Alvin and Gertrude are needed first in the Solomons and when their work is done, maybe . . . 'Would you like to go to Iran?' he asks suddenly. 'Of course, Shoghi Effendi, every Bahá'í would like to go to Iran,' says Gertrude.

On the table the Guardian unrolls the original map of his Ten Year Plan, 1953–1963, a plan developed to spread the Faith to every country, island and territory in the world, explaining each move in detail. Gertrude and Alvin huddle close, peering over his shoulder at all that has been completed and what is still left undone. Shoghi Effendi speaks at length to them about the importance of the Pacific islands. The Solomons, he says, will become an important link between Australia and Japan, the two magnetic poles of the Pacific.

Shoghi Effendi picks up a beautiful piece of parchment. It is exquisitely water-marked with delicate oval floral designs. 'I got it from Florence,' he tells them. "It will be used for a Roll of Honour and include the names of the pioneers. I would like your names to be on it.' The Roll of Honour, Shoghi Effendi has explained to all Bahá'í communities around the world, is 'designed to perpetuate the memory of the exploits of the spiritual conquerors', those Bahá'ís who have left their homes to become 'pioneers' in countries and territories of the world where so far there are no Bahá'ís at all. Those souls who have risen to the challenge in this first year of the Guardian's Ten Year Plan will be known as 'Knights of Bahá'u'lláh'.

Alvin and Gertrude make eleven pages of notes of what they have just heard. They write it down quickly, not wanting to forget any of the details. Many pilgrims have taken such 'pilgrims' notes'; they have no authority but can be shared as the personal experiences of the pilgrims. Gertrude and Alvin record how Shoghi Effendi has said it is going to be difficult for the Arab world. 'Islam is not a force as a religion, it has now become a political tool and this process is going to develop.'

The East, too, will be confused, they also write down. It is gaining in material wealth, but it is copying the ways of the West. The Bahá'í Administrative Order that is only just beginning to arise will eventually evolve into the World Order of Bahá'u'lláh. Most importantly, they note, he emphasizes the need for pioneers to persevere with their postings.

From Haifa, Alvin writes a letter to his friend Hugh

Blundell in New Zealand. In it he briefly explains that he and Gertrude will not be returning to New Zealand and that they will be leaving for the Solomons directly from Sydney. Hugh is to take the air tickets he is enclosing and exchange it for a ticket to fly me to Sydney. All he wants of our family possessions is a trunk that contains underwear and linens.

In a second letter sent from Colombo my father outlines where furniture is stored and what is to be sold. He also explains that he has written to Miss Crowe and that only the few summer clothes I have been given to wear are to be sent with me. 'We plan to take Keithie with us to the Solomons,' he writes, 'but if we find the place is not suitable for her will send her back either to Ranui or someplace in Australia.'

* * *

Auckland Harbour, January 1954

I feel the wetness creeping through my best shoes. My short white socks are soon sodden and cold. I am seated on the ground floor of the flying seaplane bound for Rose Bay in Sydney. The excitement of seeing my parents again is fast being replaced with an escalating anxiety that the plane will sink. Water is seeping through its old rusted base, turning the floor into a small pond. This is the last seaplane that will fly between Auckland and Sydney.

My parents' New Zealand friends have written my name and contact details on a piece of cardboard. It is strung around my neck like a dog collar. I stare down at my chest and flip the board to read my name.

Since I was punished for stealing food to eat at boarding school, angry red bumps that burn and make me want to scratch have been erupting on the surface of my skin. I am not yet sure what they are called, but I know that they began showing up around the same time that some of my certainty about the world being a good and safe place left me.

* * *

Sydney, January 1954

I see my mother's face in the distance. Her long hair is swooped back in a pretty French roll and she is smiling at me with her glistening green eyes. My father dashes forward, scooping me up in his big arms and hugging me tight. I throw my arms around his strong neck and cling tight. For the first time in many months I feel happy and warm.

A friend has lent us a holiday house on one of the small inlet islands of Sydney's many waterways. We get into a little boat to row across to it. That night my mother cooks a beautiful stew. It tastes more yummy than I can ever remember. I gobble it up fast, smiling at her in between my slurping mouthfuls.

As I am getting ready for bed I do a little dance. I feel so light and free again that I don't think to complain about all my recent ordeals. When I wake up I run through the house singing good morning to my parents.

Soon my father receives news that we won't be granted visas for the Solomons. No explanation is given. He strides around the house, huffing with frustration. I watch him making laps round the small living room. Finally, he stands still. 'Gertrude,' he announces, his hands on his hips. 'I'm going to Canberra.'

Alvin is kept waiting a long time before he is able to meet with the visa officials. When he finally is given an audience, he shakes hands with a smile, sublimating his frustration. They meet him with experienced impassiveness. Alvin becomes increasingly restless with their questioning. Eventually, the dam bursts. 'Look,' he says, raising his voice, 'there wouldn't be a Solomon Islands if it wasn't for our boys. Thousands of our boys died so that we could hand the Solomons over to the British on a silver platter. And you are denying me going up there?'

The room goes silent. One official's blank face flushes with shame. Another fiddles noisily with the papers in front of him and clears his throat. 'Well then, Mr, er, Blum,' he says, capitulating. 'Perhaps we can arrange tourist visas to assist you. But they will only be for two months.'

'I'll take it,' says Alvin.

When he returns, his triumph becomes clouded by a different kind of pain that is growing inside his belly. I have never seen my father bent double and groaning. I rush to his side to try and comfort him, my little hands stroking his cheeks and arms. He grabs them and plants snuffly kisses in my palms. 'I'll be alright,' he tries to reassure me.

Alvin is booked into hospital for a kidney stones operation. My mother begins to pray in earnest. I try to be as good as I can. From the hall, I can see her on her knees in her bedroom. As she cooks I hear her saying the Greatest Name over and over, in a breathy, almost silent, voice.

On the day before they are to operate, my father passes the stones. He and my mother never doubt for a second that this is anything other than divine intervention.

10

A Divine Purpose

There are four qualities which I love to see manifested in people:
first, enthusiasm and courage;
second, a face wreathed in smiles and a radiant countenance;
third, that they see all things with their own eyes and not through the eyes of others;
fourth, the ability to carry a task, once begun, through to its end.

Attributed to Bahá'u'lláh
(Furútan, *Stories of Bahá'u'lláh,* no. 60)

MV Malaita, February 1954

He hears someone in the crowd down below yelling his name. Alvin swings around sharply, knocking his elbow on the gangplank rails. A hand is waving at him and he traces his eyes down its arm until he sees the face of a Bahá'í friend. 'Telegram!' his friend shouts, glad he has been able to catch the Blums before they sail to the Solomons.

Alvin walks back down the long gangplank. The cable contains four simple words: 'LOVING PRAYERS SURROUNDING YOU. SHOGHI.' When he shows it to Gertrude, she gasps and clutches it to her heart. He watches the light returning to her face.

Since hearing about the high incidence of malaria and other insects in the Solomon Islands my mother has been worrying about my well-being. Instead of going away, the boils on my body have spread, forming new lunar-like clusters of cranky welts. An apprehension has been building inside her. Alvin responds by quickening the pace of his decisions, not stopping to allow for her doubts. My father is aware the stakes are high. They have packed up their comfortable lives for a very uncertain future. For both of them this cable from the person they trust and revere most has arrived at the right moment. It acts again as a divine confirmation for the new life they are about to embark upon.

My father looks back up at the *MV Malaita*. It is a hulking old grey tub of a passenger and cargo ship owned by Burns Philp that also served as an Australian troop ship during the war. 'We never get on these super duper ships we see in advertisements in the magazines,' my father quips. My mother smiles, squeezing my hand and slipping an arm through Alvin's.

My father has already heard about the ship's Captain, Brett Hilder. When he is told that Hilder is known for being salty and turning the air blue he chortles to himself. Brett, like his watercolour artist father J. J. Hilder, paints and draws, producing watercolour landscapes of the South Seas and portraits. A Bahá'í friend has been an artist's muse for Brett. She has written a letter of introduction which she hopes might pave a smooth way in our relations with the Captain.

After reading the letter, Hilder pulls himself up to his

full height and lets out a loud sigh. 'Well, I don't much like having missionaries on board,' he says. 'They always bring the worst storms.'

'Oh Captain Hilder, but we're not missionaries,' Gertrude pleads, quickly falling for his bait.

Brett catches my father's eye and winks. Alvin wipes a hand across his face to cover his smirk. It is the beginning of a firm friendship that will last the rest of my father's life.

* * *

'Owwww,' I holler from the bathtub. My squeals wrong-foot my mother. She stumbles, then rushes across to see what is the matter with me. 'Owwww, Mummy,' I yell again. On board the *MV Malaita* we have to bathe in seawater, then use a bucket of fresh water to rinse off. The salt has popped open seven of my boils. It feels like someone is running burning candles over my skin. My mother sees the cause of my distress and tries to comfort me. She dabs at me awkwardly with a towel. She only has the use of one hand as she too is sore and in trouble.

The *MV Malaita* makes a number of stops on its three-week journey to the Solomons: the first being Norfolk Island, next Vila, then Santo in the New Hebrides. When we anchor off Norfolk Island, the ship lowers a dinghy for passengers to go ashore. On our return journey back to the ship, the seas turn terrifyingly rough. When the dinghy reaches the ship, you have to grab hold of the rickety gangplank lowered down the side and yank your way up to the deck of the ship. People squeeze forward, rushing to get off the dinghy. Gertrude is forced to grab hold of the edge of the dinghy to balance herself and as the dinghy hauls high against the boat, the chain of the gangplank crushes her hand, stripping the flesh from her finger and tearing ligaments from bone and muscle. There is a doctor on board who treats the wound daily, but it has become infected and she suffers terrible fevers. The doctor gives Gertrude painkillers, but it is clear further treatment is required. When we anchor at Port Vila in the New Hebrides, now known as Vanuatu, Gertrude undergoes an operation at the mission hospital of Paton.

The presence of Mrs Bertha Dobbins, a fresh pioneer to the New Hebrides from Australia, is a welcome distraction. Bertha, who has been named a Knight of Bahá'u'lláh, has been having a most difficult time and is lonely and tired. When my parents see her living conditions they invite her on board to have meals with us. She unburdens her trials to them, from the everyday difficulties of sourcing food to frightening encounters with rebel gangs.

Bertha spends much of the two days we are in port on board the *MV Malaita.* When she finishes her last meal, she puts down her knife and fork and says, 'My God, this has been a bit of heaven. Oh, I wish you could stay here a bit longer and I could get some more of this good food.'

An hour later a crewmember announces over the loudspeaker that the ship's engine turbine has broken down and we will be staying another day as it is fixed. 'Bertha,' my father hoots, 'there's divine intervention. You'll be able to enjoy another three meals with us.'

At other meal times Brett Hilder often joins us, staying with my parents late into the evening. Alvin has met his match. Together they spar with each other over world politics, the economy, religion. These great, long battles are interspersed with suggestive schoolboy humour and uproarious giggles. Gertrude sits quietly, staring out as if seeing something beyond what is here in the room. Occasionally, she injects a sage-like remark into the conversation. Often it has little to do with what the two men are talking about. Alvin raises his eyebrows, and lifts his fingers from the table with a smile and a small shrug as an apology to his new mate.

When the *MV Malaita* pulls into Santo, my father walks into town and comes across a Mauritian Frenchman called Donald Gubbay. Gubbay is a businessman who is involved with a Japanese fishing company and brings Japanese fishermen to Santo as employees. Alvin connects with his entrepreneurial spirit and finds it interesting that Gubbay is already working with the Japanese, so soon after the war, in these parts. Soon events will develop to unite them in an unexpected way.

* * *

Honiara, 1 March 1954

My father hoists me high in his arms. 'Dad-dy,' I giggle as I pretend to topple over his shoulders. It is four o'clock in the morning on the first day of March and my parents have gotten me out of bed to join them on the top deck of the boat as we pull into the harbour just off Honiara on the island of Guadalcanal.

We peer through the dark trying to get a sense of our new home. I listen to my parents saying prayers as we wait what seems a very long time for an outline to emerge in the cool of the dawn. Mountains, rich with volcanic soil and shrouded in green, rise precipitously, almost from the water's edge, with small houses dotted here and there. My mother's first impressions of Honiara are of how fresh and verdant it looks.

My father goes in search of Brett Hilder to say farewell and thank him. Alvin thrusts a book of Bahá'u'lláh's writings into his hands. 'Read this and we can argue about it next time we meet,' he says. Brett laughs heartily, shaking Alvin's hand. 'Look forward to it,' he smiles. 'Alvin,' he adds, bending close like a conspirator, 'as much as I'm fond of Gertrude, I don't think she understood any of our jokes.' Alvin smiles back, slapping Brett's shoulder as he goes.

A dinghy rows us across to the beach. I watch the morning sun make sparkly diamonds on the blue water. How pretty, I am thinking. I have no idea that we are crossing what is known as Iron Bottom Sound and that deep down beneath this sweet surface lie sunken World War II battleships and the countless bodies of doomed men, unable to be raised from their watery grave.

There is no wharf for disembarking, but when my parents step onto the sand they are triumphant. My father lifts me up again and we all hug. The glory of the moment is short-lived. 'My love, do you think there are any taxis?'

Gertrude asks Alvin. He is stumped. For a while we stand a forlorn threesome with our two small bags. A passing priest sees us. 'Hello, do you need a lift?' he shouts getting out of his car.

Father Norman Palmer is a wonderful man who will later become Archbishop Palmer. I stick my head out of his car window and feel the lukewarm breeze on my face. It is only early morning but already the wet tropical heat of the day has begun. My mother stares out too with a slow, sinking feeling. The place looks like nothing she has ever seen before. In fact, it looks like nothing. There is no town, just a Shell company sign, a garage, and a few half-moon-shaped, corrugated iron huts, known as Quonset huts, that were left behind by the United States Army.

Honiara is the new post-war capital of the British Solomon Islands Protectorate, but there is little to distinguish it as such. It is also a little desired colonial outpost. Journalists of the time describe it as 'essentially a British headache'. The town of Honiara has been created out of war. The scars of this are a still open wound in its lack of development.

The British first arrived in the Solomon Islands in 1893 in an attempt to restore order over the series of reprisals and massacres caused by the harsh, often brutal, recruitment of islanders for sugar plantations in Fiji and north Queensland, a system known as 'blackbirding'. Before the war, the capital of the Solomons was across from Honiara on the island of Tulagi in the Florida Island group and Guadalcanal was populated only by a few scattered plantations and islanders.

During World War II the British Administration closed down their administrative offices and evacuated many of the expatriates, as the Japanese roared down through the Pacific in an astounding show of their naval and air strategy and took over the then capital Tulagi in early 1942.

A number of the British and Australian administrators decided to become 'Coastwatchers', a term coined that basically meant spies. This small group of extremely courageous men were accompanied by groups of Solomon Islanders, known as 'Scouts', many of whom had been police officers before the war. These men went deep into the hilly terrain around strategic areas of the Solomons with only a shortwave radio and minimum supplies, relying on the islanders to feed and shelter them. They would make frequent contact with the American bases in nearby Santo, giving Japanese positions and updating them on developments.

The Coastwatchers reported that a strategic airfield was being built by the Japanese near Lunga Point on Guadalcanal. The American High Command knew that if the Japanese were allowed to complete the airstrip, certain defeat of the Pacific and Australia was imminent. A fleet of ships carrying the US First Marine Division landed at Red Beach, Guadalcanal at 0700 on 7 August 1942. Their arrival caught the Japanese by surprise, and the Americans were able to walk the two miles to the airstrip and secure the field with relative ease. The Japanese Navy, now alert to the American invasion, came in and pounded the navy vessels that were unloading supplies for the Marines. The US Navy had to withdraw immediately, leaving the Americans with little food or ammunition. It was a precarious situation.

Both sides were ill-prepared for the punishing conditions of Guadalcanal; the humid heat, the thick tangle of jungle, the drowning rain that left them constantly wet, almost afloat, in their foxholes. The Japanese never imagined that the biggest enemy they would face would be the great hoards of tiny insects, known as the Anopheles mosquito, which carried the deadly disease malaria that infested the island. The American code name for Guadalcanal was Cactus.

The thinnest of margins stood between failure and success. Victory flopped back and forth between sides in a fierce and prolonged struggle. The narrow airstrip, known as Henderson Field, became the scene for one of the bloodiest battles, the strategic turning point of the war in the Pacific. By day the Japanese pummelled it from the hills with field guns. At night, planes dropped flares, creating a daylight that left nowhere to hide from the bombardments of Japanese warships lurking offshore. In one twenty-four-hour period, fifty-three Japanese bombs and shells hit Henderson.

Control of the airstrip eventually remained with the Americans, and when enough blood had been spilled, and the Japanese, sick, hungry and desperate, their supply lines thwarted by bombardment, eventually retreated back up the 'Slot', a narrow waterway, to New Guinea, the battle for Guadalcanal, a place that no side really wanted, ended on 9 February 1943. Both sides had suffered terrible losses. By the end of the war, in 1945, the Americans had lost over seven thousand men, and the Japanese twenty-two thousand in this region alone.

The American army turned Honiara into their own base to fight out the war in other islands further north. They developed a town consisting of administration huts, a hospital and a string of cinemas, mostly open air with log seats, to entertain the nearly twenty thousand troops remaining on the island as support.

In August 1945 a Peace Treaty was signed between Japan and the United States. When the British reluctantly returned to the Solomons, they shifted the capital from Tulagi to Honiara on Guadalcanal, installing themselves in the makeshift iron dwellings, known as Quonset huts, that the US Army had left behind and stubbornly refusing to pour money into anything new. They turned down an offer by the United States to build a road around the island in return for a small stipend of around US$10 per truck and $50 per grader. The Americans, irritated by the bloodymindedness of the British and unable to ship the equipment back to the United States due to the high cost of the freight, drove all of it into the sea.

By the time my family arrives in 1954 there are about seven thousand Solomon Islanders on Guadalcanal and about one hundred thousand in total scattered throughout the nine main provinces of the Solomons. Europeans number around three hundred, comprising British Government workers and missionaries, and there are around five hundred Chinese, former indentured plantation labourers who have chosen to stay and make a living as traders and shopkeepers.

* * *

My mother bumps her finger, still sore and healing, against the car door. She moans softly, then drags the rest of her body up out of the priest's car. He has dropped us at the Woodford Hotel, named after Charles Woodford, the first British High Commissioner, and situated on the present site of the Mendana Hotel. This is the only accommodation in this town. It has nine rooms that were once United States officers' sleeping quarters and little has been done to them since. Arranged in a 'V', the rooms look like a collection of horse pens.

Our room is utilitarian and bare. It is too small for the three of us and I already feel cooped up inside the boundaries of its handkerchief-size rectangle. I make up an obstacle course, bouncing on beds and back around to begin again. I am seven years old and full of energy. 'Keith Wilma, hush,' my mother gently pleads. I stand still for a moment, watching her slow struggle to unpack our few belongings. The urge to wriggle creeps back up through me. I want to go outside and run and play. I bunny hop across to the window and wrap my fingers over the top of the ledge to rest my chin on its wooden frame. Suddenly, I see something very strange.

There is a very dark woman working outside near our window. She has enormous fuzzy hair as well as big hoopey rings through her ears and through her nose. A skinny smoking pipe sticks out of her mouth. Most amazing to me is that she is wearing no top. She has big bare breasts the shape of watermelons, and only a skirt sits below an enormous belly that I'm sure must have a baby inside, and there is another baby tied to her back. Every time she swings her axe to chop wood, her breasts sway side to side in rhythm. Her mouth and teeth are red. Later I will learn this is from chewing betel nut and she has what is known as a billum bag slung around her neck that stores the betel nuts

I am glued to the window. Gertrude can't believe her very active little girl can stand still for so long. Eventually, I peel my eyes away to turn back to my mother. 'I think she's very, very rude, mum,' I say sternly. 'Very, very rude.'

Soon I learn that all Solomon Islander women show their breasts and they wear skirts because for them showing their legs is rude. The men wear a *sulu* (wraparound skirt) and no shoes. They have big, broad strong feet and wide toes that help them climb high up into the steep mountains. If they are working for the Government they wear a shirt with shorts or a *sulu* and maybe some flip-flop sandals. Sometimes, if they've just arrived from the bush they might only have a little loincloth tied around their hips. Many have decorations through their nose and ears and they wear a little basket around their neck to store their betel nut or shell nut. Betel nut is regularly chewed by the Solomon Islanders. Together with powdered lime it acts as a relaxant and hunger suppressant. But I notice something else: the chewing of betel nut also leads to the unpleasant habit of spitting out a red juice. It creates unsightly red stains wherever it lands.

* * *

My father pushes open our hotel room door and it shuts hard behind him. He sits on the edge of a bed balancing his elbows on his knees and his head in his hands. 'Oh, Gertrude,' he exhales, wiping his fingers down his face as he looks back up at his wife. I can see a large damp patch on my father's back where his shirt is sticking with sweat. Alvin can feel himself quickly tiring in the tropical heat. It compounds his worries about how he will get a job in this place.

My mother takes his hand in her one good hand, holding onto it without saying anything. She too is struggling with conditions she wasn't made for. Each day she has to walk several miles down the road in the ninety degrees heat to the hospital to get her finger dressed. It offers the most basic of services and still bears as its name the army area it was given – No. 9. 'Alvin, this place needs a taxi service,' she says one day after she returns.

Alvin is already aware of this. He can see plenty of things this town needs but what he needs first is a job. Since we arrived, Alvin has been on the lookout for work each day. He approaches it like a job: up early and out the door. He introduces himself to as many people as he can around town searching for opportunities. The owner of the Woodford Hotel, an ex-Australian Coastwatcher called Ken Hay, has already told him that there is no work for him. The only other jobs going are with the British Government. It already has become rigidly clear that Americans are very unwelcome and will not gain employment.

The British Government is still somewhat irritated and

annoyed by the way the US Army had the resources and equipment to defend the Solomons. The resentment has only grown deeper with the uprising of Ma'asina Ruru, also known as Marching or Custom Rule.

During the war the Solomon Islanders watched the Americans bring in a stream of cargo – planes, ships, supplies, trucks – and rapidly erect buildings. They had never imagined such wealth. Nor had they ever seen black soldiers. The US Army was largely segregated but islanders looking on only saw how black men wore the same uniform, ate the same food in the mess room and slept in the same type of tents as their white counterparts. The Americans were also very generous, giving the islanders food and gifts in payment for their scouting services in assisting the Coastwatchers. Between 1942 and 1945, over two million Americans passed through Guadalcanal and they became known to the islanders as 'Joes'.

When the British Government returned after the war, the islanders didn't want to go back to the boy/master relationship that had previously existed. 'We don't want you to rule us,' they declared. 'We want the Americans to rule us.' A series of revolutionary strikes and civil disobedience threatened to overturn the British Administration. It was contained when the British Government brought in a war ship as a show of strength and leaders were rounded up and put in prison at the end of 1948.

At the time of our arrival in 1954, these tensions are still felt most powerfully on Malaita, a large island to the north-east of Guadalcanal peopled by fiercely independent warriors. It was here in 1927 that Commissioner Bell of the British Administration was murdered when collecting taxes from the Kwaio people of East Malaita, and in the mist-shrouded mountains at its dark centre, cannibalism is still practised. The British Administration has the slimmest of holds on this island. It introduced a district council in 1953 to give some semblance of authority to locals but relies on the Christian missions to keep social order.

Two weeks after our arrival our fortune changes. My father is called across to see the hotel owner Ken Hay. 'Blum, my manager has resigned and he's leaving on the next boat. It will be six weeks before I can get anyone else in on the next ship, how would you feel about taking over as manager?'

Alvin says yes immediately. He already knows he and Ken have a different mindset. No Solomon Islanders are allowed to stay in the hotel. But it is the first time he has been offered any sort of foothold that will enable us to stay in Honiara.

On 21 March Shoghi Effendi, Guardian of the Bahá'í Faith, includes 'Alvin and Gertrude Blum, Solomon Islands' in the list of pioneers inscribed on the Roll of Honour. They are named as Knights of Bahá'u'lláh.

* * *

Before he sits down he looks at a large, wide folder piled high on the desk of the Head of Police. Alvin sees the name Blum written on the front in thick letters. He glances across at Gertrude. 'It's got our name on it,' he says simply. 'Oh my,' she whispers.

In the next room there are two voices discussing something in a low tone. Among the many words that are muttered they decipher one: 'Bahá'í.' Alvin sees the colour draining from his wife's face. It has become obvious that they have been thoroughly investigated. He tries to make light of the situation. 'Well, we'd better come clean,' he mutters in a stage whisper.

My parents have been called in by the police who want to speak to them, ostensibly, about their tourist visas. In an odd twist of fate, the Chief of Police was previously head of police in Haifa during the war. He likes the Bahá'í gardens on Mount Carmel, but his knowledge of the Faith is thin. He thinks it is a Muslim sect. 'And you're Jewish, aren't you?' he says. It isn't really a question. 'How are you mixed up with this faith? They're supposed to be enemies aren't they?'

'No, no, it's not like that at all,' says Alvin easily. He passes him a photo taken at the end of the conference in India. Pictured are people from England, America, Europe and India. 'It's not the Muslim faith at all,' he says; then he points to the diverse ranges of colours, shapes and sizes in the picture. 'As you can see, it's a world religion.'

The Chief of Police exhales heavily and peers at them through narrow eyes. He tells them he knows about Lilian Wyss having her visa cancelled. He tells them he knows that they are friends. Gertrude wants to steal a glance at Alvin, but doesn't dare.

'Why do *you* want to stay here?' asks the Chief of Police.

'We'd like to build up a business here. I've been here during the war and I know that the place has been devastated and there are no amenities here. I'm a businessman,' Alvin says confidently, 'and I can really help build up the Solomon Islands. And we're here to promote unity. Racial unity.'

The Chief sighs, often and rudely, as he listens to Alvin explain the Bahá'í message. It is beyond his immediate comprehension why these Americans, particularly with a young child, would want to come to this godforsaken place for any other reason than to gain some advantage. The details of which, he is convinced, will emerge through his continued interrogation.

He combs his eyes beadily through the papers as Alvin speaks. Gertrude feels as though the tiniest aspects of their lives and faith are being dissected; their outer and inner worth judged and weighed. She no longer hears the hostile questions being directed at them. Alvin can deal with the answers, she trusts. Her best role, she has decided, is to pray.

They are there for hours. The sun continues to heat the Quonset hut, adding to the pressure cooker ambience of the Chief of Police's office. Beads of sweat are emerging on his brow, his cheeks flaring. Finally, he flings himself back in his chair. Alvin views it as a small sign of surrender.

'Well, the hotel can't be left without a manager,' he says gruffly, tapping the table with the bottom edge of the pile of papers he is clutching with both fists. 'You can stay for now, but I'll be watching you, Blum. Do you hear me?'

* * *

In his sleep he thinks he hears the thunderous clap of artillery. Alvin wakes with a start. He hears the noise again. Two men are hammering on the door of our hotel room. 'Open up the bar, Mr Blum,' they slur.

'Boys, go away,' he shouts sleepily. 'It's 5 a.m. I'm not opening the bar for hours.'

In 1954, Solomon Islanders are not allowed to drink in public bars, and this will remain unchanged until nearer independence in 1978. Only expatriates, including Fijian and Chinese nationals, can go to the few bars that currently exist in the town.

The men keep banging on the door, waking my mother and me. My father gets out of bed and opens it. He sees two Fijian workers from last night in the bar. 'Look, boys,' Alvin says, pulling himself full height. 'Go away, sleep it off, come back later.'

This is beginning to become a regular occurrence. The drinking past bar hours, the banging on the door. 'Alvin, we can't stay here,' Gertrude whispers. 'Keithie . . .' She trails off when she sees Alvin nodding his head wearily. 'I know, Gertrude. I know.'

For weeks my father has been looking for a house for us to live in. The majority of homes are owned and occupied by the British. The few others are all occupied. One day my father hears of a plantation house on three hundred acres that has suddenly, and unusually, become available on the outskirts of the town. The Setons, Australian planters who are the owners, have said the tenants are moving out and are willing to rent it out again shortly.

My parents go to view the house, inching up the near vertical climb in the second-hand station wagon Alvin has bought. The road is made of dirt and the constant rains have bored deep holes into it. 'Oh my. My word,' murmurs Gertrude as the car makes another sideways lurch. Her spirit sinks further when they see the house. The land is an overgrown knot of creepers and littered with old army refuse. The house is an old dilapidated army mess. When she walks on the floorboards she hears them sag creakily beneath her feet. On the windows the wire netting is torn and rusted. Cobwebs hang from the ceiling. There is no running water or electricity.

'Oh my,' she says again. Alvin puts an arm around her shoulders. They walk outside to the edge of the property. Through the denseness of vines and palms they spy something quite amazing. From up on this hill, all of Honiara and its harbour rolls over at their feet. It helps them to see beyond the desperate state of the living conditions and they agree to take the property on.

Alvin is concerned about the way his finances are dwindling. Each week he pays twenty-five pounds for our tiny room in the hotel. Our stay, however, has allowed my father to begin to develop two business opportunities. Already, he has taught an islander how to drive his car and put in place Honiara's first taxi service. He also notices that guests are having trouble getting their laundry washed; it comes back late, often ruined. He writes to the Chamber of Commerce in Australia to find out how to acquire a commercial washing machine. They send him a trade magazine advertising availability of large machines and Alvin puts in an order. He now has to find a building to house the laundry.

While Gertrude oversees the cooking in the hotel kitchen, Alvin tends to the overall running of the place. The 'boys' bar' that is attached to the hotel continues to cause them unnecessary grief. It is the drinking hole frequented by Fijian, Indian and Chinese workers. As a Bahá'í, Alvin is tolerant of other people drinking, even though he himself abstains. What he finds more difficult to tolerate is the excessive drinking of the workers.

Officially, closing time for the bar is 10 p.m. Unused to long days in the heat, Alvin often takes himself off to bed before closing. The Chief of Police, to his word, has been keeping an eye on Alvin. My father is given warnings about breaking the liquor licensing laws and not closing down the bar at the required times.

When Ken Hay returns back from a trip to Australia, the Chief of Police doesn't hesitate in telling him of my father's lax action. Hay is also upset about my father's taxi service offering to take guests to dinner at the Lantern Bar Restaurant in Chinatown, owned by the Chan Wing family who today own Honiara Hotel. While my parents view this as an opportunity for guests to experience a change in menu during their stay, Hay sees it as syphoning money from his restaurant. In July he fires both Alvin and Gertrude.

The Seton house for rent becomes available just as we have to vacate the hotel. My parents view this synchronicity as yet another answer to prayer. But it is not long before they face another test. The Chief of Police has been informed of my parent's unemployed state. He calls them demanding a bond of five hundred pounds if we are going to stay.

Alvin sends a cable off to Horace Holley, their old friend who is secretary of the National Assembly of the Bahá'ís of the United States, to pass on the request for five hundred pounds to the National Spiritual Assembly of Persia which oversees the Solomons. The money is cabled and the Chief of Police agrees to let them stay. In the very same week, the Setons demand that we either buy or vacate their land. Alvin sends off another cable. This time it is to the Asian Teaching Committee requesting five hundred pounds loan for a downpayment on the house.

My parents try to work out their finances over the dinner table. I lie in bed listening to my father's voice rise and ebb over my mother's even interjections. Eventually, I hear their voices relax into a rhythmic whisper and I know they are praying.

Help arrives in the form of the District Commissioner of Guadalcanal, who has initially been quite cold and unfriendly to us. Our friend Hugh Blundell in New Zealand was a close friend of the officer's father, who also knew Alvin during the war. He has written to him to introduce my parents and the Faith. The Commissioner's attitude towards us has suddenly become very friendly and he has put in a good word to the Administration. This goes some way towards proving that my parents have no intention of being subversive.

The Commissioner contacts my father and advises him that the Setons have no right to force us to buy. 'They owe so much back taxes on the land and they've violated the lease, so we're taking it away from them,' he explains. 'We've got plans for the land, but if you want two or three acres along with the house we'll sell it to you.' Alvin smiles broadly, clasping the man's right hand between his two and shaking it hard. It is his first friendly encounter with a member of the Administration. They are issued with a ninety-nine-years lease on 2.5 acres and a deal is negotiated allowing my parents to pay off the house and land at ten pounds per week.

Our new home sits high on stilts and is riddled with white ants. Soon after we move in I am skipping inside and I fall through the floor. My parents work very hard to make it livable, replacing the floorboards, repainting and rescreening the mosquito netting in windows. It is some time before they realize they must hitch on to our nearest neighbour's electricity and water which is half a mile away. Eventually we have running water and electricity that is available for only six hours each day. In 1955, there are one hundred telephones in Honiara. We apply and are given the phone number 5.

The overgrown land needs to be cleared, new trees planted, and some basic landscaping of the area established. Painstakingly, work begins on the property – cutting down the long grass, chopping the dead trees, making paths and establishing the garden. One gardener helps my parents, but it is hot, hard work and takes years to get it into proper shape. In their mind's eye, they already see that this beautiful area will make a wonderful Bahá'í Centre and they keep dedicating their efforts to bring about this vision.

* * *

Gertrude stares at the sequins on the expensive gown, now dull, shrivelled discs. She presses her lips together hard, but her emotions are too strong to be held back. All the pressures of the past few months burst forth in great, gulping sobs.

When a Quonset hut became available on Mendana Avenue, the main street running through Honiara, Alvin and Gertrude viewed it as yet another sign of Bahá'u'lláh's blessing. Rental space in town was a rare coup. In 1955, Mendana Avenue had only three or four trading stores. The only other buildings were the American Quonset huts that were used by the British Administration as their offices. They would now be able to offer the town its first laundry service with the washing machines that already had arrived before they left Woodford Hotel.

In his head, Alvin had already worked out that the business could expand with the offer of dry cleaning. The British operate with unbelievably '*pukka pukka*' formality. Despite the heated conditions of this tiny colonial outpost they insist on keeping up appearances with stiff white shirts, dinner jackets and white monkey suits at their social whirl of cocktail parties and formal occasions, while their wives dress in glamorous gowns of silk and satin.

Refitting the Quonset hut with windows and setting up the business has taken two months, draining their personal finances of two hundred pounds. Alvin has launched the business with headed stationery outlining their services. 'Honiara Taxi and Laundry Service', it says, announcing that 'Something new has been added to the community life of Honiara. A complete laundry service is now available for your convenience.'

They offer services for the family and for the bachelor, adding 'men & women' in brackets beside this term. They also have a long list of prices per item from baby nappies to socks. 'All deliveries subject to strikes, power cuts, government regulations and acts of God,' Alvin can't resist adding to their service statement. It also informs the public that a dry cleaning plant will soon be installed.

Alvin buys a dry cleaning steam iron presser from New Guinea and orders in a magazine that shows how to make up your own dry cleaning equipment. This involves filling one forty-gallon drum with sand and charcoal, then setting it atop another forty-gallon drum. White spirit dry-cleaning fluid is pumped through the sand and charcoal, cleaning the clothes below. They are able to do up to seven garments at a time.

The British still harbour suspicions about the Americans with the strange faith. Business has been terribly slow and Alvin spends much of his time waiting at the wheel of his 24-hour cab service trying to keep his small family afloat. One day the wife of the High Commissioner favours us with one of her sequinned evening gowns to be dry-cleaned.

Gertrude knows the importance of this single garment. If the High Commissioner's wife, Mrs Gutch, is satisfied she will talk about it and our custom will be established. She allows herself a little daydream, imagining friendly people and easier times.

'Don't you iron this one,' Gertrude instructs one of their islander staff. She will look after the gown herself, turning it inside out so as not to damage the sequins. When she returns to the laundry the next day, she sees that the boy has not listened to her. He has already steam-pressed the gown, destroying the sequins.

It is some time before Gertrude is able to stop her tears. Alvin is out on a taxi run. She wrings a hankie in her hands, wondering how she is going to break this latest news to him.

When the knot in her chest has grown so tight that she can no longer breathe, she lets out one last sob and begins to pray. Suddenly, she remembers something. She hurries to the back of the hut where she has stored a sari someone gave her in India. When she pulls it out she holds it up against the gown. The sequins are identical. She sits down, carefully unpicking the sequins, then transferring them to the dress of the High Commissioner's wife.

That night I watch my mother performing this painstaking process. The next morning when I wake up, I hear my mother singing 'Summertime'. I know this means that she must be feeling happy. She always sings light opera and popular songs when things are going well. When she needs help she sings Negro spirituals. From her clothes I can see that she has not had any sleep, but the dress looks beautiful hanging from a hook. 'Oh, Mummy,' I exclaim. 'It's so pretty.' My mother smiles back at me through tired eyes and begins to sing again.

When Mrs Gutch takes delivery of her gown she has no idea of the trials it has caused. She is thrilled with the results and my parents' name gets chatted around the cocktail and tea party circuit as the provider of an excellent service.

For the shortest time it looks like our circumstances may be beginning to change. However, our Quonset hut is sold and the new owner, Ho Kee, who is a Chinese merchant and builder, wants to take it possession of it.

'Why don't you find a piece of land and I'll build you new premises,' offers Ho Kee.

My father shakes his head. 'We can't afford it.'

'Find the land, and we'll work something out,' says Ho Kee.

Divine timing occurs again and Alvin is able to secure land next door. While Ho Kee builds, we are able to stay in the Quonset hut and, for a small downpayment and monthly payments, pay off our building.

My mother is beginning to see a pattern emerging. On the surface, our lives often seem calamitous. It is as though we are being pushed from one crisis to another – only, each stumbling block turns into a stepping stone, offering my parents a new opportunity to turn the situation to our advantage. In later years Gertrude will view this time as the greatest spiritual adventure she and Alvin ever had.

* * *

At night as I lie in bed I hear them coming, a distant hum at first. Soon, the mosquitoes make it through the netting and I am held hostage by their high-pitched sirens. There are so many bites that sting and hurt me. During my sleep I blindly scratch at their puncture marks. By morning new sores are tattooed on my skin.

I am carrying many open wounds, including the most debilitating of all, a lonely heart. I am still only seven years old and my new school is for the white European children of the British Administration. Their parents have warned them about my family being American of Jewish background and members of a strange religious faith. They refuse to speak to me. The school is very small. There are only fifteen or twenty children that I have to win over, but the more I try to play games and make them laugh, the more they ignore my presence. I no longer exist for them.

My daily march through the school gate is that of a shattered soldier. I drag my feet in the dirt, kicking stones. The boils on my body won't go away. They reappear, reinfecting themselves, over and over. A collection under my arms is so violent in its attack that I have to go to hospital and have them lanced under anaesthetic.

My mother knows that I am lacking something. She spends a lot of time worrying about the food she is able to cook for her family. Fresh food is scarce in Honiara. There is a supply boat that comes into Honiara about every three months, and with erratic electricity to man the freezers, frozen food only lasts a few weeks. The islanders who live by the sea are known as the saltwater people. They paddle out for fish, but because of the sun they have to eat it as soon as they return. There are no wild animals for the hill people to eat and they haven't developed farming skills.

The American soldiers taught the islanders how to grow salad vegetables. My mother has started to try and cultivate her own small garden too, but the climate makes it difficult to grow a wide variety. Sweet potatoes are the main staple for Solomon Islanders. Every Tuesday, a small ten-metres-square fenced market is held down on the main road in town, where the market is still situated today. A huge queue forms early and they rush through the gates when they open at seven. The few tomatoes, peppers and shallots are snatched up quickly.

There is a Government Trading Scheme store where we can get some tinned produce and tinned butter, but the packaging is unreliable. Sometimes we only have a few potatoes for dinner. Often I am very hungry. My American relatives send me packages filled with pretty clothes, making me the best-dressed poor girl in the country, but I wish they would send us some food instead.

As they wait for their new building and businesses to take off, my parents are finding it hard to make ends meet. On my eighth birthday, a small ball is my only present. My father hears about a temporary position of manager at the British Solomon Islands Trading Scheme store. 'Gertrude, I think I'll go down there and offer my services,' he says cheerily. When he returns home he whistles. 'Well, I got the job. It's only for a few months. I'll be in charge until the new storeman arrives from Australia, then I'll train him to take over.'

11

Developing the New

Courage is a special kind of knowledge:
the knowledge of how to fear what ought to be feared
and how not to fear what ought not to be feared

David Ben-Gurion

Point Cruz, February 1955

He wipes his forehead as he steps outside the Government Trade Scheme retail store, hoping to catch a small sea breeze. The store, like most things in Honiara, is housed in an old army Quonset hut. It is merciless in the heat of the midday sun.

Across the beachfront he can see the huge fishing nets laid out to dry. A group of men sprawl on the beach beneath a palm, waiting for the big tuna fish to arrive. Alvin raises one arm to acknowledge them. The men look back at the white man in his jacket and bloomer shorts, and begin to talk in Pidgin amongst themselves. It is a conversation that will later be written down by Lysander Opani'ira Opaka.

'Yu pela savi dis witemun hem worka lon har?'

(Do you know the white man who has come to work here?)

'Ya, me savi, me gogo long huwse blong algeta yea.'

(Yes, I know him, I have been to his house.)

'A'e! Turu? You save gogo long huwse blong witemun yea? Yu no liar mun? Yu me native hard for gogo yea!!'

(Really? You have gone to the house of the whiteman? Are you telling me lies? We native people, we never go inside whitemans house!!)

'Turu Heven!, Ye no giamun!'

(I am telling the truth, I am not lying!)

'Mun alsam yu yea, yu go tere for wat yea?'

(Good heavens, what did you go there for?)

'For hem stori lon mission blong hem long me fala. Mission blong him hem good too much – hem telim al geta loto hem saem saem no more ya.'

(He told me about this new religion – it is a very good message he brings. He said all the religions are one, from the same source and we should all be brothers.)

'Yu fela kai-kai to?'

(Did you have something to eat?)

'Me wanem stori long time me fela must kaikai yea. Custum alsam too, no stori dry no mor.'

(We talked for a long time and I had some food. It was the white man's custom to give food when talking long time.)

'Meri blong hem, hem gud misus too?'

(Was his wife there – was she good too?)

'Se man! Meri him savi cooki gud to mus. him, redim and sharem kakai.'

(Wow man, his wife was a really good cook and she made a good meal that she shared with me.)

'Meri hem gud misus tru, no matter pikinini him cry, hem no wori al geta.'

(His wife was kind, even when the child cried, she did not mind.)

Alvin can't hear what they are saying, but he knows islanders throughout the town have begun to talk about him and Gertrude – and it's not just because they are Americans.

When they were still at the hotel, Alvin would go to the King George VI Agricultural School to buy the flowers. He introduced himself to the head teacher, Belshazzar Gina, saying, 'Hello, I'm Alvin Blum,' and shook his hand. Belshazzar stared down at his own dark hand entwined with Alvin's white hand. His eyes widened, trying to make sense of it. It was the first time he had experienced a white person shaking his hand here in Honiara. 'Bill. Bill Gina,' he finally replied.

As a boy, Bill Gina was the favourite of Reverend John Goldie, the leading Methodist missionary on the island. Before the war, Goldie sent the bright and curious young Bill to New Zealand to receive a good education. When he returned Bill became Goldie's protégé, acting as a lay preacher throughout the islands. Amongst the islanders he held an elevated status, but it could not make up for his treatment by the Europeans. He was told he was not allowed to play tennis. 'It's a white man's game.' When he held out his hand to Reverend Metcalfe, another missionary, in front of a large crowd, his hand was refused. At the time it was reported that Bill said he would 'get even' with him or some other European.

During their first meeting, Bill held onto Alvin's hand. Each week Alvin would return to collect more flowers, greeting him and shaking his hand. As their discussions grew, Bill felt an old wound deep inside him gradually begin to heal. This man who spoke about a religion that said black men were equal to white men fascinated him.

Later, when we were settled in our home, Alvin invited Bill Gina home for a meal. This was unheard of in the boy–master divide that was the custom throughout this missionary-dominated British Protectorate. Bill ate Gertrude's stew from the same dinner plates and drank their tea. In between mouthfuls, there were many questions he wanted to ask Alvin and Gertrude. Through their answers, their laughter, their simple generosity, he began to sense that their spiritual lives ran deeper than what had been drilled into him as a boy.

The news of this event soon spread through the village networks. The sharing of the white man's food would become the biggest curiosity.

* * *

The young white man coming through the store entrance looks lost. It reminds Alvin of how he felt standing on the beach after being dropped off by the dinghy from the *MV Malaita*. He glances at the date on his ledger. It reads, 'February 7th, 1955'. It's not even one year since we arrived, he realizes.

'Alvin Blum, pleased to meet you,' he says holding out his hand to the man.

'John Mills,' says the young man, shaking it. 'Pleased to meet you too.'

John Mills has just arrived off the boat from Australia to take up the position of retail grocery storeman. They step outside the front of the Government Trade store; it was originally on the beachfront near where the present Yacht Club is today. The fishermen are casting their huge nets into the sea. John takes in the dream-like scene. 'So,' he says turning to Alvin, 'Are the islanders friendly? Are you allowed to talk and shake hands with these people?' 'Sure, if you feel that you'd like to,' breezes Alvin. 'But John, I'd like to tell you something,' he says, looking directly at him now. 'You're here in a very insular European community and they will observe you very discreetly and you will get a reputation. Whatever you do, you will get a reputation, and it's up to you what sort of a reputation you want to have.'

John senses the gravity of Alvin's delivery. But, he wonders, 'How can I decide what reputation I want to have, when I'm not even sure what I stand for, what I believe in?' Life's biggest questions have been lying unanswered inside him for some time.

In his hometown of Sydney, John felt the same dislocation. His friends had all married. If he could put what he was feeling into words he would say he was feeling lonely, unsatisfied. He had looked at all the Christian churches. They would all say, 'It's nice of you to come.' But they would take great pains to tell him that they were right and everyone else was wrong. He never trusted any of them, nor perhaps himself, enough to choose to believe in any of them. What if everyone was wrong?

A girl John was interested in turned out to be a

Catholic. They dated a while and he knew she was looking for some kind of commitment. 'So what's this business with Catholics, why do you just keep having children?' he asked her. 'You have four or five or six children. It's too many.'

'When you get to three or four children, you can stop having sex, so you don't have any more children,' she answered. To John, that sounded like a strange marriage, though he never said it.

The girl went to her priest and told him she was going out with a Protestant. 'The priest wants to see you, John,' she told him. John realized the girl was getting serious. 'Alright,' he decided, 'you ask the priest one question and if he answers it satisfactorily, I'll come along and I'll learn and I'll be a Catholic. Here it is,' he said looking at her directly. 'If you become a Catholic and then you go to war, there's lots of other Catholics in other countries, so you have to go and kill Catholics. If I become a Catholic that will be more important to me than being an Australian or an Italian or a German or whatever and I wouldn't run the risk of killing another Catholic. So where does that leave me?'

The priest was unable to give the girl an answer to take back to John. It was not so long since the Australian Catholics and Italian Catholics and German Catholics had all been fighting in Europe.

John began to dream of bigger places. Perhaps he could have a street stall in London, he mused, but that would cost money. He would play a game with himself: going through job advertisements in the newspaper and thinking about whether he could get them or not. One time he saw the word HONIARA in big bold type. He rolled the word around with his tongue, saying it aloud. It sounded good to his ear. Euphonious. The ad below offered a two-year contract as a retail grocery storeman, with three months leave in perpetuity. After that, he had already decided, he would be in a position to go to London. He didn't really know exactly where the Solomon Islands were but this time, almost as a lark, he answered the advert. To his surprise he was accepted, and arrived in Honiara in February 1955.

From the moment they meet, John likes Alvin. He likes storytellers and he regards Alvin as a brilliant raconteur. Alvin spends a lot of time telling John about things he's never encountered or thought of. Morning tea is delivered daily from the trade scheme office in a Quonset hut across the road and it becomes a good discussion time. A few weeks after he arrives, John notices that Alvin isn't drinking his tea.

'Why aren't you having morning tea?' he asks.

'I don't feel like it today,' Alvin says.

'Do you mind if I have one?'

'No, go ahead.'

It is only later that John finds out that Alvin is fasting as part of his religion. John asks Alvin to tell him about it. He listens as Alvin tells him how the Bahá'ís fast for nineteen days each year from the second to the twentieth of March, and that food is only taken after sunset and before dawn. It is when Alvin tells him that the Bahá'í Faith is a world religion that John begins to listen hard.

The fact that this religion doesn't accuse other religions of being wrong is important to him. He has been reading Harry Overstreet, who held that the greatest sign of a mature mind is the ability to follow through and do unto others as you would have them do unto you.

The Bahá'í Faith seems to encapsulate and eclipse the threads of thoughts and philosophies that have been occupying his mind. It makes sense to him in a way that he can imagine calling himself a Bahá'í and being happy telling other people about it. It sounds as though the Faith has a wonderful set of universal principles that he can find no fault with. It is not long after Bill Gina has decided to become a Bahá'í that John declares himself as a Bahá'í too.

* * *

Now that John has arrived at the Government Store, Alvin is free again to get involved with other ways to earning a living. When he goes to see John at the trade store, there is a renewed quickness in his step. My father has a new plan.

Alvin's dark eyes are twinkling. 'John, what this town needs is a bakery,' he announces.

He's absolutely right, John is thinking. Nobody is providing bread, the staff of life. 'Well, I used to be a pastry cook on Friday nights and Saturday mornings. I don't say that I'm a professional cook,' he cautions when he sees Alvin's excitement building, 'but I know where to get all the stuff and all the advice.'

Alvin sees this as a green light. 'Well, John, would you look to being a partner.'

The costs of mounting such an operation add up quickly in John's mind. 'Yes,' he says slowly, 'I'll think about it.' Even as he says it, he already knows that his friend won't hear any doubt.

'But let's do it,' presses Alvin.

John rolls his eyes heavenwards and laughs quietly. He has learned quickly that Alvin is a 'do it' person. It's one of the things he enjoys about the man. One of Alvin's maxims is: 'Anybody can do it with money, the trick is to do it without money.'

'Yes, Alvin,' he gives in wryly, 'let's do it.'

John has three hundred pounds in his bank account, and that is all they have. Undaunted, they decide that John will see out his contract with the Government working at the trade store while Alvin spearheads the bakery project. They go to see Ho Kee about creating extra floorspace for the bakery.

'Look,' says Alvin to the builder, 'we want to tack another building onto the laundry but,' he tells him straight, 'we haven't got any money.'

Ho Kee is getting used to Alvin's big ideas, but knows he's good for follow-through payments. 'Well, my workers are idle at the moment and I don't like to keep them idle too long because it's hard to get them back down to work. If you give me one hundred pounds now, then you can pay the rest whenever you get going.'

The three men shake hands on it and Alvin and John head off to the British Trade Scheme to ask for a loan. It is the freshest idea the bureaucrats have heard for getting business going in this town. They give them a six thousand pounds line of credit.

When they walk out the door, Alvin slaps John on the back. 'Hey, hey,' he chuckles. The pair go into setting up their business swinging punches. They send off to Sydney for brochures. Their biggest order is for two electric baking ovens. Each is capable of baking twenty-six loaves at a time. The only thing they economize on is a dough mixer. 'Those things last forever,' insists John. They buy one secondhand.

There are great delays in getting the equipment shipped to Honiara. Alvin is unable to make any payments. Thirty days becomes ninety days and the bureaucrats who have approved the Trade Scheme loan are beginning to get edgy. My mother is also very anxious. The Depression has left her with a lifelong fear of debt. She doesn't understand why Alvin places this burden on the family. Spending a penny to make a penny in business makes no sense to her. Her caution is at odds with Alvin's 'can do'. It creates a barrier between them that can't be dissolved through discussion.

Alvin wants to leap into life. Gertrude wants to step slowly and surely. One morning before school my father and I are waiting in the car for my mother again. His fingers hammer crankily on the dashboard. He honks the horn and yells out the window. 'Hurry up, Gertrude!' His breathing is short with huffing and puffing and huge sighs that grow louder the more time that passes. 'Honestly,' he eventually bursts, 'if I'd known that woman was so slow, I would never have married her!'

John notices the tension between them. He is aware that when it comes to business Alvin sees him as more of a confidante than his wife. 'Don't worry, Gertrude,' John urges encouragingly, 'once we have the first shilling coming over the counter we'll be clear.'

A letter arrives that provides a temporary shift of focus. 'Well, I never . . .' Alvin mutters as he reads its contents. A young Bahá'í girl of Persian and Indian descent called Ruhangiz Yaganegi, who introduced herself to Alvin and Gertrude at the conference in Delhi, has written to see if she can now pioneer to the Solomons.

When Alvin and Gertrude agreed in Delhi that she could come and stay with them, he hadn't expected to hear from her again. Her parents' hotel in Poona is half a world away from the Solomons and he knows her parents were against their daughter pioneering, preferring her to stay in India and marry the cousin who had been picked for her. A compromise was reached: Ruhangiz would finish high school first before she left for the Solomons.

Alvin is surprised by her courage and tenacity. He writes to Ruhangiz, telling her that she may be able to help in the newly established bakery. However, he advises, she first must obtain her visa. 'Whenever you get your visa you're most welcome to come and stay with us as our daughter,' he adds.

Ruhangiz applies to the Police and Immigration Department. She has enclosed a photo of herself. She is beautiful and delicate with dark eyes shining out of pale caramel skin. When John sees her photo he becomes smitten. He is not alone. The Assistant Police Commissioner, who acts as hangman for the Protectorate, has also set his sights on Ruhangiz. Everyone is surprised by how swiftly he grants Ruhangiz her visa. Only later will it emerge that he perhaps had seen the little oriental beauty as a future wife.

Alvin sends a cable to Ruhangiz. 'Visa granted, Blum,' it states simply. The Guardian in Haifa has given her his blessing and she convinces her parents to let her use the money they have been saving for her wedding to pay for her fare to the Solomons.

Finally, the two big bread ovens arrive by ship. My father is very excited when he sees them installed in the new building. He has managed to obtain a little red book used by the Australian army that explains how to bake bread in a field kitchen. I watch as my parents prop the book up and begin to carefully measure out ingredients to form the dough. They read the instructions out loud as they go, determined to follow the recipe step by step. Neither of my parents has ever baked bread. I have never seen my father even boil an egg. I cover my mouth with my small fingers and giggle through them as I watch him plant his big fists into the dough.

They pull the first loaves of bread out of the oven. They are beautiful, golden humps nestling inside their baking tins. I see my mother's lovely smile returning to her face. She throws her arms around my father and together they do a little jig.

* * *

After her long journey from India, Ruhangiz is a much welcomed and wonderful addition to our small family. She wants to start helping immediately and is soon assisting in the bakery.

Through the dark I see her get up out of bed. I know that it must be four in the morning. That's the time Ruhangiz gets up to get ready to go down to work in the bakery. Ruhi and I share a bedroom together. She is eighteen years old, ten years older than me. I am enjoying having a big sister; it helps break the loneliness of being an only child and counters the silence I am experiencing at the local expatriate school from children who have still not spoken to me in all these months. She calls my parents Mum and Dad. I don't mind because I know that she loves them. Ruhi is very kind, but she has weird eating habits. She puts really hot chillies that burn my mouth in everything she eats.

I hear the engine of John's car. He comes each day to pick her up and drive her down to work. I think he must be sweet on Ruhi to make himself wake up in the dark. I watch her outline slip out of our bedroom to meet him.

A new routine has formed around the bakery. Ruhi along with some of our other staff bakes the first load of bread. Soon my parents wake up and say their prayers. Then they go down to the bakery around 8 or 9 a.m. and Ruhi will come home to rest. Everyone is home for lunch between 12 and 2, and then my father will go back down until dinner. Ruhi will also go down later with my father to make more bread for the evening crowd. In this part of town there are cinemas situated in the old army

Quonset huts that were left here by the soldiers. After the cinema, the islanders like to come and buy more bread. The bakery doesn't close until 10 p.m.

The bakery is a huge success. George, who was the cook at the Woodford Hotel, has come to join us along with some of his Malaitan friends. None of them can read. Literacy in the Solomons is about two per cent overall and in Honiara there is only one school that islanders can attend. Gertrude trains them how to cook. She lays out all the ingredients in order and points to number one saying, 'First you cream the butter, then you put the sugar, then you put the eggs . . .' until she has finished along the line. Even though they are not educated the men are very bright and they pick up baking skills quickly. Gertrude praises Peter, a gentle Malaitan man with large graceful hands, telling him he has hands like an artist. She loves to watch him knead the bread, seeing his hands caress the dough as he moulds it into the 'staff of life'.

They produce many kinds of breads, including pumpernickel, raisin and wholemeal. They also make meat pies, donuts, scones, sponges and cakes. Rock cakes filled with raisins are snaffled up by the Solomon Islanders. The Europeans' favourite is Gertrude's cheesecake. Each day there is a different special like jam tarts or Danish pastries.

The Solomon Islanders have never before tasted bread nor the varieties of delicious cakes, but they love them immediately. They are very inventive in how they eat bread. For a shilling they buy a loaf and eat all the soft bread out of the middle. Next, they buy a small five-ounce tin of Japanese mackerel and tip all the fish inside the hole in the bread they've created and squish the outsides of the loaf together. That is all they require to make a brilliant and filling meal for two or three islanders.

Slowly, Alvin begins to be appreciated by the British for the services he is bringing them. The bakery also opens up a new rival. Quan How Yun, a local Chinese businessman, has begun boasting that he will have Blum out of business in six months. He brings in big factory equipment and begins to make bread on a much larger scale. But the bread is mass-produced and can't compete with the quality of what my parents are offering.

* * *

1956

The declaration of Bill Gina as a Bahá'í brings almost insurmountable trouble for my parents. So moved by the teachings, Bill has wanted to share them with his people and has begun translating them into Roviana, one of the main spoken languages on his home island of Gizo in the Western Solomons. He hands a pamphlet to the Chairman of the Methodist District Mission here. It is not well received. The Methodist Mission has put much money and effort into Bill's education, spiritual and otherwise, and he is an influential leader. They react as though they are about to lose not only their star pupil, but their entire flock. Pressure is put on his family and

Bill is told that it is his duty to return to the Methodist fold or there will be consequences.

The Government is also concerned. Unbeknownst to my parents, Alvin and Gertrude have become a subject in secret intelligence reports. The Government has misgivings about the influence my father might have in the Western Solomons. They are aware that Bill can give him access to the local leaders, and view the Bahá'í Faith as a rival mission, fearing that the Bahá'í teachings of equality and fairness will draw many into their congregation.

When Collis Featherstone, a prominent Australian Bahá'í, arrives to visit my parents in January he is called in to see the Superintendent of Police. Alvin has tried before to explain that Bahá'ís are required by their teachings to obey the government of the land and live within the prescribed laws, but he is well aware that this has not yet been clearly understood by the authorities. Alvin decides to head off trouble and invite the Superintendent to come to the 'firesides' or discussions that they will be hosting with Collis nightly for one week. The Superintendent comes along for one night and sends islander policemen to attend on other nights. They see at first hand that there is no threat to the Government.

Other churches also feel threatened by the Bahá'í Faith when they hear that their members are attending these meetings. My parents are denounced from most pulpits. The relevance of other religions to the Bahá'í teachings is completely overlooked. As is the fact that each week I attend the Sunday Schools of various denominations so I can learn about other religions.

Learning about other religions is one of the basic tenets of the Bahá'í Faith, which encourages independent investigation of truth. Being part of the Bahá'í Faith is not something that happens automatically through birth. Children of Bahá'ís are taught about all the world's great religions.

Soon after their public denouncement, Alvin and Gertrude are drinking tea early one evening. They hear a noise on the front porch steps. Alvin gets up to see what it is. At first he can't see anyone. He stares out through the dusk. In the dimming light he can see an islander poised edgily beside some bushes.

'Hello there, what can I do for you?' Alvin calls out. The figure edges forward on one foot, then retreats again.

'Hello,' Alvin calls again, 'do you want to come in and have a cup of tea?'

Slowly a small muscular man comes towards him. He stops a few feet away.

'Hello, I'm Alvin Blum, what's your name?' Alvin puts out a hand. The man stares at it and after a short while grabs it and shakes it back. 'My name is Hamuel, Hamuel Hoahania,' he says softly.

'Well, Hamuel, why don't you come inside and have a cup of tea?'

Hamuel shakes his head, still looking at his feet.

'Please, come in, be our guest,' urges Alvin.

Hamuel has never been invited inside a white man's house. Eventually, he sits balancing himself on the window ledge. In Malaita where he lives, a lot of people have been talking about the Blums. George Kwota and

Bethuel Bama, two of the Malaitan cooks from the bakery, have become Bahá'ís. Mostly Hamuel has heard about them from his friend Gideon Susu who attends the Agriculture College in Honiara. He has heard how the Blums will let you sit with them and give you a cup of tea or even a meal. But Hamuel hasn't come across from Malaita for a meal. He wants to know more about this new religion.

During the time when blackbirding was practised, Hamuel's grandfather was taken to work in the Queensland cane fields and became one of the first to bring Christianity back to his people. Hamuel has become interested in the concept of brotherhood. He hears the other missions talk about brotherhood, but then they treat the islanders differently. Hamuel is hoping that maybe this new religion is different. He asks many questions in a short time. When he is done, he asks if he can take some pamphlets back with him to read. Alvin and Gertrude say 'Of course', and give them to him. They don't press Hamuel for details about who he is and it is some time before they hear from him again.

* * *

The phone rings. It is late at night. 'Mr Blum, you'd better get yourself up the hill, you're taxi driver's stuck at the top.' It is a local policeman. Alvin gets into his pick-up truck and drives up to the top of one of the ridges above Honiara. He sees his taxi, its front bonnet tipped forwards and balancing precariously.

Alvin opens the driver's door and peers inside the car. The air is filled with loud, pungent snorts. His driver is slumped over the wheel, dead to the world, asleep. Beside the man he can see a bottle of local home brew. Alvin puts both hands up against the roof's edge and sighs. It's been another long, hot day and he's too tired for this. 'Come on son, let's get you out of here.'

He tries to heave the man out of the vehicle. His body is heavy and slack with sleep, making it difficult for Alvin to manoeuvre. The car is wedged over a large rock sitting on the side of Kola Ridge. If Alvin makes a wrong move, the driver, car and he will all end up at the bottom of the ravine. His heart pounds hard and he feels the sweat forming across his face.

When he has finally hauled the man out of the car and they are both sitting safely by the road, Alvin starts to weigh in his mind whether he should bother with this taxi business any more. Someone else has already copied the idea, so bookings are thin and he doesn't have the time to keep watching over the driver. The bakery is established now and our basic needs are being met. Alvin looks across at his driver, still slumped and snoring, and back at the car still teetering on the edge of the ridge. He decides our family can survive without all the headaches of the taxi business.

Reliability of his staff sometimes adds to the difficulties of running businesses. Language is a further barrier. There are seventy-five languages spoken in the Solomon Islands. On Guadalcanal there are at least five languages, not just dialects, but completely different languages. Out of this melee, the main language of communication that has developed is Pidgin English. Its descriptiveness that lunges towards wonderfully dramatic and overblown lyricism causes much confusion.

When Alvin was starting the laundry business a worker didn't turn up one day.

'Is he coming?' Alvin asked another worker.

'Oh mun hemi no cum woki, hemi gutum big kil – hemi di lidel bit!'

Alvin's eyes popped wide. 'He was killed?'

'Oi yeh, hemi catsum big kil.'

'Well, have you told the police?'

'Oi no, hemi olrite, me no telum police.'

'What killed him?' Alvin asked, concerned.

'Oi une big pela fite. Big pela fite.'

The next day the 'dead' worker walked through the door. Alvin rushed over to the man, pleased to see him. 'Hey, I was told you were killed.'

'Oi ye mun, me getum kil. But me no ded, di, finish. Me fela just getum kil no mor ya.' (Not dead, only hurt.)

Alvin soon learns not to be so alarmed by what they say. '*Kil*' means that someone is just hurt. Only when you say '*kil, ded, di, finish*' does it mean someone is truly gone.

My parents don't speak Pidgin English. My father speaks a few words as shorthand, but my mother doesn't see the need for it. She believes that if it is spoken slowly it is just like English.

I learn how to speak Pidgin very quickly. I love how expressive and inventive it is. It makes me laugh. One day I am lying on our lounge room floor listening to a radio broadcast of the Queen's Birthday Parade in Honiara. Billy Bennet, an ex-Coastwatcher and now the main announcer over the Solomon Broadcasting Corporation, is describing the parade in Pidgin as the High Commissioner inspects the police.

Big pela mun blog u me. Dis pela mun High Commissioner. Mun blog England. He be look smart for good! Calico blog hum. Alsam wite al wae. Gogo long shoe lon feet blon hum, hemi wite. Gogo truser blog hum. Hemi strate for gud an hemi wite. Sa coate blon hum, hemi wite to. An mun, stacka medals, front lon hum. Makim hum look smart for good. And gogo. mor, hemi getum wun fela big wite hat. Heme sit lon top, long hed blon hum. Me suprise for good, on top lon big pela hat stop stacka feathers on arse lon cockarocko.'

Translation: The British High Commissioner, all dressed for the pomp and ceremony of the Queen's Birthday Parade, was very smart in his white outfit.

Shoes, starched trousers, jacket with medals and lastly his high pith helmet . . . the surprise being the feathers of the arse of the cockarocko (chicken) sitting on top of the pith helmet!!

I laugh so hard when I hear him describe the chicken plumes in the High Commissioner's hat that my small belly bumps up and down on the floor.

When the Trans Australia Airlines (TAA) inter-island air service begins in 1956 they describe planes as '*big pela bird. Dat mun hemi savi sit lon beli belon him.*'

Translation: big birds that men can sit in its belly.

The pianos brought by the British are described as '*big bokus, taem yu pela pusem teet blon hum hemi sing ote*'. Translation: like a big box, when you press the teeth (keyboard) they make a big noise.

I am told a story about when the first telephone line went into Auki on Malaita, where 'islanders are suspicious of the white man's invention. The first line installed was between the hospital and police station. When it rang for the first time, the male nurse jumped away from it and ran to the District Doctor standing nearby.

'*Hae, bokus hum crae ut!*' said the nurse, pointing back at the little black phone. (The box made a noise!)

'*Yeh, hum crae ut – dis taem nu yu putem lon ear belon yu and herem taek taek lon bokus.*' (Put the phone to your ear and hear the voice talking.)

The Doctor lifted up the handle of the telephone to show the nurse what to do and the person on the other end said, 'Hello, hello, hello.' The nurse jumped back again saying, '*Heh, hemi crae ut! Hemi taek, taek to!*' Then he ran away again and wouldn't have anything to do with it.

At my new school I speak Pidgin with my friends in the playground. After seeing how unhappy I had become my mother took me out of the Red Cross school for European children. I now go to the Catholic mission school called St Johns at Rove, on the outskirts of Honiara. The American nuns who run the school live in nearby Tanagi Mission. They cycle three miles each day into school. I have lovely early memories of their white habits billowing gracefully behind them as they make their way riding to and from school.

The children who go to this school are mostly of mixed race. Because I am European, the children often defer to me. It is as if in being wholly white I am somehow more complete than they are. Having been so ostracized at my last school, my latest audience renews my exuberance. I become very outspoken and bossy. 'You go there. You there and you there,' I command my obedient playfriends as I organize them into groups for games.

The family of one of my schoolfriends, the Wickhams, live in a house up above ours on the top of Kola Ridge. I often climb up a little track to go and play with them. As the European children won't play with me at all, I also make friends with local children. Isaac, who works at my parent's laundry, often comes up to our house to do our ironing. One day he brings his son, who sneaks off with his father's cigarettes. Crouching low behind the back door, I watch him blow big rings of smoke out of his mouth. 'Can I try too?' I ask. 'Sure,' says my co-conspirator, 'I'll show you how.' Soon we have smoked all of Isaac's cigarettes.

'What are you children doing!' Isaac's voice booms behind us. We jump when we hear him. Isaac tells my parents what we have done and my father is very angry. He grabs me and whacks me on my bottom very hard with his belt. I am in shock. My father has never raised a finger to me in my life. I am used to getting away with all kinds of nonsense.

My parents have always encouraged me to be outspoken and have the confidence to try things out and do what I feel. Sometimes their belief in my capabilities is rather stretched. When my mother takes ill one day, there are two orders for birthday cakes at the bakery.

'Oh well, you can decorate them,' says my father.

'But I don't know how,' I plead.

My father raises his eyebrows and looks at me over the dark rim of his glasses. 'Well, learn,' he says.

I can't believe what my father is asking me to do. I am only nine years old. When I have made up the icing I pick up my mother's pipes and write 'happy birthday'. Then I put swirls and squiggles around the edge. I take a step back and look at what I've done. I think my cakes looks quite good. Apparently, others do too. It helps to soften the crankiness I am feeling with my father, but I am still unaware that he is trying to teach me a valuable lesson in self-belief and self-reliance that I will come to lean on in later life.

* * *

A cable has arrived for Alvin. As he reads it his face becomes serious. It is from Donald Gubbay, the Frenchman he met in Santo on his way to the Solomons in 1954, who runs the fishing cannery on Santo. Eighteen of Donald's fishermen are due to go home to Japan. Their boat has broken down and they are stranded off Honiara. Donald is asking if Alvin can give them a place to stay until he arranges another boat or charter plane to take them back to Japan.

Alvin wipes a hand over his face and holds onto his chin as he thinks about how he is going to handle this. No

Japanese have set foot on Guadalcanal since the war and the Solomon Islanders are still harbouring deep wounds from their treatment by this foreign force. During the war, the way the Japanese sought to gain authority was by killing people. When they first landed on the north-western edge of Guadalcanal in early 1942 the saltwater people gathered on the beach at Visale, east of Honiara, to see what was happening. Only a few scattered plantations were in existence and they had little experience of foreigners.

In one story, villagers told about how they were lined up by the Japanese. A little boy of seven stood holding his grandmother's hand. They shot her and two other people. The rest of the saltwater people ran away and sought shelter in the hills. Below them their village and gardens were taken over by the Japanese. With few natural food or water sources available, the villagers survived on leaves and roots. Many people died. When the Americans found them a few months later they brought containers of fresh water and food to them. In return, the Solomon Islanders passed on what they knew about Japanese movements.

At no point does Alvin stop to consider that it is only a little more than a decade since the Japanese were his own official enemy. Nor does he consider how prophetic it is that he, the only American serviceman to return to the Solomons, should now be asked to help the first returning Japanese.

He goes down to the police station and explains the situation, asking for both accommodation and police protection. At first the police are reluctant to help. Alvin goes in harder. 'All right, Blum,' they grudgingly surrender. 'There's a disused house up on Kola Ridge above your place. They can stay there.'

The men look in a poor way when they arrive at the house. They haven't washed or showered for days. The smell of oily fish is caked into their clothes and mixes with their sweat. I screw up my nose and block my nostrils. Only one of the Japanese men speaks a little English. He acts as a translator. My father tries to make them welcome and shows them hospitality and kindness.

Soon Alvin swings into organizational mode. He arranges for the men to have showers and for their clothes to be washed. Then he goes down to get some groceries to put inside the house where they will be staying. When he returns, the police tell us that the house is ready for them. Kola Ridge, where the house is located, is so named because that is where the Americans and Japanese fought many battles, leaving the place strewn with empty bottles of Coca Cola. Nobody has time to take in the irony.

It is not long before we start receiving calls at our home. My father picks up the phone, often in the dark of the night, and hears an angry voice saying that he will shoot the Japanese if he sees them. Each time, Alvin reports the calls to the District Commissioner of Police. I can tell by the look in his eyes that my father is concerned, but he has decided to ignore any threats. For him, the humanity of the Japanese is the overriding factor: they are people in need of help.

Alvin goes up to the house each day to make sure the men have enough food. After ten days, the plane arrives to take them home. Alvin and Gertrude go with them to the airport and see them off. As they walk across the airfield with them, the site of one of the bloodiest battles during World War II, they can feel the Solomon Islanders watching them interact with the Japanese. They hope it goes some way towards helping to ease the fears and the tension that exist between them.

Shortly after this, I see the courage of my father in action again. He has picked me up from school and we are nearly home when we hear people from the fishing village screaming on the beach. My father stops his utility van, or ute, and runs up to the frenzied group.

'What are you screaming about?' he asks.

People point to the water and yell, 'Shark!'

Alvin sees the torso of an islander man shooting out of the water and back under. His arms are flailing each time he resurfaces. 'Why aren't you helping him?' my father shouts. He is already ripping off his shoes and socks.

'It's against custom,' one whimpers back. The people from this fishing village are from an area on Malaita called Langa Langa where they worship sharks. They believe that if they go out to rescue the man they will bring a curse on themselves. If the man has been attacked, they tell themselves, it is because he has done something wrong.

My father keeps stripping. 'Custom be damned,' he growls.

When he is wearing nothing but his undershorts he

Hamlyn Walker, Hamuel Hohanea, Gertrude and Alvin, Honiara, 1958

Hamuel Hohanea, the first Bahá'í on Malaita, visiting the Shrine of the Báb, Haifa

Hand of the Cause Collis Featherstone and family,
with Keithie, in Adelaide, 1960

1961: Keithie arriving back in Honiara, aged 15

Teddy and Grace Saunders, with Gertrude
at Bruce and Keithie's wedding, Sydney, Australia, 1966

Keithie and Rosemary Scadden at the fashion show
on the veranda of the Mendana hotel, 1969

Formation of the first Veterans' Association, 1967,
with the wives of the High Commissioner and the Chief Justice

Alvin and Gertrude greeting US Marines, 7 August 1967, the 25th anniversary of World War II

Alvin with Sergeant-Major Vouza at the 25th anniversary

Sergeant-Major Vouza with a General of the US Marines at the 25th anniversary

Sergeant-Major Vouza meeting Prince Philip, Duke of Edinburgh, 1972

'Blum's Hometel', 1960 (now King Solomon Hotel)

Café at the Blum Motel (now the Bamboo Bar, King Solomon Hotel), with Alvin on the right

Pa Ariki, Queen of the Cook Islands (*centre*), with Gertrude and Peter Titi, the first Cook Islands Bahá'í

Alvin in the Cook Islands, 1967: the last photo before his death in 1968

Amatu'l-Bahá Rúḥíyyih Khánum and Violette Nakhjavani with local Bahá'ís at Alvin's grave, 1984

runs down to the water and swims out to the man. All his old army training comes back into sharp focus. He quickly hauls the man away from the shark and back into the beach. When my father pulls the man out of the water he is still alive but he is missing his legs. Long, ragged strands of bloody tendons drip from his torso in their place.

Alvin manages to get the shark attack victim into the back of his ute. I sit goggle-eyed and silent as my father drives as quick as he can to the hospital nearby. When we arrive my father calls for help to get the man inside. The man, a government worker in his thirties, later dies from shock and loss of blood.

I never hear anyone say thank you to my father for his bravery and I never feel comfortable swimming in the ocean again - anywhere. Ever since we arrived, Iron Bottom Sound has been a dangerous swimming area. When all those ships went down during the war, the bodies of dead men drew in schools of sharks. The waters have been infested with them ever since.

* * *

June 1956

Ruhi is wrapping a white sari around her body. A small slither of sun comes through the window. The sari shimmers with its light. Today Ruhi is getting married to John Mills. I have never seen my 'big sister' look more beautiful. A lot of men in Honiara think Ruhi is very pretty.

Once a chief came all the way across from Malaita and offered my father two hundred pounds to marry 'his daughter'. My father laughs his big belly laugh when he tells that story.

Ruhi's parents, who are also Bahá'ís, are very surprised at how soon their daughter has wanted to get married. It is not even a year since she arrived in the Solomons and they are yet to meet John. He is not the Indian her parents had imagined their daughter marrying. My parents have written to assure them that John is a Bahá'í and a good man. Rúḥíyyíh Khánum, the Guardian's wife, has written to say that if Ruhi says she loves John and John is a Bahá'í then let them get married. After this, Ruhi's parents finally sent their consent. They haven't been able to make the long journey to come to the wedding, but they have sent the wedding sari for Ruhi to wear.

John and Ruhi are officially married in a civil ceremony because Bahá'í marriage is not yet recognized in the Solomons. Afterwards, a few close friends and other Bahá'ís come back to our house where a Bahá'í marriage ceremony is performed. This is an important event; it is the first time two Bahá'ís have been married in the Solomons. My father gives a short talk on how it is possible through the Faith to bring together a person from the East and one from the West.

My mother has arranged for Mrs Chandra from Fiji to prepare an Indian-style luncheon. Soon around one hundred and twenty-five other guests arrive from all parts of the community. There are Solomon Islanders, Europeans, some Fijians and some Chinese. A man is sitting in a corner broadcasting a description of this event in Pidgin on the radio. A bamboo band play their music and my mother has made lots of her beautiful cakes and treats.

A picture of Ruhi and John and a small account of the wedding are published in *Pacific Island Monthly*, the largest circulating magazine in the Pacific. A lot of people talk excitedly about the Bahá'í wedding, but there are some who start more rumours against my parents. John gets wind of the latest. Some people believe that my father has bribed John into becoming a Bahá'í. 'First he becomes a Bahá'í, then all of a sudden this beautiful girl comes out and they get married. Ah,' they say, 'that's how he's done it.' John and Alvin have another good laugh over this one.

I am a little sad that Ruhi will no longer be living with us. The British Trade Commission where John still works has given them a house in which to live. My bedroom suddenly feels bigger and emptier than it ever has before. I find myself spending more time with the people who always come to sit on the front porch with my parents, drink tea and find out about their faith.

By this time we have become more accepted into the European community. The '*pukka pukka*' system of social niceties is still quite formal and my mother organizes my play time by writing and answering little notes. 'Could Keith Wilma come and play with so and so at such and such a time?' She always remembers to write a thank you note.

When my mother isn't working, she is often tied up in her office typing minutes from meetings and other administrative duties connected with the Bahá'í Faith. Her voluntary work as an original member of the Red Cross Association also occupies much of her time. She is often down at the hospital working with occupational therapy and taking patients magazines or cakes. When she hears that someone has died, she is always the first to go to the family and offer them comfort.

Sometimes I go with my mother and watch her holding their hands and soothing them with her beautiful voice. Even as a young child I can sense there is something different about the way my mother speaks. She infuses her words with a spiritual quality that changes the light in other people's eyes. The islanders are particularly grateful for the white woman who will bother to bake them a cake, often at two in the morning, and sit with their black hand in hers. For her own part, Gertrude looks forward to a time when it's not the colour of her skin that distinguishes what she regards as her small kindnesses.

When I turn ten, my mother organizes a birthday party for me. It is a small window in which their finances seem to be riding smoothly. I blow out the candles on the cake my mother has made me and dictate the games my friends will play. I am so excited to be having a birthday party, I do not realize that this will be the last birthday I have with my family for many years to come.

12

Change and Separation

If we sat in a circle and put an object in the centre of the circle and we all described what we saw, everyone would see different points of views from each other. Some would even see opposites because they would be sitting on opposite sides of the circle. In other words, you don't have to see what I see for you to be right. In fact, everyone in the circle is right based on their own point of view. If we are willing to listen to everyone's point of view, then we can get a more accurate description of the object in the centre.
Let us put our minds together as one.

Irving Powless, Sr.

Leaving Honiara, January 1957

My mother's arms are around me. She pulls me in very tight. I can hear her heart beat, faster now, beneath my right cheek. When she loosens her hold I look up into her eyes. They look wet but she doesn't cry. I am too young to understand what it is costing my mother to send her only child away. Gertrude has decided not to show me her heartache. It's best that way, my parents think.

Education in the Solomons does not yet stretch to secondary schooling. My parents' options are few. They do not have the money to send me to boarding school so they have found people through the Bahá'í network in Australia who are willing to take me in.

The prospect of going to school in Australia does not entirely upset me. I have developed a deep sense of loneliness. My local friends are very sweet but because I am the only European child most of them have ever associated with, they are also subservient to my every wish. I am only ten years old but I have been allowed to become the kingpin. What I desperately need, although I don't realize it, is to be brought down to size. To be challenged.

The Trans Australia Airlines (TAA) DC3 arrives to take me away. It is one of the old US wartime planes that has been converted to a commercial plane after World War Two. It should take two days to get to Brisbane via Lae in Papua New Guinea. I sit in one of the canvas seats that line the sides of the plane facing inwards and place my hand luggage on the floor in front of me. Through the window I see my parents waving me off. They honestly trust that God will look after me, as if I am some divine bounty.

First the plane stops in Yandina, then Munda and Gizo in the Solomon Islands. We then cross the Papua New Guinea border and fly into Buka, Kieta, Rabaul and, eventually, Lae. In Lae I step off the plane, go through customs and get onto the TAA bus. It takes me to a collection of pretty cottages up on a hill which makes up the TAA Transit Mess. When I wake up the next morning I pick up my little bag and catch the bus back down to the airport for my onward flight to Brisbane. When I arrive I am told that the plane has been overbooked and I will have to come back tomorrow.

I shrug my shoulders at the news and get back on the bus that takes me back to the Transit Mess. I go to the office and ask them to cable my parents. 'Been delayed, am going tomorrow,' I tell them to write.

The next day when I arrive at the airport I am told the same thing. This will happen every day for the next seven days. Each I time I ask for a cable to be sent to my parents. I remain unaware that the office at the TAA Mess is not passing on any of my cables, and to all intents and purposes, I have disappeared somewhere between New Guinea and Australia.

My father is first aware of this when he receives a cable, not from me but from Viva and Geoff Rodwell who are to be my new houseparents in Brisbane. They tell him that I have not arrived in Brisbane.

Outside communications are still very poor in the Solomons. The only option my father has of enquiring of my whereabouts is to cable every location along my route. He doesn't receive any communication back from TAA. Alvin cannot face telling my mother that I have gone missing. Gertrude has already been grieving for me since I left. He keeps his upset to himself.

After a week in Lae the next flight from Honiara arrives. I see familiar faces arriving at the Transit Mess and all the emotions that have been bottled inside me burst open. 'What are you doing still here?' they ask. I tell them of my trials. 'Right, we'll see about that,' they say. I am relieved that someone else is taking command.

The next morning, my rescuers from Honiara accompany me down to the airport. 'Look,' they say, 'this child has been offloaded for a week now. You'd better get her on board or there will be trouble.'

Soon I am flying to Port Moresby. When I get there I change planes and catch a DC6 to Cairns and, finally, I arrive in Brisbane. When my father learns what has happened he is furious and lets TAA know it. There is an investigation and a number of people are fired over the incident.

The next year when I am flying back to Brisbane from Honiara after school holidays, the same thing happens. Only this time I am a full twelve months older. I am eleven years old.

'I have a confirmed booking for this flight,' I say.

'Yes, but we're overbooked.'

'Well, how many hostesses on this flight have you?'

'Yes, we've got eight hostesses.'

'Well, offload one of them and put me in her seat.'

'We can't do that.'

'Yes you can,' I tell them in my biggest voice. 'You did this to me last year. For seven days I was caught up here and I'm not going to let you do it again.' I make myself as tall as I can. 'Offload one of the hostesses and let me sit in her seat,' I command. The TAA staff stare back at me – this tall, skinny kid with pigtails, buck teeth and glasses. Eventually, they decide it is easier to find me a seat than to put up with the consequences. This is my first lesson in assertiveness, and in my memory there was a full complement of hostesses when we took off for Brisbane.

Geoff and Viva Rodwell have four children, two girls and two boys, who are at university. They also have another girl living with them, Betty Hindson. She is the first Aboriginal Bahá'í, and is studying at university here. A few months after I first arrive, I start having rigours, also known as 'the shakes', accompanied by high fevers and then periods of cold sweats. Viva thinks I am homesick and takes me to a psychologist who makes me 'look at a spot on the wall' to relax. I start to shake again with another attack.

Viva writes to Gertrude telling her the symptoms. 'Have her tested for malaria,' my mother cables immediately. Sure enough, malaria is diagnosed and as soon as the treatment takes hold, 'looking at the spot on the wall' becomes a bit of a joke for everyone.

After my malaria incident, my mother is anxious to see if I am fully cured and settled in. She visits me in Brisbane and also takes me to the dentist. It is the first time my teeth have ever been checked.

* * *

Honiara, October 1957

Gertrude arrives back from Brisbane to find Alvin in hospital. My father has had to have an operation due to complications that stem from the diabetes his body has been developing since we arrived. He is told he is now a diabetic and is given pills to try and keep it under control.

At the same time a Persian family arrives from Iran. My parents have been asking the Guardian to send them some help. Their businesses keep them tied to work and there is little time left to visit people who want to know about the Bahá'í Faith. For nearly a year they have been trying to secure visas for the Safajous that will entitle them to work for Alvin. At last they are granted the visa. The Safajous have a two-and-a-half-year-old daughter. At first they live with my parents, but it is too uncomfortable for them all together. My parents move into the tiny room in an outhouse they have been using for an office and give the larger house to the Safajous

'Sacrifice' is an integral part of one's life as a Bahá'í pioneer. My parents' greatest bond is their faith and they have a shared understanding of what they are willing to do in their quest to help unite the world. They are prepared to tolerate the extreme heat, the poor living conditions, the difficult communications, the enormous cultural and language differences, the extreme loneliness and the absence of their only child. This, Alvin and Gertrude understand, is not something everyone can adapt to. After a few months, the Safajous find this is all too hard and leave Honiara to go back to Iran. They subsequently move to Australia, where most of the family live today.

Pressure has also kept building on Bill Gina, the first Solomon Islander Bahá'í. He writes a letter saying that his wife will not accept any other religion than Methodist. Bill Gina's father was the first Methodist convert and brought the religion to his people. He says he must be loyal to that. What Bill doesn't add is that it appears that the church mission has promised him re-ordination if he returns and that his house and his children's education will be paid for. He leaves the Faith, taking five others with him.

* * *

My father receives a phone call. A group of Japanese priests has arrived in Honiara. It is only six months after Alvin and Gertrude looked after the Japanese fishermen. The fishermen have gone home and talked to the priests about my parents and how they were assisted and well treated by them. The priests, sensing an opening, have now come to hold prayer services for the dead on Guadalcanal and to make peace with the Solomon Islanders.

The reception they are given is still somewhat hostile, but their robes, perhaps, protect them from worse. Alvin and Gertrude are the only people to receive them. They invite friends along, hoping somehow that their earlier encounter with the Japanese fishermen might soothe some of the fears of the locals. The Solomon Islander Bahá'ís are particularly curious. They have never met anyone of such a foreign faith.

'So can you tell us about Buddhism?' asks Alvin.

There is an awkward silence as the priests look at one another. 'No, no,' says one, 'we are Shinto priests. We don't talk about our religion.'

'Never mind,' says Alvin, undeterred. 'Let's have some tea and talk about the world.' They are so touched by the hospitality that they give us several beautiful Japanese dolls in glass boxes and many other small gifts. I am thrilled when I return home and discover them.

After the horror of Guadalcanal, the Japanese arrived at a new way of writing the island's name. The characters, delicate fine-haired strokes, carried the weight of something grave and sinister. The name translated as 'hungry ghosts'. The beloved relatives of those soldiers who died in battle here were still alive with the sort of constant fear and upset that awoke them in the quietest hours, sweaty and trembling. They worried and fretted about the bones of bodies that lay lost and unburied without proper rites. Would these hungry ghosts be doomed to walk the earth eating its waste? For many Japanese this was a real spiritual question.

How the priests felt, the way they were welcomed by my parents, by their friends, stayed with them when they returned home. With simple gestures of friendship, the backbone of anguish that still existed between the Japanese and Solomon Islanders was beginning to be broken down.

From these first two encounters, more Japanese priests will arrive on peace missions, conducting ceremonies and apologizing for the war and what had happened. They burn incense and leave little pieces of wood with Japanese markings sticking out of the soil that covers souls now laid at rest. Still, many years later, I will see relatives arrive, often with meticulous maps of where bones have been buried.

The establishment in the 1970s of the Taiyo fishing company – a joint venture between Japan and the

Solomon Islands Government – has also gone a long way to cement normal relations between the two countries.

* * *

Gertrude watches her husband jump out of the ute. His arms pump at his side as he strides quickly back into the bakery. Even before he speaks she knows Alvin has a new idea. She recognizes the visible happiness, like a current of electricity, running through him. He becomes light on his feet, as if he no longer feels the merciless heat that is wearing him down.

A little sigh of resignation evaporates from her lips. Gertrude sometimes feels that she can barely keep up with all of her husband's ambitions. Alvin is a man of the future, always seeing what is ahead. She is both energized by his vision and exhausted by it. Whatever his new project is, she knows she will be the one to keep it running. Sometimes it seems like she is stuck with only the drudgery of work, not that she ever would say this to Alvin. Most days she accepts her calling graciously.

She stops icing the cake she is decorating to listen to him. Alvin has heard about a man in New Guinea who wants to sell off his soft drink bottling business. 'I think I'll go down there and see him about it,' he tells her. Gertrude smiles back at him. 'That sounds like a great idea.'

The man in Port Moresby is so eager to get out of his business that he sells all the machinery at a very reasonable price. By the time Alvin makes it back to Honiara, he already has a soft drinks business mapped out. When the equipment arrives he and Gertrude have to work out from scratch how to balance the syrups, the sugars, the colouring, the flavours and the carbonating. On the first night they are up until three in the morning, studying the various manuals they have bought from the Australian Chamber of Commerce.

Eventually, they work out a process where they use stubbies of 4X beer; they sterilize the bottles by hand, then pour in the syrups and flavouring before carbonating them and putting lids back on. Alvin will later expand the business from selling drinks only in Honiara to shipping bottles to the outer islands in copra sacks packed with sawdust to protect the glass bottles

He begins to make ice blocks, filling tubes of plastic with a cordial mixture and sealing them at the end. For the young, they offer sweet, frozen relief from the daily heat they endure. Children happily sucking on Blum's Ice Blocks become a familiar sight in Honiara. They are just as popular as Blum's Ice Cream that my father has already made renowned with one of the first radio advertisements in the Solomons:

'*Where are you going?*' a small child's voice asks.

'*I'm going to buy a Blum's ice cream*,' another answers.

'*Where is that?*'

'*Oh that's down in Blum's store in the main street*.' The businesses in town are so few that no further directions are required.

My mother continues to be obsessed about not having enough food. Getting protein into our diet is still difficult.

Meat is shipped in about every six weeks, but it is all gone in the first week, leaving five weeks of trying to live on something more than vegetables.

In 1956, when the first regular air flights started, the Agriculture Department brought in day-old chicks to try and stimulate a chicken industry. In an effort to improve our nutrition, my mother decided to have a chicken coop built. She purchased some chicks; they grew well, but she could not understand why no eggs were being produced.

One evening around dusk, our gardener began yelling at us to come and look. There in the coop was a six-foot-long python consuming our few precious eggs. The eggs, swallowed whole, formed a lumpy outline in its long frame. The gardener leapt across and cut off the snake's head, but it continued to slither, moving swiftly around the base of my legs. I remember the feel of its slimy, damp, headless body wrapped around my feet and lower legs. To this day I cannot look at a snake without shivering. Suffice to say, our egg supply improved after the demise of the python.

Gertrude reads in the *Pacific Island Monthly* that an ichthyologist has established Tilapia fish in ponds in the rice fields of Malaysia and is introducing the fish into Vanuatu. Tilapias are omnivorous, thriving on things that breed in dank, dark places. Gertrude particularly likes the fact that they feed on mosquito larvae – anything to reduce their bites. She writes to him asking him to establish the fish in the Solomons. He visits, bringing the initial fish for a pilot programme.

Fish ponds are dug in the garden outside our house,

under the supervision of an expert from South Africa. As water is being pumped up and into them, the town plumber comes racing in the drive. 'What are you doing up here?' he yells. 'We've got no water down in the town because you are draining the supplies!'

Water becomes a stumbling block for the project. The Public Works Department install a meter monitoring its supply and then quote an exorbitant fee for the usage. Alvin has already spoken to the Government about supplying them with free fish to distribute to other islands. He has heard the reports of how the people of Rennell Island, a coral atoll unsuitable for agriculture, suffer deficiencies caused by undernourishment. An Acting Senior Agricultural Officer argues his case in a letter to the Chief Secretary, asking for Alvin's water levies to be lifted in return for his free service.

The Administration still refuses. Alvin has no energy to keep his argument going. Without any cooperation from the Government the project is too expensive and he shuts it down. My father hates saying goodbye to a visionary idea. He decides to pass on what fish they do have to the Agricultural Officer who has been helping him, so that they can be put into Lake Tengano on Rennell Island and will hopefully become a new source of food for the people there. The project is successful and today the people of Rennell and Belona have millions of Tilapia fish to provide their protein. The project is also taken to Malaita, where the King George High School dig ponds and stock the fish. In this way, what has not been successful for my parents becomes a source of feeding others.

Gertrude is still searching for more sources of food. Much of the burden of organizing other small farm animals falls to John Mills. John has now left the Government Trade Store and is working with my parents. They have arranged a house for him and Ruhi to live nearby. John builds Gertrude a more secure chicken house. She soon has the idea of getting some goats.

John manages to buy a couple of goats and they multiply like rabbits. One day a Chinese man rings up Alvin. 'Mr Blum, the goats are running over our ancestors' graves in the cemetery,' he cries. John is sent out to round them up. It is such an ordeal that it is quickly decided that the goats have to go. They are given to a man who owns a plantation on another island. John loads them into a bus and takes them down to one of the inter-island boats.

The building of a house for ducks brings more problems. John leaves a small space above the door for the ducks to breathe. One night he wakes to the sounds of duck quacks and banging iron. Someone has threaded a small child through the gap over the top of the door and into the duck house. The child stands inside handing the ducks back out. At one in the morning John finds himself chasing a man carrying a noisy gaggle of ducks down the road. He never catches him.

Alvin decides that he will solve the issue by importing the first frozen meats and fish into Honiara. He commissions Ho Kee the builder to fill in the front of the bakery and he turns that into a general store. An old GI freezer that Alvin locates needs fixing up, but it will act like a walk-in frozen storeroom. By this time the electricity is running eighteen hours a day – enough to keep and store frozen food for longer periods.

* * *

In April 1957, almost three years to the date my family arrived in the Solomons, the first Local Spiritual Assembly of the Bahá'ís of Honiara is formed. A photo of the members is taken to record the event. John is smiling broadly, Gertrude is sitting next to George Khota, holding a sign that bears the Arabic symbol for the Greatest Name. It is a momentous achievement for my parents, and they look serious but quietly happy, aware of the sacredness of this moment. This institution can now decide upon activities of the fledgling Bahá'í community in the Solomons, and the shared collective decision-making takes a burden from the heavily loaded shoulders of my parents.

Alvin reads through the letter he has just received from Hamuel Hoahania, who lives on Malaita. He remembers the man, eager to hear about what he called a 'new religion', but anxious about sitting down on their furniture and having tea. 'Don't you think it's time to come here to establish a mission in Hau Hui?' Hamuel writes. Alvin raises an eyebrow when he sees the word 'mission'. He realizes they still have some work to do before Solomon Islanders truly know that they are not here to set up another mission. Bahá'ís have no clergy, and no 'career' opportunities. They don't have any resources to set up health clinics or any other services. In fact, they have no financial backing from their religion at all.

Since he first met Alvin and Gertrude, Hamuel has quietly been studying Bahá'í teachings by himself. He was formerly a member of the South Seas Evangelical Mission, but found such things as having to close your eyes to be close to God in Heaven quite hard. When he wanted to feel closer to God he used to stand on a table to pray. This was at the beginning of the idea that there was something better in the Christian and something bad in traditional religion, and for a long time Hamuel was unhappy with the unequal treatment being given to Solomon Islanders by the Christian missionaries. The more he reads about the Bahá'í Faith the more its sense of equality breathes new hope in him. Community and oneness are paramount to the Melanesian way of life. They organize themselves into Wantoks or 'One Talks' – extended family villages. So much division has happened in their society since the missions came. Hamuel finds he can no longer preach a religion that talks about loving one another when they are told that those who have not accepted Christianity are heathen and bad people and you should not associate with them.

Already, he has started speaking about the unity of this 'new religion' to family and friends. When John Mills goes to visit him early in 1958, he finds that his people do want to know more about the Bahá'í Faith. He also discovers that Hamuel is a big chief. Born in AreAre, he is the traditional owner of large allotments of land at Hau Hui on Malaita. Hamuel also has a successful copra production operation, one of the most prolific on the island of Malaita.

This news comes at a good time for Alvin and Gertrude. The Guardian's sudden death in London a few months earlier has hit them hard. He was only just over sixty, and still had so many plans to fulfil. Alvin and Gertrude have never felt so isolated. They are used to relying on his letters and cables. These would suddenly turn up, often in times of crisis and just at the point when they were ready to give up – sick, exhausted by the heat, and weary of winding their way through the convolutions of the Government Administration's bureaucracy. In between the lines of encouragement from the Guardian they could reconnect to the sense of purpose in what they were striving for. It gave them fresh energy to go forward.

The Government still makes it difficult for Europeans to visit Malaita. They patrol activities throughout the islands with caution. Much of their intelligence reporting carefully weighs the balance between the power held by the missions and the potential uprising of Ma'asina Rule – the political movement that has emerged since the war, based on the rejection of European rule and assertion of independence for Malaita. However, the Government knows Malaita is sorely in need of development. There are very few services on the island, except those that are provided by the missionaries.

Alvin instantly sees the opportunity when he hears that the Government is opening Malaita up to new business. He decides that they will build a store, bakery and theatre. John and Ruhi will manage it.

Land is bought at Auki on the west coast and John begins making the trips across to oversee the building.

The journey to Malaita takes twelve hours by small inter-island boats. Often the seas are rough, the crews inexperienced, and the boats old. Many of the crossings are terrifying. On one occasion John's boat slices through the side of another boat mid-crossing back to Honiara. In the middle of the night it is dark and it takes a desperate effort to get the people from the sinking boat on board.

Another time, John and Laurie Lake, a Bahá'í who has come up from Australia to help him in Auki, are heading for Malaita when a big pile of masonite shifts and puts the ship off keel. 'Oh, we're lost! We're lost!' a young boy starts yelling. John has to grab hold of the wheel from him and is able to straighten up the ship. On yet another stormy crossing, the ship's captain is drunk and staggering around the boat. This time John has been through so many dangerous experiences that when he sees that the coxswain has control of the ship he goes down below to sleep. 'If I'm going to buy out this time, so be it,' he decides.

* * *

Pacific Ocean, 1959

She can feel the scratch of his stubble, crusted with salt from the sea air, as he brushes her cheek with a kiss. 'Welcome back aboard, Gertrude,' chortles Brett Hilder. Gertrude smiles at him. It is such a different greeting from the one they received when they first boarded the

MV Malaita, almost exactly five years earlier. Brett rushes her and Alvin through to meet his French sister-in-law. 'Meet my brother Alvin,' he says proudly, then adds: 'I was just telling my sister-in-law about our religion.' Alvin chuckles when he hears this. He remembers how on our original voyage to the Solomons he had some lengthy talks with Brett and left him with some Bahá'í books to read. Brett Hilder has still retained his roguish ways and a special aversion to missionaries but Alvin is glad to see that he has never put the Blums in that category and has obviously taken time to study the Bahá'í teachings.

In the years since Alvin and Gertrude arrived in Honiara, Brett Hilder has been coming to visit them each time he pulls in with the *MV Malaita*. He's watched them build up their businesses and services to the community. 'I've been sailing into Honiara for years and years and nothing happened until the Blums came,' he says, one day out of the blue. He asks to paint Alvin's portrait, a homage reserved for his most respected passengers.

Two Solomon Islanders and members of the Local Spiritual Assembly of Honiara, Shebual Mauala and Bethuel Bama, are accompanying Alvin and Gertrude on a momentous trip. They are the two elected delegates to attend the formation of the first Regional Spiritual Assembly (RSA) of the South Pacific to be held in Suva, Fiji. The RSA will be the regional administrative body that includes Bahá'í communities in New Hebrides, Samoa, Fiji, Tonga, Cook Islands, Nauru, Gilbert and Ellice, New Caledonia, the Marshalls and the Solomon Islands.

They are on board the *MV Malaita* taking them to

Sydney, from where they will fly to Suva. The wind is chopping up the sea, crowning each broken wave with white froth. Gertrude stares out into the blue, but she doesn't really see the waves. Her mind is busy with the significance of what they are about to embark upon. She thinks of the distances involved, and how far-flung the people of islands such as New Hebrides (now Vanuatu), New Guinea, Solomons and Fiji are. But it is more than that. There are many hundreds of languages and customs and races, some traditional rivals, that will be brought together to cooperate as a single unit for the first time. A small surge of excitement ripples through her. She turns her face up towards the sun, closing her eyes, allowing its light to wash over her.

* * *

Malaita, November 1959

Several months later my mother heads out of Honiara on a small boat, making the first of many trips to the island of Malaita. John Mills is accompanying her. She watches him talking to the captain as the boat wends its way through the tricky passages. In Auki she sees their bakery, cinema and store being cobbled together out of Quonset huts. Many of the forty thousand inhabitants of Malaita have never seen a film before. For a moment she thinks about the vision she and Alvin have for the cinema: along with popular movies, it will also screen films by the United Nations for free.

It is eight hours from Auki by sea to reach Hau Hui where Hamuel and his family live. Gertrude breathes in deeply, bringing all her senses alive before stepping into the dug-out canoe. It is long and skinny and built for small, nimble Malaitans. My mother has grown larger and more unsteady on her feet. It takes all of Gertrude's concentration to keep herself balanced and seated during the long journey. Her head feels heavy with the effort of it when she eventually greets Hamuel, but she never lets him know it.

While the western world has had some impact on their governance and spiritual life, little has been done to improve the conditions of everyday life for Malaitan villagers. Gertrude has never been in a situation where she is required to go to the toilet on the beach. At night she carries a torch, shining it out ahead of her in short sweeps across the sand, keeping watch for crabs. In the morning she washes in the river. This is so alien for a woman brought up in New York, and in her ageing years, but her sense of spirituality and detachment overcome the discomforts she is willing to endure for her belief in unity.

Gertrude has brought bags of flour and yeast to teach the women how to bake bread. Jabin, the government-appointed headman, is the only person who has an oven. He is not willing to share it. Gertrude improvises with ovens made out of forty-four-gallon drum barrels and wood burning beneath them, and the women learn to make damper, scones and rock cakes.

During Gertrude's visit there are ten people who want to become Bahá'ís, including Hamuel. A few months later Alvin also visits Malaita. Hamuel has been speaking to the people of Su'uhara about this religion that says black man is equal to white man, and they want to hear more about it. To reach them Alvin wades through crocodile-infested waters with a battery-operated slide projector clamped tightly under his arm. He shows slides of the Bahá'í Houses of Worship around the world and of the many Conventions held, depicting the diversity of peoples, races and languages.

* * *

Honiara, 1960

They come towards him in a pack: six men in various states of undress and decoration. Alvin doesn't really know them, but he can tell that they are from Malaita and are men of standing within their culture. They come into our store on Mendana Avenue.

'Mr Blum, we want you to come and help us,' says one of the men. 'We've got some cargo. It's very, very heavy.'

'OK, I'll come,' Alvin says automatically. My father is one of the few private people in town who has a truck. He is also very willing to help Solomon Islanders with what they need. Our shop is not far from the wharf, so it is not unusual for them to ask for my father's help in this way. Sometimes they give my father a little bit of money. But in many cases Alvin just drives down there whether it is day or night.

My father fails to realize that his random acts of

help and kindness are building his reputation amongst Islanders he has never met. They also admire his commercial success and see him as someone who is there not just to bring benefits to Europeans but to the whole of the islander community.

At the wharf, seven enormous tin trunks squat on the jetty. It takes ten men to lift one of them onto the back of the truck. 'Woah there,' says Alvin, 'what have you got in these things? I don't think the truck will take more than two if they're all this heavy.' 'This is for you, Mr Blum,' one of the men says. 'This is all yours.' He opens a trunk. It is full of gold and silver coins. Alvin is confused. 'What do you mean, this is for me?'

'We've decided you're to be our new leader,' one announces. 'You're going to be our new boss. You're the only "Joe" who came back and we know that you came back to be our leader. This is our money for you to start this.'

The six men are all chiefs from the Are Are and Marau Sound areas on Malaita and Guadalcanal. They represent the most independent of tribes still clinging to the thinnest threads of custom rule. For years the trading schooners have been going to their shores for copra, giving them money or goods in exchange. When the war came they were given more money by the Americans. There are no banks on Malaita so they would bury it in tins around their houses. Alvin stares at what he recognizes is years of buried money that has been collected up. He sighs inwardly. 'Come on, let's sit down,' he says to them. They find some logs to sit on.

'Now, I didn't come here to be your leader with all this money,' Alvin says clearly. 'That's not what I came for,' he says it again. 'I came here to develop the people of the Solomons, make a small living for myself, but I'm not here for any political reason.' The men have no words. Their faces wear the look of disappointment, but they bear it like proud men, silent and upright.

'What do you want in your area that will help your life, improve your life?' he asks them, filling in the silence. The men look at each other. They begin, slowly at first, to discuss their needs together. Alvin leaves them to work it out. Finally they are ready to speak.

'We want a boat.'

'Why do you want a boat?'

'Because the Chinese come and they trade with us, take our copra and our goods and we know they're not giving us fair prices. We want to trade ourselves and to have our own boat. We've got bosuns and captains and we've got crew, we know the sea well. We can do this.'

'All right,' says Alvin. 'Let's take this money to the bank and get it counted.' There is only one small Commonwealth Bank in Honiara, situated where the Bank of the South Pacific, opposite Central Bank, is located today. The six Australian bank boys spend nearly a week sifting through the mountains of coins in varying currencies. When they finish it totals several thousand pounds. The money is still short of what is needed to buy a boat and an engine. Alvin agrees to guarantee the remainder.

The Government has already heard rumours that a

company is being formed. They are particularly concerned when they hear that Waiparo, the chief of Takataka and the most rebellious adherent to custom rule, is involved. A line of fear has been running through British administration intelligence reports that Waiparo thinks the Bahá'í religion will help him with tax. Alvin cuts through the rumours by informing the Government exactly what is going on.

Alvin baffles the High Commissioner, John Gutch. In his reports he writes of my father with a mix of grudging admiration and bewilderment. 'Blum is a shrewd and intelligent businessman, and he has used the same characteristics to infiltrate the Bahá'í Faith into the Solomons,' he writes, then adds, 'He has been meticulous in observing all necessary formalities and in most respects is an excellent citizen.'

It is two years since the High Commissioner appointed Alvin to the first Honiara Town Council. It was the first sign of acceptance from the Government. In the years following Alvin is asked to become President of the Hospital Board, with specific regard to building new premises. He also becomes a charter member of the Works Committee established to build up Honiara town, and of the Boy Scouts, as well as being appointed to the Civil Aviation Committee, and an adviser to King George VI Secondary School.

Alvin thinks of himself first as a businessman. He filters his actions through his faith and the straightforward ideals of humility and service he learned from the heart of Howard Colby Ives over twenty years ago. Alvin believes that you have to treat people with fairness and justice and equality. If business is going to develop in this town, he decides, it needs a voice in the Government.

Off his own initiative he organizes the first Chamber of Commerce. The Solomon Islanders also need enormous encouragement with developing agriculture. He wants them to believe they can do it themselves. Setting up the Financial Farmer's Club is one way he sees can help. He also acts as an adviser to the Young Farmer's Club on how to set up commercially viable schemes. And like Howard, his mentor, in setting up all this Alvin gives little thought to his personal well-being.

* * *

Ageing usually happens gradually and subtly. You seldom notice the extra pounds someone is carrying, the wrinkles that begin to deepen the lines of their expression, the grey strands fading their hair. Nobody sees what living here is doing to my parents more than I do. Each year I come home from school for five weeks of summer holidays and it is a new shock. It is as if they have aged ten years in one and it breaks my young heart to see them grow older in this way. I know their trials and tribulations and wish I could do more to ease their many burdens.

Somewhere in the deepest recesses of my childhood memory I have an image of my mother. In it she is frozen in time, always very neat and slim and stylishly dressed. I like her smell. It is clean, like soap. My mother no longer resembles my personal snapshot. Her body has become swollen and heavy and she moves more slowly than I can remember. When I am older I will learn that her thyroid has become underactive. My Aunt Molly, Abe's wife in New York, is particularly concerned about my mother's loss of her 'beautiful figure'. In her letters she hopes Gertrude is losing weight and sends tins of Metrecal, a meal replacement drink for dieting that she buys in Macy's.

My mother is too busy to care too much about her looks. In any case, shops and style are now unavailable to her. Sores emerge on her legs like open bruises and her feet are engorged with fluid. She wears flip-flops for simple comfort. Once dapper and fashionable, my father has developed his own version of a business outfit. It is a beige, short-sleeved safari suit. He wears it every day, like a uniform.

My father's little leaps in the air, the glow of his grin, have grown dim in my mind. There is his business work, then there are all the other activities in which he is involved. Every time I come home there is something new in their lives. My father has just opened a hole-in-the-wall fish and chip shop at the front of the bakery. He sends out his own fishermen to get the catch for the day and wraps up them up in butcher's paper with chips made out of local sweet potatoes. My mother has expanded the shop with a delicatessen. She cooks up hams to be sliced off the bone and even makes pickled herrings.

But there is something more that is wearing my father out. It is the challenge of trying to get anything done in this part of the world. It is as if Honiara is too small and too slow for my father. He gets an idea and he wants to set it in motion. Here, every attempt at something new is mired in obstacles. John Mills even suspects that they often hold up my father's goods in customs, sometimes letting food spoil on the wharf, just to make the 'pushy American' wait.

An insect bite and the slightest scratch make my father terribly sick, but he pays little attention to his health. He is bored by the detailed care involved in living with diabetes. Often I see him wolfing down donuts and soft drinks out the back of our shop, as if they will offer him a soft landing for all of his trials.

One day he declares he's fed up. 'I'm going off to Gold Ridge,' he tells my mother. He sets off with six Solomon Islander men in his truck. He climbs high into the mountains away from the mummifying heat of Honiara in search of cooler air, driving as far as his truck will take them. From there they walk on foot to the Gold Ridge area and find an abandoned hut for shelter. Alvin passes days reading *Thief in the Night,* a Bahá'í book on Bible prophecy in the form of a detective story, written by William Sears, while the men dig for gold.

When they leave, the men are happy, they've found their gold. Alvin is pleased for them, but he is still searching for a different kind of gold. Spiritual gold. The rains have caused the river to rise. The engine of his truck gives out when the water from the crossing gets through to it. He walks to the nearest village in Roroni. My father is always courteous and goes to find the headman to ask permission for he and his men to stay. He has some extra food, so a big feast is cooked up to share with the headman. As they are eating, a young local teacher whose leg has withered from polio comes up to him, hobbling on a crutch.

'Mr Blum, tell us about the principles of the Bahá'í Faith,' he asks in perfect English.

Alvin's eyes brighten. He is surprised the young man has heard of him, this area is so deeply missionized. He remembers the pamphlets he stashed in his bag – just in case. For six days he's been looking for the opportunity to show them to someone who might be interested. Alvin asks the boy's name. 'Stephen Matango,' he replies. Stephen's name becomes synonymous with opening up the area to this new religion. It is not long before a Local Spiritual Assembly is formed.

The world vision of the Bahá'í Faith is also beginning to permeate my own thinking. Conversations with my parents often revolve around global events and I am beginning to find it very interesting. I have moved to Adelaide to go to high school and am now living with the Featherstone family. When I am thirteen years old we are discussing the Aboriginal problem. My classmates are calling them 'black rubbish' and degrading them in the nastiest way.

'I think the Aborigines have been treated very unfairly,' I hear myself say as I stand up. 'Their own society has been destroyed by the whites and what we see now with all the drinking are people who have no hope.' The class goes silent. My teacher, Miss Anders, smiles at me. 'Thank you, Keithie.' Miss Anders is fond of me and writes to tell my parents how impressed she is by what I have said in class. She doesn't know that in the playground the children have begun to tease me. I am called 'black lover'.

The universality of the faith appeals to me greatly. The humanitarian and spiritual solutions to economic problems make sense in my mind. I have never come across anything that better answers the problems of today. Growing up in the Solomons I have seen the great divisions inside the Christian Faith through the way the missions are organized. They seem to operate as rivals, each making grabs for everybody's souls. Even at my young age, I can see that the principles of the Bahá'í Faith, if enacted, would bring more stability to the world.

When I am fifteen, I declare myself a Bahá'í. I am not a deeply philosophical child and quickly adopt my father's approach to his faith. While my mother spends many hours in prayer, my father says his prayers on the go. Like my father I believe that life is about living and getting things done. About wanting to make a difference by helping people to help themselves.

* * *

Malaita, 1962

For years Hamuel has been working as a Government 'dresser' or medical attendant, travelling through the Are Are area dispensing medicine. The most serious cases are reported back by him to be seen by a doctor who tours the islands on the Government medical boat. Many Malaitans have now heard of this chief who talks about a new religion that accepts all people of all faiths. Other village chiefs come to visit Hamuel and he tells them how the Bahá'í Faith can make things much clearer and that custom and culture can live together.

There are still enormous divisions on Malaita. The missions brand the people who find they are unable to accept Christianity, 'heathens'. They also tell their flock to stay away from them. The 'heathens' are the ones who are most watched by the government Administration. They are considered the most likely to stir up trouble.

As Chief Waiparo lies dying in his village at Takataka he tells his people to watch for the man who brings the Bahá'í Faith and to accept it. This causes a flurry amongst both the missions and the Government. Jabin, the Government headman, who opposes the Bahá'í Faith, hears that the Bahá'ís are on a crusade. He takes this news to the Government, believing that it means the heathens will soon join with the Bahá'ís to kill all the Christians in the Solomons.

A few months later, in August, Jabin threatens members of the Hau Hui Spiritual Assembly with jail. Members of the South Seas Evangelical and Roman Catholic missions begin to stalk Hamuel. One time, when he is speaking to a group, they begin to talk over him. 'The Roman Catholic Church is the first of all churches in the world and the only right church in the world,' yells one. The crowd doesn't want to hear about separation and begins to turn on the mission people. 'Please. Please stop,' begs

Hamuel. 'Remember we are all God's children. God is peace and we must be at peace and love each other.'

The condemnation by the missionaries has the reverse effect. People are tired of the squabbles and the separation. My mother and John are invited to visit villages in the Hau Hui area. Gertrude finds that eighty more people want to become Bahá'ís.

In Hamuel's village she notices a lot of children running around instead of being at school. The Malaitan mission and government schools refuse to take Solomon Islander children until they are eight, and it is very unlikely that any girl will be encouraged to attend. Illiteracy is still rife throughout the island. Gertrude speaks to Hamuel's son Dick about the situation. Dick has only had five years of education himself, but he is confident that he can teach pre-schoolers. Gertrude decides to organize a teacher's wage for Dick. His little school is the first to equally encourage both boys and girls to learn.

After my mother leaves, stories about the European woman who sits down with the islanders to eat *kaikai* (food) and talks about all religions run through the villages. In November, more than three hundred 'heathens' are saying they want to welcome in a new age as Bahá'ís.

13

All Things in Time

If we cannot end now our differences,
at least we can help make the world safe for diversity.

John F. Kennedy

Honiara, 1962–1963

In the giddiness of being invited to Government House, the presence of my parents at this event fades into the background. It is the first time we have all been invited to a formal dinner party by the new High Commissioner David Trench. I am too busy enjoying flippant repartee with the smart set of Honiara to register the significance of this discreet nod of acceptance to my parents, and the fact that it has taken almost a decade of involvement with the community for it to happen.

I have never been to such a formal occasion. I study the movements of ladies around me, watching how they use their cutlery for all the different courses. When the dessert plates are removed the High Commissioner's wife stands up. 'Well, come on ladies, we'll go and powder our noses,' she announces.

The High Commissioner clears his throat and places his napkin on the table. 'And gentlemen, we'll visit Africa.'

Visiting Africa sounds so much more interesting to

me than powdering my nose. 'I think I'll visit Africa with the men,' I say in a loud voice. The eyebrows of the High Commissioner's wife shoot up. She rushes across to me and firmly tucks her arm under mine, leading me into the powder room. 'My dear girl,' she says. 'Visiting Africa is only for men. It means the men are going to puff on cigars and do a wee in the garden. It is not the place for a young lady.' I feel a crimson heat creeping up my face. It is my first foray into the protocol that will surround me much later in my life.

I have finished my schooling and have returned to live with my parents for a year. Honiara has opened itself up to me in a totally new way. I am sixteen years old and have grown tall like my mother, only more fine-boned. My mother tells me I get my stature from her father. In personality, I am my father's daughter, wanting to take on the world and able to talk my way in and out of any situation.

The colonial boys of Honiara consider me a beauty. I am no longer ostracized. Most of the European girls have been sent off to finishing school so I have little competition. I revel in being fêted by a round of boyfriends, experimenting with makeup and new hairdos, piling my long hair high on my head. It turns out I have my mother's gift for creating glamour on a shoestring. When the navy boats dock in the harbour my party card is full.

During the day I work in my parents' businesses doing the paperwork and accounts. We no longer do dry cleaning and laundry, but the long line of services with the grocery, bakery, fish and chips, soft drinks, ice blocks and ice cream keep us enormously busy.

My father still pushes himself at full pelt. My mother is a slow, shadowy presence as she struggles to keep up. Late at night when my father is trying to shut up shop, my mother's attention becomes absorbed by some small detail. She dawdles and fusses as he waits impatiently at the door. Finally, his brow collapses against its solid surface. 'Please Gertrude,' he pleads in a deflated voice. 'Come away from the shop. Let's go home.'

Alvin decides that Gertrude will now only come down to the shop in the morning. In the afternoon there are plenty of Bahá'í secretarial and administrative duties that need to be attended to. I am too self-absorbed to give too much thought to what this says about my parents' relationship.

In a way the decision makes sense to me. I know how much my mother enjoys anything to do with the Bahá'í Faith. Our house is an open house. There is a constant stream of guests, mostly islanders, who arrive for friendship, food and spiritual sustenance. My parents are always giving informal talks on their porch, often lasting long into the night. I watch my mother's elegant hands, animated as she speaks. Her voice is a languid croon that drifts on the tropical breeze. My father's voice, an energetic contrast, rises and falls along with hers. In matters of the Faith there is a gentle rhythm that binds them. It provides them with a sacred space where their shared passions and ideals can come together. It is only much later that I will realize it has become their only connection.

My father has agreed to teach me to drive. It never occurs to me that this gesture might cause Gertrude pain. For years she has been at Alvin to teach her to drive but he has always refused, viewing her slow reflexes and etherealness as a potently dangerous combination behind a wheel. It is hard for me to imagine her frustration. I am skittish like a young colt, unrestrained and encouraged to go hard for what I want, no matter what the obstacles.

I am to be taught on my father's old ute. It is huge and unwieldy on the boggy, cavernous dirt tracks that still form the majority of roads in Honiara. Its engine whirrs as it heaves in and out of deep potholes. The gearbox resonates with a heavy clunk with each enforced change. 'Dad, why don't you teach me to drive on one of the better cars?' I ask, irritated as I wrestle with the heavy steering wheel. 'Because if you can drive this you can drive anything,' he reasons with typical Alvin logic. I roll my eyes in a huff, still unable to appreciate my father's way of building me up.

The nuts and bolts on the wheels are obviously worn. Often the ones on the front left wheel work themselves loose and the wheel runs away from the truck. My father is not alarmed by the sight of it spinning down the hill ahead of us. 'Put your clutch in and take it down into first and pump the brakes while pulling over to the side,' he instructs me calmly. The truck eventually stops. I get out to collect the itinerant wheel and my father shows me how he puts it back on. I much prefer it when Michael Marriot lets me practise on his swish new VW. This is often difficult to arrange because he is a much older boy who is courting me and my father doesn't like him very much.

A European police officer from England is the examiner for my driving test. We are in the ute going down Langakiki Hill when the wheel comes off again. I glance across at the examiner's face. It is stretched white and both hands clutch the door handle. 'Don't worry,' I say breezily, 'I know what to do.'

I double clutch down to first and pump the brakes like my father has shown me. Eventually the ute hobbles to a halt on the side of the road. I hear the door handle squeak open. 'You've passed,' the police examiner says, jumping out. 'What about the three-point turn?' I sing out to him. 'You've passed,' he calls back over his shoulder. 'I'm walking back to the police station.'

My driver's licence expands my sense of freedom and my burgeoning social calendar. I am always flitting off somewhere, especially on weekends. 'Hey Keithie, what have you been up to?' my father asks. Alvin has always asked me questions about my day since I was small. When I was at school he asked, 'What did you do in class today?' or 'Who did you play with?' and I would answer him. I am older now and don't always want to tell my father what I'm up to. I view his questioning as an intrusion upon my exploration of the deeply exciting territory of adolescence.

'Dad, why do you ask me so many questions about what I'm doing?' I say one day. 'Why are you so interested?' My father gazes at me for a long time. In his eyes there is something I've never seen before. 'You know,' he says quietly. 'I grew up in a household where nobody asked me any questions. My mother and father were busy with the business and the other children. Lillian was my special sister.' He looks away and runs a hand along the store counter. 'She brought me up and I would have loved someone to have asked me what I did, but no one was interested.' He turns back again, looking at me with soft eyes. 'I just wanted to let you know that I am interested because I care so deeply for you.' I stare down at my feet in silence.

My father has never spoken so intimately with me. I feel both humbled and a little closer to him. Years later when I become a mother I will still be moved by the tenderness in my father's words brought on by long-held feelings of hunger and loss. It will make me try very hard to always be intensely involved and alert to my children's needs. 'You don't miss a trick, do you Mum,' my youngest daughter Monique will tease me.

In the November of 1962 a cable arrives. When my father reads it all the colour drains from his face. I can tell something dreadful has happened. A sickly anxiety forms in the pit of my stomach. 'What's the matter with Dad?' I whisper to my mother. My mother is brief. 'He's just heard some bad news.'

My father goes home and shuts himself away in his room. He prays all day for the soul of his sister and her husband. His beloved Lillian and her husband Frank are dead. They have fallen into terrible financial difficulties that neither of them could see their way out of and decided together to end their lives.

Alvin goes over and over the circumstances of their deaths in his mind but finds he cannot wrap their action into an explanation that he can make sense of; that he can take comfort in. He is a man who has also been to the brink and stared hard into the financial abyss. Prayer and his belief in creating a better world have always carried him forward. My father does not show me his tears, but his distress is palpable.

* * *

London, 1963

My father makes his way down to the centre stage. He takes a deep breath and looks back up at the crowd. More than six thousand Bahá'ís from all around the world have come together at the Royal Albert Hall to celebrate their first International Bahá'í World Congress. My father has been asked to give a speech. It is the third great honour he has received. Being named as a Knight of Bahá'u'lláh was the first. The second was being invited, as an elected member of the National Spiritual Assembly of the South Pacific Islands, to go to Haifa to elect the nine members of the first Universal House of Justice – the international governing council of the Faith, as laid down by its founder Bahá'u'lláh.

As he speaks his words are animated with excitement. The crowd is captivated, silent, as my father's voice soars up through the stands. He tells stories about his life, some of which make the crowd laugh with him and some that I am hearing for the first time. He talks about the secret of pioneering, a question he is often asked.

'The secret,' he says, 'is being willing to give everything of yourself. The secret is willing to be sick, be lonely, willing to cry, give up, give up yourself and be willing for God to help. That's the secret. Believe me,' he continues, 'you go into strange places. You're hungry, you're tired and you're just fed up. But if you have the faith, everything works. The power of prayer, friends, is dynamic. You can't believe what has happened.'

I've heard my father talk about 'sacrifice' before, but I have never heard him speak about what that has meant in his own life – what it has given to him and what it has cost him. I don't realize that he is speaking like a man who has travelled far and fought hard and is nearing the end of the road.

London is swinging and I don't want to think about sacrifice. I am exploding with the wonder of everything I am experiencing. When my father flew to Haifa before going to London, my mother and I boarded the P&O cruise ship *Strathallan*. I was invited to a party by a gorgeous young man on the first night, and partied every night after. In Egypt I rode a camel and saw the pyramids, then travelled through the Suez Canal, stopping off in Marseilles, then on to London.

All the well-bred boys and girls from Honiara are home in London. Eddie, a boyfriend whom I hang out with in the Solomons, takes me to his family home outside the city. On other days I saunter down the fashionable streets and into dress shops, wide-eyed and soaking in the latest trends. My father joins my mother and me a few days later in the Earls Court apartment we have rented.

John and Ruhi are in London too. Alvin takes John to meet Bruce McComb, one of the three young boys he met in the print shop in New Zealand during the war, and later lent four hundred pounds to fund his dream of having a stall in London. My father often lends money to people. Sometimes he never sees it returned, but his belief in supporting ideas, especially imaginative or bankable ones, is irrepressible. Bruce now operates an art shop and has a thriving business, buying prints from homes that are being auctioned and reselling them. John smiles, thinking back to his own youthful dreaming in Sydney of having a stall in London. 'Well, my idea wasn't so silly after all,' he thinks to himself.

John and Ruhi have left my parents' business and won't be returning to Honiara with us. They have two small children, Jalal and Louise, and they are concerned about their future education. It is three years since they tragically lost their first son Leroy in an accidental drowning in India. Leroy was just a toddler and the experience left both John and Ruhi, and my parents, who adored the small boy like a grandson, grief-stricken. Now, having watched how difficult it was for my parents when I was sent away to Australia to attend school, John and Ruhi have decided they want to stay close to their children. After London they will start their new life in Sydney.

My father tries hard not to show his sadness. From the beginning, John accepted and understood Alvin in a way that others in Honiara would not or could not. He appreciated and learned a lot from his unconventional approach to money. Alvin never worried about it. John admired the dangerous amount of credit Alvin was prepared to rack up for his belief in what the bakery would bring to the town. Like a Musketeer, John took an enormous leap alongside Alvin, throwing in his life savings. They have been through a lot together – financially, spiritually and as friends. John knows Alvin will miss having someone to talk to. In some ways he feels like he is letting him down.

* * *

New York, 1963

It is a very different America that my parents return to after sixteen years. JFK has been elected President two years earlier. He is young and handsome and everybody, it seems, has a pin-up of Jackie. There is a great sense of excitement about him. He has begun the space race and started the Peace Corps. It feels like the dawn of a new age. The jaded hearts of the post-war era are now filled with hope.

I am experiencing for the first time what it is to be part of an extended Jewish family. I am totally spoiled. They take me out and buy me beautiful clothes and I visit delis, eating foods I've watched my mother cook. Schwarz New York cheesecake is my favourite. My parents have taught me about Moses and the Torah but I have no understanding that to be Jewish is a way of life. I make terrible *faux pas*. One night we are having dinner with my mother's family. I ask for ice cream after a meat meal. Nobody says anything and I am brought some as dessert. Like a good girl, I wash up the dishes, inadvertently mixing the plates of meat and milk in the same water. I have no idea that according to Jewish law I have just contaminated them. My mother's family are very good about it, they watch on in silence. After I finish, all the china is thrown out. I feel dreadful.

I go with my mother and Aunt Rose to visit my grandmother Rebecca. Her life has never expanded beyond the ever-decreasing Yiddish community in lower Harlem, where she lives alone. In the sixty years she has lived in New York she has never learnt to speak English. Now in her eighties, Becky bears her life like a terrible burden. Age has fragmented her spine, and she is bent over as if some great weight is holding her down. She does not occupy much space in this world.

I have only encountered my grandmother through photos of her younger, more upright self. The same eyes stare up at me now through more deeply fissured skin; a sad mouth smiles the wrong way around. She is stroking my face and saying something in a language I don't understand. 'She's telling you how beautiful you are,' my mother says. I have no Yiddish words to offer my grandmother and struggle to find a connection.

It is only much later in my life that I will discover how much disconnection my Aunt Rose has felt with her family background. My mother has long passed away when I go to visit Aunt Rose at her home in Florida around the year 2000. I ask her about being Jewish. A boy cleaning the pool overhears me and my Aunt is furious.

'I don't want you to ever mention that I have a Jewish background in front of anybody else,' she screams. I feel my heart stop a beat. I am shocked. I have never seen my Aunt so cross. 'Why?' I stammer. 'I'm not interested in discussing it,' Aunt Rose snaps back. 'That's a part of my life that I completely ignore.'

I will have no idea of the extent to which my Aunt has gone to follow this through until her son, Robert Roy, contacts me years after our meeting. My Aunt Rose has died in 2006 and Rob has been researching his family tree. Brought up as a Presbyterian, his mother a pillar of the church, he has only recently discovered, at the age of 72, that his family is in fact Jewish on both sides. I will hear how his family name was changed and how he grew up unsuspecting about the mythical background, full of heroic characters, that was handed down to him.

* * *

My father's cousin Elsa Sobo has arranged a family gathering for us. Her brother Lester is there. I watch Lester and my father ribbing each other as if they are still young bucks. It feels strange hearing Lester and my father speak in this way. I want it to stop. Lester says something very crude. I climb high on my horse and say, 'Nobody speaks to my father like that!'

Elsa cannot believe how much her favourite cousin has changed, though she never says this to him. Alvin seems a quieter, more serious version of his old self. But it is not just the years spent in a difficult place that have changed my father. Nobody, including Elsa, realizes how much my father is grieving for his dead father and sister.

After his wife Pauline died in 1957, Oscar was a lost man. He was still charming and full of big vision, but working on his own mediocre real-estate projects. With his gift for stories, he managed to talk his way into another marriage, but it wasn't long before his new wife realized that the promised money didn't exist and Oscar was alone again. A man unused to having to bend his ideals for the next generation, he wore out his welcome with various relatives who couldn't really understand him or what he was trying to do with his life. Three years later, in 1960, he isolated himself back in the apartment he last shared with his wife in New Jersey and there he died alone.

Alvin seems terribly troubled by the knowledge that no one was with his father, perhaps including himself. The recent loss of Lillian compounds his anguish. It ferments inside him until, unexpectedly, it erupts in great, gut-wrenching sobs. I am shocked to see my father grieving in this way, openly broken and inconsolable.

My father never talks about what is going on inside him and I don't dare to ask. We travel down to Florida where my cousins Richie and Martin live and where Lillian and Frank are buried. Again, it is a sad visit. Alvin feels an acute sense of loss, helplessness and isolation. He prays frequently through this ordeal, drawing on his deep spirituality to sustain him.

I feel for my father, but after a week or so I can't wait to get back to the big city glamour of New York. It is as if a whole new world is waiting for me there. I see how different my parents' lives could have been, how different my own life could be, if we had stayed in the States.

I have already decided that I will study nursing. My decision has largely been financial: my parents don't have the money to house me anywhere, and nursing or teaching offer free student accommodation. One of my Aunts insists that I stay with her in New York to do nursing. I imagine all that might happen for me here and decide to accept her offer. I tell my parents that I will travel with them to Los Angeles to see the rest of our relatives, then return to New York. They put up no opposition to my new plan.

When I am in Los Angeles, I suddenly decide that I don't want to stay in America. Something doesn't feel right, although I don't have the words yet to express what that is. I have this sense that my life will probably change forever – and not in a good way. Without understanding it, I am a bit frightened of the American way of life. It is fast and materialistic and I sense an emptiness in a way I cannot explain.

I write to my Aunt to tell her I have changed my mind and I am going to continue with my original plan and study nursing in Cairns in Northern Queensland.

* * *

Solomon Islands, Malaita crossing, 1964

Alvin can no longer see what lies beyond the bow of the boat or to either side of it. All lights for navigation have been knocked out by the storm and the crew is panicking. My father is making a night boat crossing back from Hau Hui in South Malaita. The boat is small: twenty, maybe thirty, feet. It heaves to the right. Waves crash against the side, their torrents of water rushing in furiously over and across the deck, toppling some of the crew.

My father hauls himself along a handrail to the front of the boat. The Captain has been steering the cutter back and forth, searching for the mouth of the canal that transverses Nggela Island on the way back to Honiara. Alvin knows they need to reach the calm of the passage now before the boat either goes under or runs out of petrol. He hears the voices of men behind him, high-pitched with fear. The seawater blasts his eyes with stinging salt, but he keeps them open in the inky black. He prays hard for some sort of sign; shouting out his words, as if making sure he is heard above the deafening rages of wind and sea.

Alvin's answer comes after an almighty crack, then a thunderous roar. The sky opens up with lightning. He looks around, convinced something divine has turned night into day. The moment of light is long enough for Alvin to see that the boat is nearly alongside a narrow passage opening. He swings his whole body around. 'Turn now,' he yells as loud as his lungs will carry. The boat turns into the Bole Passage that cuts through the island. The calm of the passage allows them to take stock and settle cargo the storm has scattered.

As they leave the passage, Alvin can see the distant lights of Honiara. The boat limps into Honiara on the last of its fuel. Alvin rests his full weight on the side rail, his head bent forward staring into the murky nothingness. The intensity of the experience has almost drained him of his own reserve.

This trip to Malaita has come suddenly, after receiving a letter from Hamuel saying he was in need of urgent help. Years earlier Hamuel allowed the British Administration Government to build a school on a parcel of his land for free. This worked until recently, when the Government announced it wanted to charge the parents school fees. In response, Hamuel said that he wanted the Government to pay rent. The Government did not like being pushed into a corner and pressed Hamuel to sell them the land. Hamuel refuses, so the Government has now closed the primary school and moved the building to the village of Su'u.

Alvin has arrived here with roofing to build a new school as quickly as he can, but already there are problems mounting for Hamuel. Some of the parents in the village are blaming him for the loss of the school. They don't understand that he has been trying to stop them being taken advantage of.

When Alvin sees Hamuel, he hugs him. It is the first time he has met up with his friend since he gave his speech at the Congress in London. There he acknowledged all that this man had given of himself. 'He's the big daddy in this area,' Alvin said. 'He's the sparkplug; the cause of hundreds of believers in his area coming into the Faith.' These are mostly people who do not want to have anything to do with the missions that wrote them off as heathens. Alvin is sure these Malaitans have a big future. 'They're intelligent,' he told the Congress. 'They're smart and they know what they're doing. We offer them nothing either,' he added. 'We have nothing to give them.'

Hamuel's son Dick still has no proper premises and the number of children in his pre-school has grown to sixty-three. Under pressure, Hamuel has decided that he needs a fresh start, both for himself and to build a new school. He moves both his family and the school location to another piece of his land at Tawaimare. It is about two kilometres away.

Over the next year my parents will help Hamuel search for proper teachers to staff the new school. It is a difficult task to find fully trained people who are willing to come to such a far-flung and undeveloped location for a pittance of a wage. They search through the Bahá'í community. Eventually, there are two volunteers from Australia – the Simpsons. At first Mr Simpson is rejected by the Government because he is suffering from the early onset of multiple sclerosis. On appeal, he is granted his visa, but it will be early 1965 before they arrive.

An American architect, Mr Grunewaldt, has also just arrived to help with the building of the schoolhouse. My mother will write how the mothers of children, so eager to help, carried sand, gravel and leaf for the native-style building. The school soon opens, teaching the government curriculum but run according to Bahá'í principles. In 1968 it becomes fully inaugurated and accredited to the Solomon Islands Education Department.

14

A Sudden Leaving

We work and pray for the unity of mankind,
that all the races of the earth may become one race,
all the countries one country,
and that all hearts may beat as one heart,
working together for perfect unity and brotherhood.

'Abdu'l-Bahá, *Paris Talks*

Honiara, 1964–1965

Alvin watches the well-dressed Melanesian man pacing. The man treads an unseen tightrope, back and forth, across the front drive of the Hotel Mendana. At each end-point he stops, shakes his head furiously and turns on his heels again. A small group of locals recline languidly against a nearby fallen tree trunk. The man has become their theatre, the trunk their viewing platform. Their heads turn, left and right, with each pass the man makes.

'You look very upset, is there anything I can do to help you?' Alvin asks the man.

The man stops mid-line. 'Well, I did have a booking at this hotel, but now I've got here and there's no room for me, and I've got nowhere to stay,' he says, bundling his words into one breath.

My father is shaking his head now. Ken Hay, the man who first hired, then fired my father from the Woodford Hotel all those years ago, has upgraded the hotel to become the Hotel Mendana, adding another fifteen rooms, but little has changed about his policy on accommodating islanders.

'Don't worry,' my father tells the man. 'You come home with me and stay with us for the night.'

Some of the stiffness relaxes out of the man's shoulders. 'Well, I'm leaving the next day for Vila, so I just need accommodation for the night. I'd be very grateful,' he says, shaking my father's hand. 'Thank you very much.'

Gertrude cooks dinner and they all sit down together. When my father hears the man's European-sounding name he understands why his booking was initially accepted by the Hotel Mendana. Of course, it has been a different matter when he has presented his dark-skinned self in person at reception. The man is unused to being treated in this way. He is a respected doctor from Vanuatu and is on the return journey from attending a United Nations conference in Australia.

Alvin lies awake and alone with his thoughts. The more he thinks about what his guest has had to go through the more incensed he becomes. Alvin is used to his body cramping at night – it is one of the side effects of years spent living with diabetes and strained kidneys – only now, the adrenalin pushes more chemicals around in his body, compounding the pain he feels in his rigid muscles.

My father has developed a routine involving the Hotel

Mendana. On Tuesday nights the hotel turns into a social meeting point as guests disembark from the DC3 plane making its weekly run from Lae in Papua New Guinea, while those who are leaving the country on the return flight are being farewelled. Alvin goes there as much for a chance to socialize as for the mail and magazines the plane delivers.

As he thinks about what he can do, tiny capsules of blood pulse inside his temples. Finally, a solution pushes its way through the anger. In the morning he gets out of bed early. He strides through to the breakfast table and his hands slap down on its edge. Alvin grins broadly at Gertrude and his guest. 'I'm going to build a hotel,' he announces. 'I want to build a hotel where anyone can stay. Any colour, race, religion, creed, it doesn't matter.'

Gertrude smiles thinly back. She can see what Alvin is trying to do, but in the pit of her stomach she wonders and worries about what new edge he will stretch their finances to. She prays that they won't topple off.

After he drops his guest off at the airport, Alvin goes to visit the Commissioner of Lands, Brian Toomey, at the Lands Department. His friend listens to him intently as he outlines his plan. 'Alvin, I'll tell you what,' Brian says when he has finished. 'I've got just the piece of land for you.' It's the kind of news Alvin likes to hear. He slaps his friend on the back. 'Let's go!'

Brian walks him down a dirt track. It is cross-hatched with old army issue Marsden matting that has been laid down to stop the grass growing and give it traction when it turns to mud with the wet season rains. 'In the future, this is going to be a main thoroughfare, Alvin,' Brian says confidently, 'and this is going to be an excellent spot for your hotel.' Alvin believes in his friend's foresight, which will later prove correct when the road is sealed. Today it is Hibiscus Avenue, one of Honiara's main thoroughfares.

In a surprisingly short time Alvin manages to raise the money to buy the land and build the hotel. In many ways, this proves the easier part of the process. It is much tougher than even Alvin imagined to get all the materials needed to construct his vision. I do what I can from my Cairns base in far North Queensland, Australia, sourcing taps and other specifics to be sent up. The delays on goods arriving are both unavoidable and intentional, with customs often impounding them for weeks.

I don't see how the frustrations of making the hotel happen are wreaking havoc with my father's health. He has become large and overweight, his old jaunty bounce is now a low hop, as if something is pressing him into the ground. Away from Honiara, I delight in my choice of different rainbow colours to paint the front doors of rooms. In my mind's eye I can already see how they will blend beautifully with the low slung, sleek hotel lines that are the fashion of the day.

When the hotel is built my parents call it Blum's Hometel. Hometel is a word Alvin and Gertrude invent themselves to describe how they want people to respond to the ten rooms that each contain a kitchenette, a bathroom, bed and sofa bed. A home away from home – a hometel.

* * *

Sydney, 1965–1966

There has been some difficulty at the Cairns hospital where I am studying. There is no official tutor sister and many of the girls are failing their prescribed academic courses. I am not one of them but I realize, after nearly two years of studying, that I need to transfer to another hospital. I decide to continue my nursing studies at the Rachel Foster Hospital in Sydney.

Ruhi and John are living in Sydney, and I have been given the address of my parents' friends Eva and Fred Grant. They are Czechoslovakian Jews who have become Bahá'ís. I knock at the front door of their apartment in the beachside suburb of Coogee. 'Hello, who are you, young lady?' I hear a voice ask. I turn and see the face of a handsome young man with a cheeky grin and a naughty glint in his eyes poking his head out the window of an apartment that is below where my parents' friends live.

When nobody answers my knock at the Grants' residence, he invites me inside. His name is Bruce Saunders and this is not the first time Bruce and I have met. When I was living in Adelaide during high school, his mother Grace was very sweet and kindly took me under her wing. I remember Bruce as a tubby teenager without much dress sense. I cast my confident fashion eye over him now, appraising the man he has become. He still has shabby dress sense, I decide, but he has slimmed down and is dashingly debonair and quick-witted.

I suspect immediately that it is this last quality that has already charmed my father. During the early 1960s my father has been meeting up with Bruce when he comes to Sydney to do business and pick up more films for our theatre in Auki. As a young Bahá'í, Bruce is full of admiration for Alvin – a Knight of Bahá'u'lláh - and is more than happy to drive him around to his appointments. Alvin takes Bruce out to Jewish restaurants and gives him free movie passes that his agents hand out to wholesalers.

I have never held back from telling my parents about my boyfriends in Cairns. My father would ask me many questions about them, but they never quite measured up. 'You know, in Sydney there's a very nice man called Bruce Saunders and he looks after me when I go down,' my father would say to me. I am young and rebellious and not interested in my father's choice of beau. 'Well, if you like him,' I would reply, 'he must be the biggest square out.'

Bruce works with Nationwide Food services. He is only twenty-three but already he is managing the catering for eight cafeterias and factories. He is also one of the young men about town. Instead of cooking at home he has many girlfriends whom he visits and gets free meals from. After we begin dating I am in his apartment one day and open the fridge, thinking that inside there will be all sorts of gourmet delicacies. Instead, I find a typewriter and six books.

Needless to say, the fridge is not functioning; it is used as a storage cupboard. Bruce usually eats at work, where the adoring ladies in the kitchens take pity on their young boss and cook him meals. With his flatmate John Walker, a brilliant insurance executive who frequently makes the 'young entrepreneur list', both young men enjoy the delights of Sydney town in the '60s.

We are soon madly in love and full of all the possibilities in the world. Both of us operate at the same pitch – one hundred miles per hour. Bruce writes to my parents telling them that he is keen for us to be together. My parents are delighted and so are Bruce's parents, Grace and Edward.

We are to be married after I finish my nursing training, but our plans soon change. I have contracted hepatitis. It is my second long bout of illness, having had glandular fever in Cairns. I don't seem to have the physical stamina required for the nursing standards of the day. Often there are only two nurses on a forty-bed ward. Even though I have only one more year to complete in my four years of training, I decide to quit. My parents are dismayed, but I am in need of nursing myself. I go to Adelaide to recuperate with Grace and Teddy, who is in the midst of a long battle with Parkinson's Disease.

My father can no longer ignore his own health. He is ordered to go down to hospital in Sydney for tests, and Bruce and I visit him in hospital daily. When I first see my father it is a shock. His skin and eyes are stained a sickly yellow by something foreign that is ruminating inside him. At first the doctor believes he will have to operate, but tests show it is not my father's usual problems with his kidneys or gall bladder that are causing his illness. A germ has burrowed its way inside Alvin's liver, swelling it to twice its normal size and blocking the functioning of the surrounding organs.

My parents' only forms of communication are cable and letter. Alvin cables Gertrude to let her know that no operation is needed. When he writes a letter to explain his condition in more detail, he still has not heard from her. He knows my mother has been worrying about money and writes jauntily, 'a week more of rest will do the trick' and the savings on an operation will be at least 150 to 200 pounds.

Building the hotel, on top of all his other businesses and activities, has drained my father both of his health and his finances. Bruce and I are to be married in two weeks, but my father has no money to stay in Sydney. My parents have decided that only my mother will be present. My father is distressed that he won't be at the wedding of his only child, but he doesn't show it. He is a man who keeps his emotions locked up – especially those that are connected to the people he holds dearest.

Before he leaves Sydney to go back to the Solomons so that my mother can come down for the wedding, he sits down and talks with me as a father to his daughter. He tells me about his family and about his childhood. It is only the second time I have thought about my father as anything other than a man of action, clear in his direction. For a few short hours I see the lonely boy he was: unsettled, unsure and unhappy. It is hard to say goodbye to him knowing he is still unwell and going back to the heat, tribulations and constant frustrations of the business. I try to be philosophical; life must go on, but we bid a sad farewell.

* * *

Our wedding cake arrives from Honiara ahead of my mother. Bruce and I open the box and our shoulders slump. The cake has been smashed to pieces during its journey. Both of us understand how much love my mother has put into making this cake. We pour what money we have left into getting the cake restored. It costs fifty pounds, ten times my monthly nurse's wage. Gertrude never finds out.

On the day of my wedding I go to the hairdresser and have my hair piled up and intertwined with frangipanis. Their sweet white and yellow petals and fragrance remind me of a part of Honiara I love. Ruhi's parents have sent me a beautiful white and gold sari from India and Ruhi arranges the pleats, making sure they drape in the correct way around my body. When my mother sees her nineteen-year-old daughter dressed as a bride she is overcome. 'My word,' she gasps proudly. 'I was nearly twice your age when I married,' she tells me but there are no words of advice. She has never been motherly in that way. Instead, she smiles broadly and the love radiates out of her.

We are married at Judy and David Hassall's home in Strathfield on 5 February 1966. We cannot afford a sit-down wedding breakfast, so a friend caters with a light supper. Our honeymoon is a few days in another friend's shack at Bateman's Bay on Sydney's south coast. When we return we hear a call to pioneer in the Cook Islands. Bruce is friendly with an American couple, Rick and Gwen Welland, who already live there. Rick is a well-known artist and has often written telling Bruce how beautiful the islands and the people are. Bruce looks at me. 'Let's go!' he says. 'Fine,' I answer, not really minding either way. Bruce is just twenty-five years old and I am about to turn twenty. We are up for an adventure.

My mother is still in Sydney when we tell her our news. In a letter to my father she expresses her displeasure. It seems to have more to do with the fact that she cannot understand why the Cook Islands, with a population of only twenty thousand, needs any more pioneers than the two it already has. 'I know what you're thinking,' she writes, 'but evidently, the Solomon Islands is not a major goal.'

My father's opposition is more directly aimed at us. He is terribly disappointed. In a series of letters he writes how he is not well and needs our help. Help with the business. Help with the Bahá'ís. We feel that we are letting him down badly and, for a moment, we almost waiver. We talk to other Bahá'í friends and they agree with us. Bruce and I need to establish ourselves as a couple independently of home.

Our first row is over food. Since I quit nursing I have been working at WD & HR Wills (the cigarette company) in Raleigh Park Sydney as an industrial nurse. In my downtime at the clinic I study cookbooks, trying to teach myself how to prepare gourmet dinners to impress my chef husband. I rush home to set the table and make these wonderful suppers, but my new husband has not yet dropped his old habit of eating at work. 'Look,' I snap one night, 'if I'm going to put all this effort into food you'd better come home hungry.' But there is something else.

I realize that I have never learned how to cook because I have barely lived at home. My mother is famous for her food. Her knowledge has been lovingly passed on to the women who have lived with my parents and women who are close to them. They have spent time, years sometimes, following Gertrude around in her kitchen and studying how she creates wide-ranging delights out of almost nothing. I have only learned three dishes from my mother. All of them are Jewish – borscht (beetroot soup), Wiener schnitzel and a yummy New York cheesecake.

* * *

Honiara, 1966

He reads the headline. 'New Cash, New Owners, But the Same Old Policy for Honiara's Mendana'. A picture of Ken Hay, gruff-faced with his plaid shirt tucked in around his portly belly, sits beside an article that is published in the March 1966 edition of *Pacific Island Monthly* magazine. Alvin can feel a heat rising inside him. The new shareholders in Hotel Mendana don't have any issues with Ken Hay's old managerial policies, so Solomon Islanders still cannot book accommodation there or eat or drink in the main lounge or dining room.

Ken has his own justifications. 'Solomon Islanders can't stay at my hotel because they are not all at the stage where they are fit to stay here,' he argues. 'Certainly some of them are, but if I let some in and keep most of them out then that would be discrimination. I don't discriminate.

However, the sign still sits at the entrance of the hotel: 'No dogs or blacks allowed inside.'

'You can't ask Europeans to wait on some of these people,' he adds. 'My Chinese cook wouldn't cook for them. Europeans wouldn't be able to use the same bed linen.'

The comments leave Alvin both energized with anger and weary all at once. He is tired of these old ideas that won't go away. Despite his best efforts over more than a decade, the Solomon Islanders are still so far from being allowed a position of equality in their own country. And he worries. How much longer can he keep going like this?

Alvin forces himself to get up out of his chair, go over to his writing desk, and fight the best way he knows how – with reason and encouragement. His letter to the editor appears in the next edition of the magazine.

'We refer particularly to the comment of the New Guinea people who say, "Thank God you have enough guts to keep out the rabble!" ' he writes mid-letter.

'We wish to go on record as saying that this policy does not reflect the opinion of the majority of the people of Honiara. Many here are dedicated to developing the Solomon Islanders to first-class citizenship and do not consider them as rabble.

'If any of the islanders come to Honiara, including the Nauruans, there will be a place for them. "The Earth is one country and mankind its citizens." '

Alvin doesn't get much public support after his letter. It is as if nobody wants to acknowledge the deep wounds that the colonial administration has carved into this country. One day an anonymous letter turns up in the post. It is handwritten on a piece of paper torn in half from a lined paper pad and folded four ways until it forms a tiny rectangle.

'Mr Alvin J. Blum,' it begins.

> I have just read your letter in PIM (April 66) and I heartily endorse your remarks. It needs more people with "guts" like yours to speak up for these people, but unfortunately, too many of us are moral cowards – we remain silent when we should speak – in some cases, because we feel we may offend our commercial associates. I regret to say that I am one of these people and therefore leave this letter unsigned . . .
>
> Best wishes and more success to you.
>
> An admirer.
>
> (I am known to you personally.)

Alvin folds the letter back up and files it away with the all the other letters that are a record of his life. There is a meeting he has to get to at his hotel. Mr Hemphill, the Chief Administrative Officer of Australia and New Zealand Banking Group (ANZ), has arrived in Honiara to see what is necessary for setting up a branch here. For years Alvin has been working with other businessmen in the region, rallying them up, to break the monopoly that the lone Commonwealth Bank has in Honiara. Alvin has had his own difficulties with the Bank and sees this set-up as having been a barrier to wider development in the Solomons. He wants competitive banks to give better developmental opportunities.

It is three years since Donald Gubbay and a few other businessmen began meeting in earnest with ANZ in Australia. Alvin has given his own assurances that if another bank was to open a branch in the Solomons he can guarantee them fifty clients tomorrow. He shakes hands with Mr Hemphill after showing him around Blum's Hometel and agrees to provide temporary accommodation for the bank's staff when they arrive.

It is early October when the bank opens. The new bank manager is Alan Barker. True to his word, my father introduces him around to the business community and does anything he can to help them get established.

Gertrude understands her husband's excitement about the new bank, but she doesn't share it. For the first time in a long time, she feels secure. They are free of debt with any bank, and free of the Auki business: Mr and Mrs Fassy, Bahá'ís from Ceylon, have taken over the lease of the store and bakery on Malaita. For most of their marriage she has watched her husband, wanting to tell him to slow down but knowing he won't listen. In his recent decision to give up the business in Auki, she can see a change happening in Alvin, only she doesn't yet know what it all means.

* * *

His old friend has grown thicker with age, his hair is now a wiry mound of silver floss. The afternoon sun backlights it, making it appear like a bright halo around his head. During World War II, Jacob Vouza was one of a few hundred islander Scouts who along with a handful of Coastwatchers operated, often behind enemy lines, as a crack squad reporting on the movements of the Japanese.

They played a vital role in informing the Allies of Japanese military targets and supply lines. The most infamous was dubbed the 'Tokyo Express' by the Allies, a run of Japanese-laden ships carrying extra troops that regularly came down from Rabaul through 'The Slot', the long, skinny channel of islands that leads to Guadalcanal, at high speed and under the cover of night. In the Western Province, near New Georgia, two of the Solomon Islander Scouts, Biuku Gasa and Eroni Kumana, traversed forty miles of hostile waters in a dugout canoe to rescue the future President John F. Kennedy and his crew, who were found in a most pitiful state after their PT-109 had been mowed down by a Japanese destroyer returning from a supply drop in August 1943.

These brave men, known simply as 'Scouts', received little recognition and almost no payment for their services. Sergeant-Major Jacob Vouza was an exception. A former policeman, Vouza rescued a downed American Naval pilot on 7 August 1942 from behind Japanese lines. After meeting the Marines for the first time he volunteered to go back inside enemy lines as a Scout. Later that month Vouza was captured by the Ichiko detachment at Tenaru beach.

The Japanese found an American flag tucked inside his loincloth, so they tied him to a tree with vines and tortured him: bayoneting him in the arms, throat, face, shoulders and stomach. Still, Vouza refused to give them any information. Eventually they left him for dead.

Over three days, Vouza chewed his way through the vines, then stumbled to safety, refusing treatment until he had informed the Marines of the Japanese Army's movements. It took twenty-six pints of blood and twelve days in hospital to revive him. When he discharged himself he went back out behind the enemy lines in a thirty-day raid. He used to boast he was half American, with all that blood.

For his bravery, he became the most decorated Solomon Islander, awarded the Silver Star, the Legion of Merit and the British George Medal. Later, he received the Police Long Service Medal and in 1957 was made a Member of the Order of the British Empire (MBE). Alvin had long passed away when the Queen knighted Vouza in 1984. Sir Jacob Vouza became an icon of Solomon Island steadfastness and honour.

The experiences of war have bred in Vouza a love of the Americans. He calls his village, west of Tenaru, 'California'. Every day he raises and lowers the same Stars and Stripes flag he was given before he was captured. As an American who came back, my father has a special bond with Vouza. Vouza also loves his country and his people and was one of the few indigenous Solomon Islanders who was trusted enough to be appointed as a member of the first Protectorate Advisory Council in 1951. Both Vouza and Alvin have a respect for what heights the Islanders are capable of and an honest desire to see them gain their independence.

Vouza, however, doesn't share my father's ability to view the Japanese in a way that isn't attached to the horrors of war. They keep their conversations focused on the bravery of the Coastwatchers and War Scouts. Believing that this is something that should be formally celebrated, they have joined together in 1967 to form the Solomon Islands War Veterans Association.

The sun catches the row of medals on Vouza's chest as he turns around. He is wearing his old Sergeant-Major's uniform from his pre-war police force days. Vouza bears himself like a proud chief as he stands under the high native thatched roof of the Bahá'í Centre that my parents have built on their property. A group of former American Army veterans who have made a symbolic flight from Hawaii to Henderson Air Field for the 25th anniversary of the Battle of Guadalcanal gather around him.

The vets already know about Vouza's heroism. They have brought him small gifts as simple tributes: a cigarette lighter that tinkles 'The Marines' Hymn' and a Marine belt and cap. They also carry a more significant mark of respect: a personal letter to Vouza from Lieutenant General Victor Krulak, who is commanding the Marine Corps in the Pacific.

He lifts his head back, showing them the scar that rises, thick and nobbled, in a line down his throat, neck and arms. They peer in awe. Vouza grins, flashing the set of teeth that Jack Parr, the host of American television's Tonight Show, paid for in a show of appreciation when he visited Guadalcanal on the 20th anniversary of the bloodiest battle in the Pacific. It was an emotional pilgrimage for Jack Parr, who had spent twenty-eight months as an infantry sergeant in a special service company. His main job, as he wrote when he returned back home, was to try to make men laugh in a place that was one of the least funny in the world.

Jack Parr interviewed my father during his visit to Guadalcanal. He was trying to get some sense of what would move anyone who had experienced the conditions on Guadalcanal to want to come back. Alvin tried to explain about what he saw in the people, and all that he believed could be built up out of this place of hell.

Billy Bennett, another indigenous islander War Scout, is here for the anniversary celebrations too. Billy is now a popular radio broadcaster and Alvin remembers Jack Parr describing this man as 'the most cheerful soldier who ever slit an enemy throat'. He recalls an incident during the war when Billy was embedded in a village he was using as a scout base. Two armed Japanese soldiers arrived, and in trying to impress the villagers and win their cooperation they passed around their modern arms. When it was Billy's turn he accepted the gun, looking at it first with slow, careful curiosity before swinging the rifle around and swiftly shooting both Japanese dead. Jack was right: it is hard to reconcile this action with the sweetly colourful Pidgin commentary Billy gives on his radio broadcasts.

Jack has been right about something else: it is hard to live here on Guadalcanal. Nothing has changed about the humid, bug-ridden heat and rains that once drained so many men of their will to fight, or even simply to carry on. As Alvin drives back through the town, he sees the rusted detritus of war still lolling under the sun where it was abandoned and the GI equipment that's been reclaimed for buildings or fencing. There are small signs of progress that ground the hope that this country will one day be capable of standing on its own feet. But there is still the longest limp towards independence ahead, and Alvin is not sure what strength he has left in his body to help it along its way.

My mother no longer uses words to urge my father to take better care of his health. Alvin pretends not to notice her looks of concern. He continues through his days, stretching himself thin across the many parts of his life – his businesses, his community work and his faith. His beliefs still burn brightly inside him, only lately he has begun to feel as though there is something shadowing his connection to why he is here.

Something is squeezing his heart. The pain grabs him suddenly, then goes, leaving his head in a light, spinning fog. Alvin, always so acute and sharp-minded, can sense a looming danger. His doctor looks at him gravely. He tells Alvin as firmly as he can that he needs to get away from the Solomons for a while and have a good rest.

There is an Intercontinental Bahá'í Conference being held in Sydney in October. Gertrude says a small prayer of thanks; she doubts that without this event to organize himself around, her husband would consider a break. Owen Battrick, an elegant English Bahá'í who has wanted to move to the Pacific, agrees to look after the businesses while they are away.

Hamuel is with my parents when they leave for Sydney. They stay with Ruhi and John, and the boisterous happiness of their children Jalal and Louise returns some of the spark to my father's eyes. At the conference he witnesses how cities as far-flung as Kampala in Africa, Poona in India, Frankfurt in Germany, Panama, and Wilmette in Illinois can all be linked up through the modern technology of telephone satellite. His faith in a future age in which the world comes together as one is buoyed up.

It takes a week in hospital for the doctors to study what is going wrong inside my father. They decide he doesn't need a gall bladder operation. The old kidney stone problems are still there, but there is also something new. Alvin has developed angina and must carry tablets to keep him calm.

* * *

Cook Islands, 1967

I have grown used to seeing the changes time plays upon my parents. It is the softness in my father's eyes as he steps off the *Northern Star* boat launch, and the warmth in my mother as she hugs me, that I notice first. I already sense that any hurt we have caused them by not returning to Honiara has been forgiven.

My friends throw garlands of frangipanis and beaded shells around my parents' necks. I have wanted to make a great show of their first arrival to our adopted paradise. I want them to feel welcomed in a way we weren't when we made our first lonely steps onto the beach at Honiara.

Our island home at Rarotonga envelopes my parents in the same happy trance that has cradled Bruce and I since we arrived. It is the promised paradise that Guadalcanal could never be. Overseen by the lighter hand of New Zealand and being blessed with only one traditional language, Maori, it is newly independent since 1965. Our friends are a mix of Europeans and Maoris. The Polynesians celebrate love, sex and dancing. It is the opposite to the warrior-like ways of the Melanesians I have grown up with.

The island is as sensual as its people. In this languid climate, fruit, vegetables and flowers grow in abundance. As my parents walk along the road the people sing out, 'hello mama, hello papa'. Their Queen, Pa Ariki, embodies this same ease of affection. She is a fellow Bahá'í, and we have come to know her well in this small community of friends.

Alvin and Gertrude have their own emotional connection with the island. Their old New Zealand friend, Dulcie Dive, Dulcie Burns when they first knew her, pioneered here at the same time our family went to the Solomons and was also named a Knight of Bahá'u'lláh, but she has now passed on. The Bahá'ís and all our friends sweep up my parents quickly. Their days are filled with luncheons and dinners. Dancers tell them stories of vivid experiences and everyday life. Their hips writhe in a slow, hypnotic sway, then faster to the crescendo of drumming.

It is the first holiday my parents have allowed themselves in fourteen years. My mother drinks up the island's indulgent beauty; the white-sanded beaches surrounded by reefs and natural lagoons to swim in, plants she has never seen, fragrances that hang in the warm air. Later, it will form long, lyrical sentences in her letters. She marvels at the variety of foods and the island way of cooking in the ground; a natural pressure cooker that punctuates the flavours of fish in coconut cream and succulent chicken served in pieces of bamboo, along with puddings made of pumpkin, taro root and banana. She imagines all that she could do if she had such fresh, natural abundant produce available to her.

The more my father becomes rested, the more absorbed he becomes by our movements. Bruce and I have passed the stage of being little greenhorns attempting to bring some set of standards to the rundown government hotel we are trying to transform. We have become used to the light soap opera that occupies our lives: lovers' quarrels, the frequent pregnancies of the local women. I have even delivered a baby on the hotel's laundry floor.

My father is impressed by the way we have decorated the hotel and developed a café called the Banana Court that has become a popular meeting place. Like my parents, our lives have become entwined with the community. We are studying the Maori language and Bruce is one of the best tennis players of the island as well as being a member of the Junior Chamber of Commerce and two government committees. I am heavily involved with the Girl Guides, teaching the kitchen staff, decorating the hotel and making wedding cakes.

One time my parents are watching me as I am

decorating an enormous five-tier cake. My father turns to my mother wearing an expression that is half amazement, half pride. 'Where on earth did she learn this from?' he asks.

I realize that my father has no recollection of the time he made me decorate a cake when my mother was sick and I was only nine. This surprises me, as the event has been pivotal in my life, instilling in me a sense of being capable – even without learning.

'Da-ad!' I sing-song. 'You made me do it as a kid and I studied some books on the subject and went from there.'

My father grins and exhales a short gust of air as he stares in wonder at my latest creation, but he soon returns to asking more of me. He wants me to keep going further and faster.

'When am I going to see a grandchild?' my father asks in a way that is more a demand. I roll my eyes upwards.

'For heaven's sake, Dad. That's my business,' I retort.

'It *is* my business too,' he comes back indignant. 'I want a grandchild. You've been married all this time and it's not right that you haven't got children.'

For the rest of his trip he won't let the issue lie. I cannot understand why my father is being so pushy. I am just twenty-one and have only been married for a couple of years. I am busy enjoying life as a young married woman, revelling in the happiest period of my young life. It doesn't occur to me that my father might be weighing his own time, and finding it is not a big number.

After six weeks together our parting is fraught with sadness. We have no idea when we will see each other again, and we know our communication will be reduced to letter and cable. It is made more difficult by the news that a cyclone is arriving. I watch the launch carrying my parents bobbing its way through the mounting sea to the *Southern Star* liner. The seas are so rough the crew is unable to let down the gangplank. Instead, my parents must enter through a large window in the hull's side. Despite his health, my father is still agile and jumps inside. It takes four men to push my mother through the hole. She lands unceremoniously on her rear.

The cyclone fixes its eye on our island foreshore, ripping the front off our hotel and washing it away. I cower in the main part of the hotel that holds strong with its coral walls. I want to be sick, only it is not just through fear. Soon, I will find out that I am four weeks pregnant. My father has got his wish.

* * *

Honiara, 1968

Alvin paces around the outside of his Hometel. The temporary homestay has been welcomed by people of all races and walks of life – from government workers to islanders to tourists. Alvin laps up the ever-changing guests, making friends with many of them. Richard Tregaskas, who wrote *Guadalcanal Diary*, and his journalist wife Moana are among them. Richard was born in the same New Jersey town as Alvin. They spend many happy hours together, swapping stories about their childhood and their life.

It has been hard returning home from holiday to the news that their other businesses – the grocery store and bakery – have not been leased out as had been planned before they left. While Gertrude's response is to consolidate, Alvin views it as a time to expand. My father is unstoppable. He has decided to build an extension to the hotel – several rooms and a café like the one Bruce and I have created in the Cook Islands. Already he has a vision in his head of how it could be. He pushes quickly into doing things his way.

'As usual Alvin's always got something up his sleeve and its better to let him do it as he is not happy otherwise,' Gertrude writes resignedly in a letter to friends. She absorbs her worries in prayer and by giving her Bahá'í secretarial duties even closer attention. More and more she is becoming detached from the harsher decisions of the material world.

Alvin searches out the company of men. At night, he often goes down to the Guadalcanal Club. He and John Holloway, the head of the Criminal Investigation Department, enjoy long and wide-ranging conversations over a soda. They have developed a casual friendship where conversations can continue into daytime, with John stopping by during his rounds to chat with Alvin as he's out back cleaning bottles to make up soft drinks.

In the years since David Tudor-Pole saw the sign pointing to the Bahá'í Centre at the bottom of our hill and visited, Alvin has also developed a relationship with his father through correspondence. Major Wellesley Tudor-Pole is a writer, philosopher and mystic who has had the rare privilege of having the ear of the major courts of England and Europe as well as everyday people.

An innate urge to seek out what lay beyond this world led Tudor-Pole to interview 'Abdu'l-Bahá in 1908. Their meeting would later play an important role during World War I. Tudor-Pole operated in military intelligence based in the Middle East. Through the wires and through contacts, he picked up information that the Turks intended to 'crucify' 'Abdu'l-Bahá and his family if they were forced to pull out of Haifa. His efforts impressed members of the British Cabinet led by Lord Lamington, Lord Balfour and Lord Curzon to influence General Allenby's decision to take Haifa, providing bodyguards for 'Abdu'l-Bahá, his family and his followers.

Alvin knows that since 'Abdu'l-Bahá's death in 1921, Tudor-Pole has drifted away from the Bahá'í Faith, but he values his friend's insights on world peace and the afterlife. During World War II, Tudor-Pole, now awarded an Order of the British Empire (OBE), approached King George VI to call for a minute's silence, whereby at nine o'clock each night people would concentrate their thoughts on peace and freedom. Becoming known as the Big Ben Minute, ten million people began regularly observing silence. When a former Nazi Gestapo officer was asked why he thought Germany had lost the war, he reportedly replied, 'You had a weapon we could not counter – your Silent Minute.'

Many of Alvin's private thoughts get poured into his letters to Tudor-Pole. They share spiritual understandings and an interest in the Middle East. Tudor-Pole sends Alvin his books. There is his early work, *Private Dowding:*

The Personal Story of a Soldier Killed in Battle, that he wrote in 1917 using an imaginary soldier to make sense of his thoughts on the meaning of war and the conditions of life after death. The last is his just-published *Writing on the Ground*, in which he reinterprets the everyday events in the life of Jesus as signposts for a future age and writes of the Bahá'í movement. My father reads constantly. Books on the development of Israel and David Ben-Gurion now form small piles beside his bed.

* * *

Alvin walks into the National Honiara Library. He inhales the mustiness of books, made stronger by the humid heat. He places his pile of books for return on the desk and smiles at the librarian as he walks away.

'Mr Blum,' the librarian calls out, 'You haven't taken any books!'

Alvin stops for a moment and looks back at her. 'I don't think I'll need any more.' The librarian is puzzled. Alvin is her best customer. What a strange thing for him to say, she muses to herself.

He heads back up to the Hometel. The opening of the new café and rooms took place a few weeks earlier. It was a great success, with a mix of people from the Chief Secretary of the Government to fellow businessmen attending the celebrations. Alvin is not sure yet whether his latest gamble of trying to introduce something new to Honiara will pay off.

The process of building the new addition to the hotel

has brought with it the usual frustrations. This time, though, it is as if they have lodged themselves somewhere deep in his bones.

That evening Gertrude can see a weariness in her husband's eyes. She puts down her fork to say something about it to him, then something stops the words from leaving her mouth. 'I don't think I'll go to the Expo in Japan,' Alvin says, without looking up from his food. 'I think I'll go on pilgrimage instead.' Gertrude shifts back in her chair and her cutlery falls loose in her fingers. She is surprised, but again she says nothing. They have been planning the trip to Japan for the International Expo for some time. This proposed visit has developed a symbolic significance, not only as the country that went into battle here, but as the important spiritual centre 'Abdu'l-Bahá and Shoghi Effendi said it would become. She goes over it in her mind all evening, trying to make sense of her husband's sudden wish to return to Haifa.

A few days later Alvin is thinking about how he is going to lease out his other businesses. Sitting inside the office of his accountant Jim Curtain, he is aware the figures aren't adding up. He meets them with a shrug. It simply means he'll have to spend more time and energy working his way around the bankers.

Alvin suddenly feels tired in a way he has never known. His stomach churns and an acute pain strains hard at the centre of his chest. Jim immediately recognizes that his friend is in deep trouble. Alvin is rushed to the hospital where he is treated for heart attack. He is booked into hospital and ordered sedation and rest.

After three days, Alvin pushes the hospital bed sheets away from his body. 'I haven't got time for this. I've got too much to do,' he protests.

The doctor rallies himself to make a last stand. 'Alvin, you need to rest, and a few days is not enough,' he says in the firm and well-practised voice used for difficult patients.

My father checks himself out of hospital anyway. In the following days he attends to the needs of each of his businesses, beating a track down to the grocery and bakery stores on Mendana Road, then hurtling around the corner to the Hometel in Hisbiscus Avenue. There are all the deliveries and pickups to be made in between, as well as attending to his Bahá'í and community work. Trying to make new negotiations with banks and business lessees only builds the momentum.

Gertrude watches on, helpless and silent. When her husband comes home she notices his skin has turned a new shade of sallow-grey. Beads of sweat bubble in small pools across his forehead and upper lip. She turns away. For the longest time she doesn't hear Alvin move. Gertrude feels uncomfortable with the quiet and she looks back at him.

His hand is clutching at his chest. Inside, his heart is being strangled by a great unseen force. Gertrude realizes he needs help and calls for the driver to quickly get Alvin to hospital.

He doesn't feel the uneven lurches of the car as it tries to quickly make its way, in and out of trench-like potholes, along the unsealed road. He doesn't hear the frantic cries of hospital staff as they find they cannot wrench the oxygen gas bottle open. All of Alvin's senses have turned inward and are moving him rapidly through a dark tunnel. At its end he can already see the most magnificent light. His life, the endeavours, failures and experiences are flashed before him. He realizes his life on earth has ended. The spiritual journey into the next world is about to start.

* * *

Rarotonga, 23 September 1968

My husband comes through the door of our apartment which juts off the side of the hotel lounge room. I look up into his eyes from where I am sitting. They are full of storm-grey sadness. I already know that what Bruce is about to say cannot be good.

A cable has carried news into our office from Honiara. He tells me my father has died. My mind refuses to connect these words with the last images I have of him: noisy, dancing, joking, demanding. It was only nine months ago. I am in shock. Despite all his illnesses, Alvin has never really slowed down. He is only fifty-six, too young for life to end.

I look across to my baby daughter. She makes small, snuffly sounds in her sleep. My father's much-wanted first grandchild is only four weeks old. We have called our baby Natasha. Her middle name is Grace after Bruce's mother. She is sweetly blonde with clear, shining eyes like her other grandmother, Gertrude. The islanders have opened their hearts to her. Queen Pa Ariki and her Aunt, Pa Makira, have bestowed on her a great honour, giving our daughter a Maori name = *Teremoana Teriki au Moana.* It means Might of the Sky. Something sharp pinches my heart. It is the realization that my father will never see her.

There are no direct air services into Rarotonga. The runway only carries the B52s which fly in and out as they monitor nuclear testing at French Muroa Atoll. The New Zealand Government, which still handles foreign relations for the Cook Islands, puts in a request to the American Government to see if they will fly us out.

A small miracle helps us get on our way. The arrival of the next B52 has been delayed a day, allowing time for the New Zealand Government to issue Natasha with a passport. The next plane out would not have arrived for another two weeks.

We board the B52 the day after we get the news of my father's death. I am still in shock as our friends shower us with row upon row of shell necklaces. We have been told that flowers are not allowed on board. The aircrew have stuck two seats in the middle of the cargo hold. The aircraft isn't sealed for noise and we must use earplugs for Natasha and ourselves. My little baby won't stop crying. I try to breastfeed her while military men sit around the hold's edges. It doesn't cross my mind that it was the American Army that first brought my father into contact with this part of the world, and it is the American Army that is now, at his end, carrying me back towards home.

We are taken to Pago Pago, where we stay with dear

friends Lilian and Suhayl Ala'i. It was because of Lilian having her visa cancelled all those years ago that my family went to the Solomons. The next day we catch a commercial flight to Suva and then to Honiara.

In all, it is a harrowing trip from the Cook Islands: six days of constant travelling with a newborn, often in small aircraft. Natasha and I are both distraught when we finally arrive in Honiara and into the waiting arms of a grieving Gertrude.

* * *

Honiara

She looks around the Bahá'í Centre she built with her husband, the special place they envisioned, soaring and open to the air, where people of all races, colour, status and religion could meet together. There are all the people inside and the hundreds that aren't able to fit in who have gathered on the lawns stretching to the front porch of the house where Alvin has welcomed so many of them. It is a huge and diverse congregation who have come to celebrate the man with whom she has shared such an important journey.

A prominent Melanesian gets up to say a few words. 'Before Mr Blum came there was a sickness in the land. White man and black man did not come together. But this has changed now and I feel it is Mr Blum's example.'

Gertrude's face radiates love back at the man. She knows how much these words would mean to Alvin. She hopes that somehow he can see how, even in death, he has brought people together. The High Commissioner has sent his representative along with the heads of all government departments. They sit alongside all the many different members of the community who were part of Alvin's everyday life. Melanesian, Chinese, Fijian, Micronesian – they are all here. Billy Bennett is here too, providing a live broadcast on radio for those who are in some of the far-flung parts of the Solomons and unable to make it to Honiara on Guadalcanal

It is the biggest funeral for an expatriate the island has ever seen, only I am not there to bid farewell to my father. The difficulties of living in this part of the world have kept us apart to the end. It will be a week of island hopping and waiting for planes before we arrive in Honiara.

Trucks jam the road from the Bahá'í Centre down to the main road at No. 9 hospital and around to the Bahá'í Cemetery, a plot of land tucked into the foot of Kola Ridge that has been only recently secured. The Returned Services Association has draped my father's coffin in the American flag. As his coffin is lowered a lone trumpet plays Taps and the Last Post.

That night my mother sits listening to the radio. She cradles her head in her right hand. Her left arm bends back up on itself as her hand rests over her heart. She listens to the words of people, moved by my father's death, as they pay tribute to the part Alvin has played in the development of the Solomon Islands. A government official speaks, then members of the Chamber of Commerce and other dignitaries.

She bends her head further inwards, reciting words of Bahá'u'lláh that are full of lyrical meaning for her, then she turns her head towards the heavens. Her green eyes are wet and glisten in the low evening lamplight. A broad smile comes across her face as she thinks of all the distrust and suspicion she and Alvin endured when they arrived – the Americans with their weird religion. How different it is this day, everyone coming together in a state of reverence. 'Oh Alvin,' she whispers, 'What a triumph for the Faith it has been.'

Beside her is a pile of cables and messages that have come in from around the world. She reads through them slowly, taking in all the thoughts for her husband and herself. A simple line from an old friend, Vi Hoenke, herself a Knight of Bahá'u'lláh to Papua New Guinea, touches her so deeply that she knows it should be engraved on Alvin's headstone. It says, *'He died where he chose to serve.'*

15

When All is Said and Done

I have made death a messenger of joy to thee. Wherefore dost thou grieve?

Bahá'u'lláh

Honiara, 1968

I see her wave from behind the fence as I step onto the tarmac at the small airfield, which today is the golf course in Honiara. She looks a lonely figure without my father's familiar bulk in his safari suit grinning next to her. I force myself to smile as I hand my unsettled baby over the fence to meet her grandmother before going through customs.

It has taken a week to arrive here and I am unsure of what state I will find my mother in. In truth, I am not coping myself. Somewhere between the shifting datelines of our journey, Natasha has stopped feeding and my breast milk is quickly drying up with my mounting stress.

My mother tries to hush my baby's squeals, but it is a long time since she had her only child and she struggles to give me any practical advice. Much of her time is spent in prayer, reading and writing; it offers her a comforting window through to another realm where she can feel closer to my father and to God.

Days pass before she returns to the growing pile of letters of condolence. She unfolds the thin, wrinkled paper of an aerogram. It is from David Tudor-Pole. He writes how his father, Major Tudor-Pole, passed away on 13 September – two weeks before Alvin.

Sometimes life allows us to see the threads of connection between seemingly random events. It is a frequent occurrence for Gertrude and it happens for her now. First, she realizes that this is the day that Alvin told her that he wanted to go to Haifa. And then she remembers: the words of Beng Liew, the young Malaysian girl who has come to teach at the school on Malaita, and who stayed with my mother after the funeral. Sleeping in my parents' house she had a dream about my father. It was so clear, so powerful that she woke and in the morning told Gertrude how Alvin was trying to send a message that he and a friend were going to Haifa.

Soon, another letter arrives from a Swiss Bahá'í who was also a friend of Tudor-Pole. In it she writes how she has had a vision of 'Abdu'l-Bahá walking up into the Shrine of Bahá'u'lláh with Tudor-Pole on one side and Alvin on the other. Inside the Shrine 'Abdu'l-Bahá is talking to them, explaining the station of Bahá'u'lláh and Jesus Christ. As he speaks, two figures – one red, one white – rise up and merge together in a blaze of glorious light. Alvin looks on in awe, as if everything he has believed in during his life has just been confirmed. Tudor-Pole falls to his knees and sobs.

* * *

My mother cradles Natasha and sings 'Swing Low, Sweet Chariot'. The smooth richness of her voice reminds me of one of the sweetest parts of my childhood. I use the memories to warm up the greyness that has accompanied my realization that we won't be going back to live in the Cook Islands. I won't be getting the chance to say goodbye to my friends.

Bruce and I have soon agreed that we have to stay in Honiara and help my mother with the businesses. We have had our own vision of heading to Hawaii to study tourism and returning to work with the Government to promote the Cook Islands. It is now pushed aside and we do our best to keep our disappointments to ourselves.

Bruce has spent three weeks in the Cooks, packing up our possessions and trying to pass on the management of the hotel in Rarotonga. When he returns he begins to go through my father's business accounts. It doesn't take him long to become aware that my father – fast-thinking, big-picture Alvin – didn't keep records of salaries or rents on properties, or anything. Bruce cannot fathom how my father had planned to pay for the extension to the Hometel.

What money my parents have had has been churned back into their business, loaned out to all manner of needy and enterprising people or used to buy property for the Faith. When the Government Legislative Council passed a bill that incorporated the Bahá'í assembly in Honiara in 1964, properties bought in my parents' name were transferred across to the Bahá'í community. We realize that my father knew this town and would have been able to talk his way through his debts, but we are young and green.

We borrow money from my mother's family. Her sister Rose sends US$500. It is money she can ill afford, but she offers it graciously. The grocery store has already been leased out and my father has built up the bakery with contracts for all the government institutions. A Chinese businessman is already interested in buying the bakery. We find that he is a front for six other buyers when we sell. Honiara is developing and a machine-run outfit has outmoded our hand-operated soft drinks and ice cream business, so we sell the piece of land to pay off more debts.

It is an emotional time for my mother as she watches the structure of her everyday world change shape. My parents had already decided to lessen the load of the businesses before my father died, but Alvin had his own way in which he was going to do it. Now that he is gone, my mother decides she wants close involvement in the business decisions. All her frustrations about not being included by my father in the businesses they have built up together come bursting out the gate.

Like my father, I struggle with my mother's slowness. Her grip on the simplest of economics is shaky. She cannot understand why things are a different price to what they were in the 1930s. Bruce does his best. He is more understanding of her desire to feel involved in the businesses she's worked hard to sustain and patiently goes through finances, explaining them to her as he goes. Bruce is also a natural businessman and knows that you have to invest money to make it. Gertrude's fear of debt overrides most of his suggestions. A lesser man would have walked away. My admiration for my husband grows as I watch him plod on, dealing with my mother and progressively sorting out the family finances.

Soon my mother decides she wants to try again to get her driver's licence. She hasn't understood that Alvin's refusal to teach her has been for her own safety. Bruce cannot say no. The respectful son-in-law dutifully gets into the car with Gertrude at the wheel. They are driving along the main street of Honiara when someone calls out her name. My mother frequently mixes up the brake and accelerator. She turns to sing hello back and hits the accelerator, banging into the middle of traffic. Bruce is at his wits' end. He has a quiet chat to Alvin's old police friend John Holloway. John, now Chief of Police, rings Gertrude and gently advises her it may not be a good idea to continue on with driving lessons.

In the years after Alvin's death, Gertrude continues to work closely with the Bahá'í community, continuing their lifelong passion of developing the institutions and activities of the Faith. It is not long before she sees the Government of Solomon Islands giving increasing attention to her religion, with official recognition of Bahá'í Holy Days and Bahá'í marriage. In 1971 four acres of land are acquired at Panatina for a Bahá'í Temple site – later it will be swapped for eight acres of freehold land at Mount Austin. All these achievements are milestones that allow her to look both forward with energy and back with fondness to the times she and her husband worked towards this shared vision; it helps give her confidence that, even without Alvin, things will still grow.

* * *

1970–1971

Gertrude writes to her old New Zealand friends, Vera and Hugh Blundell, to tell them that our new tiny bundle has arrived ten days ago. We name our second daughter Monique Eva. We have chosen 'Eva' for my mother's Bahá'í friend Eva Grant, who lived above Bruce's flat in Coogee in Australia. My little brunette daughter is yelling noisily as my mother tries to gather her thoughts for her letter.

She tells Hugh that she feels she is almost floundering. There have been so many changes in her life. 'It's a little more difficult to adjust when one grows older,' she writes. 'Alvin always used to be the one to decide things for me, that is, the larger issues, and now I've got to strengthen my own inner sites. It's been a difficult period all round, not that I'm complaining, but a tremendous adjustment . . .'

Gertrude has been made an Auxiliary Board Member. It is a position of service that is given to some respected members of the Faith and should free my mother from the burden of daily administrative duties, allowing her to travel more. In truth, her days are still very full. Living with my mother has been like living at Grand Central Station. Locals turn up on the doorstep at any time of day, looking to have a chat and eat a piece of her banana cake. With our young and growing family we are all finding it difficult living in a two-bedroom house. My mother graciously moves into the little house where John and Ruhi used to live.

Since my father died, there have been few events that Gertrude has been able to anchor herself to. When one arrives, it is usually something she can focus her faith on. Recently there was news of trouble at Lau Lasi on Malaita. Lau Lasi is made up of man-made islands and is rich in the traditional art of making shell money. We have started a small tour company called 'Keithie Tours' and Lau Lasi has become a popular stop on our itinerary with demonstrations of shell money being made and local dancers entertaining the tourists. Because we are Bahá'ís and many of the families here are Bahá'ís, the local Catholic priest has stepped in to voice his objection to money being made from tourism.

This is an old issue. Two years earlier, not long before Alvin died, the Catholic mission school decided that it would no longer teach the children of Bahá'í families. This action necessitated the start-up of the little Bahá'í school here on Lau Lasi. When Gertrude heard of this latest objection she decided to view it as an opportunity to speak to both the Bahá'ís and Catholics about working together and unity. Forgetting her age and size, she took herself off to Auki, then hired a canoe to take her to Lau Lasi, about one-and-a-half hours away.

Gertrude felt ignited with purpose, and at Lau Lasi she counselled the islanders towards a peaceful reconciliation. Now, she has been asked to go on a speaking tour of New Zealand and is writing to Hugh of her apprehension about going it alone without Alvin. 'Oh for that oriental attitude of Inshallah' (*if God wills*), she says.

When she arrives, the New Zealand press is taken with my mother's story. In her interviews she speaks about the Bahá'í Faith, but it is all that she and Alvin have done in coming to the Solomons and building up business and the community that captivates the journalists.

While my mother is in New Zealand a cyclone hits Honiara. In the old house built by American soldiers all those years ago, the only room with a concrete floor is the bathroom. We huddle inside it and try to comfort our little family as the fury of wind rips the roof off my parents' home. We move out to the home of our friends Harry and Denise Toy. I am in the middle of icing a wedding cake, so we arrive, kids, goods, chattels and cake in tow. I finish decorating the cake, the bride is happy and the Toys very understanding. We later rent a house by the beach while we wait for our own home to be built on new land we have bought.

My mother spends many months in New Zealand speaking in cities, large and small, across its two islands. In her absence, the Government in the Solomons announces that it will recognize Bahá'í marriage certificates, and the National Spiritual Assembly of the Solomon Islands is elected in 1971 and incorporated on 26 July that same year. I think of all that my parents have given of themselves to help bring this about. Now, neither of them is here to celebrate in Honiara and it feels very strange.

* * *

Honiara, 1975

Rarely do women get much notice in Solomon Islands culture. On Guadalcanal, and in parts of the west on islands like Isabel, there is a matriarchy, meaning the land is passed through the line of women. It offers a shallow power that is in name only. On Malaita, where the patriarchy is strong and warrior-like, life is particularly difficult for a woman. 'Bride price', or the paying for a bride, is the basis of many cultural habits. When a boy decides he wants to marry, the families get together and decide how much the girl is worth: consideration of her physical strength, her meekness and her ability to bear children are given priority. Education is not always a plus, as with education comes questioning and this breaks customary norms.

The Government has only relatively recently begun to pay attention to the most basic education for women and few can afford it anyway. Illiteracy is widespread throughout the Solomons. Even the well-meaning intentions of aid agencies have focused on men. They have failed to realize that the gardeners and real producers at a family level are women. Men have been given money to put into growing cocoa and the women have been forced out to plant their gardens further away. Only now in the 1970s are the UN and non-governmental organizations beginning to notice that women need more support.

Having a voice in her own life is not something that has come easily to my mother. She is not a natural leader, but as a woman and as a Bahá'í she has done what she could to encourage women to develop themselves since she arrived more than twenty years ago. When Alvin was alive she would look out of their shop and see the girls in the street, wandering around as if they didn't know what they were going to do next. 'Alvin, go ask the girls to come in and see me,' she'd say to her husband.

With the light in her eyes and tender words Gertrude has always had a way of making women feel that each one of them has something of value that they can contribute to this community, that they are as valid as any man. In doing this she has gained her own special place in their life. Everyone calls her Mum. Mum Blum.

Gertrude gets appointed to the first National Women's Council of the Solomon Islands, but it is her solid, everyday support that touches women's lives personally. She continues her Red Cross work, often teaching sewing skills for women so they can earn an extra income, as well as her work with English and literacy programmes. The Bahá'í community also want to do more to promote the equality of men and women and decide to hold the first women's conference in the Islands.

There is no real sense of community for women, whether you are an islander or a European. I have looked for my own ways to overcome the isolation I feel as a

Old Chinatown, 1974

Honiara 1978 (postcard)

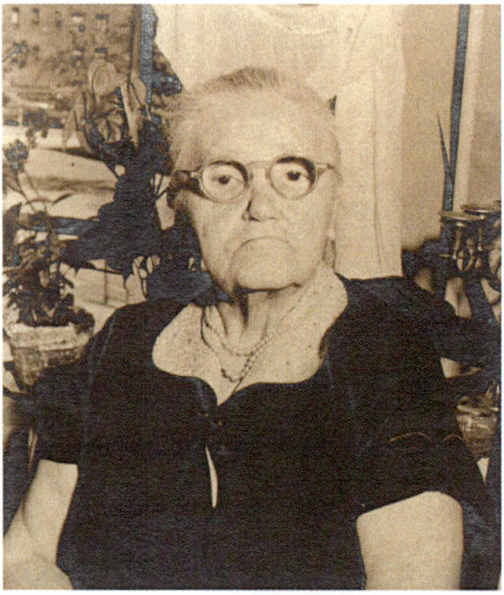

Grandmother Becky Gewertz, New York, 1963

Gertrude and her sister Rose, 1978

Gertrude receiving the MBE from the Governor-General of the Solomon Islands, Honiara, 1985

Gertrude with her granddaughter Natasha at Natasha's wedding on the Australian Gold Coast, January 1993

Keithie and Gertrude at Gertrude's 80th birthday party, Honiara Bahá'í Centre

Gertrude, two months before she died

Gertrude's funeral, 6 June 1993

The first recipients of the Blums Community Awards, 1993, with Speaker of the Parliament Paul Tovua and Prime Minister Ul'ufalu

young mother. There are no support groups and I now have three small girls. Our third daughter is a dear little island girl from the Lau Lasi community who has had a terrible eye disease. Her name is Riswan and she is the same age as Natasha.

I have a close friend, Jenny Lewis, who opened the first kindergarten in Honiara. She has had to leave as her husband has been reassigned to Hong Kong. She offers to sell me the operation but I have no money to pay her. With my usual bravado, I talk the bank into giving me a one hundred per cent loan. Looking back, I think the manager was too overwhelmed to refuse me.

With my nursing background I look to books for guidance and use many of the Montessori methods I read about. It is only much later that I will realize that I have been following the old research methods of my parents. Soon, I have five teachers and one hundred children in attendance. The bank loan is repaid in full within a year.

I am in my twenties and still hungry for things that lie outside of my style-less island world. I open a fashion shop called 'Girl Talk', then a shoe shop called 'Walk Talk' – the names play on the Solomons' community system of 'One Talks'. Expatriates are my main source of custom, but I try and get the Solomon Islands girls involved. I throw fashion parades that are open to the public. The island girls love getting dressed up for the catwalk.

My kindergarten and shops are a success. But while I am free to develop which direction I want to go, my husband is still struggling with my mother over the various businesses and the Hometel. She rejects his ideas for improvement, saying, 'It's my business,' and Bruce's confidence is becoming undermined. A call comes out from the Government to help islanders make money from their arts and handicrafts. Bruce responds, seeing the opportunity for a cooperative initiative. The island artists who have their own One Talks can't comprehend the idea of benefiting as a whole. The visionary idea is sadly short-lived and Bruce has to let it go, to continue on with his own business venture to showcase the local arts in partnership with Mariano Kelesi, a successful Melanesian businessman who will later become a knighted member of the new parliament and President of the newly formed Malaita Assembly.

The country is gearing up for independence in 1978 and the future of the Solomons is uncertain. Not long before this, Bruce decides to approach my mother about selling the Hometel so that we are cashed up and ready for what might come. Gertrude accepts the sale with surprising ease, as if she has sensed his frustration. It is my husband who in the years to come will regret not being able to find a way to make the arrangement work. Bruce is sorry for the loss of Blum's Hometel – the history of it and what it stood for in the Solomon Islands' social development.

* * *

United States, 1978

She is praying over the graves of her mother and her older half-brother Ben. The noises of everyday life become silent to her. The green lawns of Beth-El Cemetery in New Jersey are studded with the headstones of tens of thousands of Jewish families who have passed on, but the words of her childhood religion have become unfamiliar to her.

It is fifteen years since Gertrude last visited her family. In the years in between, these two deaths have resulted in her lonely pilgrimage to their graves to say a final goodbye. 'This is one of the important things I wanted to do,' she writes in a letter to me during her return visit to the United States.

My mother has written many letters to me during her latest journey, that began with a pilgrimage to Haifa. She met twice with Rúḥíyyíh Khánum, her old friend, and said prayers for the future of the Solomons just a few days before Independence at the Shrines of the Báb, Bahá'u'lláh and 'Abdu'l-Bahá. Gertrude also visited Jerusalem, the place her father longed to make his home, but her letters contain no mention of any personal connection to the holy city.

In New York she is reunited with her sister Rose. There are other siblings to see, children who have grown up and new children that have been born. It is a joyous time for Gertrude as she wanders back through the city of her youth. Rose takes her to Coney Island. It is one of the few cherished memories they can share from their childhood.

She heads up to Green Acre, her old Bahá'í retreat in Maine. In the vast open space my mother writes how it is still easy to feel the presence of 'Abdu'l-Bahá, who visited Green Acre in 1912. She meets up with old friends there.

Mildred Mottahedeh is among them. Gertrude holds her at arm's length to look at her and smiles.

All these years, Gertrude thinks, what a tremendous force for peace and unity her friend has turned out to be. Mildred is still working with the United Nations as the representative of the Bahá'í International Community to ECOSOC. She has the ear and friendship of powerful people, among them presidents and vice presidents – the most recent being Gerald Ford and Henry Rockefeller.

Mildred has also become a powerful force in the world of art and interior design. After marrying Rafi Mottahedeh, she began researching the intricate designs found in Persian pottery that she would later reproduce along with Iranian woodcarvings. Their business on Fifth Avenue, New York, 'Mottahedeh and Sons', has become immensely successful and is acclaimed as the producer of some of the world's finest porcelain. Mildred and her husband have made millions, most of their money being channelled back into social and economic projects in the developing world.

For two days Gertrude stays in Mildred's New York apartment. She walks around rooms filled with magnificent artefacts from China that date back to before Christ, and precious porcelain and sculptures from Persia and India. She remembers when Mildred visited us in the Solomons, not long after we first arrived, and laughs gently to herself. 'Where is everything?' her friend had asked as she looked around the 'one horse town'.

An idea comes to her. What if there is a way of promoting the arts and handicrafts of the Solomon Islanders here? Gertrude has already spoken to an art gallery owner about the possibility of this and she writes to tell us that she will also speak to Mildred.

When it is time to leave New York, Gertrude puts her arms around Rose and holds onto her. When she pulls away she sees the tears in her sister's eyes and more fall from her own. Somewhere beyond the immediate thoughts in their minds, both are aware that they may never see each other again.

Gertrude turns and gets on a plane that takes her back down into the Deep South. It is forty years since she set out alone in the same direction. Everything is so changed. The pictures in her memory don't match the smooth highways and tall, modern buildings. The most important difference, she writes, is that there are no more Jim Crow Laws. She marvels at what the Civil Rights Movement has achieved. 'The black people are in every kind of job and there is need for their skills,' she writes. But she can still see more has to be done. 'I know the racial thing has to be settled before the US can play the role she has to play in the world.'

In Birmingham, where she first pioneered, there are now more than four Bahá'í Spiritual Assemblies. In Greenville, despite her years spent there, the lumbering inflexions of vowels make it difficult for my mother to communicate. 'I could hardly understand it,' she writes. Little Rock, the place of my birth, is barely recognizable to her. She is touched when the Bahá'í community throw a spontaneous memorial service for Alvin. On World Peace Day she gives her own talk.

A bus takes her north to Chicago. Her time spent at the Temple in Wilmette is filled with private moments. The light in the centre of her chest becomes brighter as she circumambulates the Temple, delicately tiered and domed like a wedding cake, and its gardens. When she hears that on 23 September they are having a special service for pioneers who have left American shores, she raises her eyes towards heaven and holds her gaze as though someone is talking back down to her. It is also the tenth anniversary of my father's death.

* * *

Honiara, 1979

My mother returns home to a newly independent nation. The Prime Minister is Peter Kenilorea, a man from the Are Are tribe on Malaita who was first elected as Chief Minister in 1976 during the initial self-government phase of the Solomon Islands. In his inaugural speech on 7 July 1978 he spoke of the importance of unity. 'Regardless of our ethnic, cultural, and religious diversity, we can, from today onwards, attest to a single national identity. Today we are Solomon Islanders and we can say with humility, but also with pride, that we all belong to one free independent nation.'

Encouraging the people in what they could do was also uppermost in Kenilorea's mind. 'We are a rich country in many ways,' he said. 'We have a varied and enduring culture with its roots in the past. We have resources, many of which have not been tapped but which, when the time comes, must be used wisely for the benefit of our people.' His words make me think of my father. How Alvin would have loved this day. He wanted the people to break loose, to know that they didn't need anyone else doing things for them, to know that they could be of great service to each other.

In a gesture of solidarity with the people, my mother gives up her American citizenship to become a Solomon Islander. She has decided that this is her home and this is where she is going to die. I am feeling entirely the opposite. Earlier that year, I have felt what it might be like for my time to run out. I have had breast cancer and I want to go to the United Kingdom where I can try alternative therapies to the medicines that make my body feel sick.

But it is more than that. There are things that I still want to do, and I want to experience them today. I want to get out of my little island life. I want to absorb myself in arts and culture, go to concerts, and learn piano and cordon bleu cooking. I don't have the same zeal for the Solomons that my parents have had. There is too much trauma attached to my early life in the name of religion to lay down my life no matter what. I have already made the decision not to sacrifice my children in the way I was.

My mother has never understood why I want my children to live in a nice home. She thinks the hacienda-style home we have built is ostentatious. I remember her reaction to the gold-coloured taps in our bathroom. 'What do you want those for?' she cried. 'Mum, it's important to me to have a nice home,' I tried to explain. 'I grew up in a home where I fell through the floor and we had no electricity.' But she cannot understand. She thinks I am extravagant.

But I see how the times are now different: the Bahá'í community is established; the believers are starting to do things on their own. Each generation has a calling, and I decide mine is to bring some normality and stability into the lives of my children.

There is also the issue of the children's education. European children are unable to continue their education in the Solomons after they reach eleven years of age. The Government concentrates solely on educating Solomon Islanders through high school. I want the girls to experience a broader education and I am sure going to the United Kingdom will give them that opportunity.

My mother is devastated that I am taking the children to live in London, but my mind is made up. Nothing and no one can stop me. Bruce's largesse as a husband is very apparent. He encourages me to do my own thing and develop myself. His own businesses are starting to take off and we decide that we can manage the distance in our relationship with Bruce flying back and forth between London and Honiara.

I sell up my shops and kindergarten and we set off with my three little girls. We travel to London via New York. I meet more of my Jewish relatives for the first time and it is an amazing experience. My father's relatives shower us with their Jewish generosity. One of them owns a sweater factory. 'Come on down, honey, and take whatever you want, you're family,' he beams. In London, a cousin who owns a private bank organizes a loan to buy a place there and guarantees it. It is amazing to me how in the Jewish community family transcends all barriers.

We buy an apartment in Chelsea, mainly because it is cheaper than renting, and I immerse myself in what I consider to be the centre of the cultural universe. For two-and-a-half-years I don't look back, and then one day I wake up and realize that I have to face the fact that our future is in the Solomons. Suddenly, I feel a deep sense of responsibility for all that my parents have done. There are many times that I don't want to go back because all it represents is pain and suffering. But I find myself asking the eternal spiritual question: what am I here for? I am beginning to understand the reason for my parents' dedication and sacrifice.

* * *

Honiara, 1984

Two men stand at my mother's side. They help her pick up a shovel and place its blade into soil. It is the thirtieth anniversary of our arrival in the Solomons. The Bahá'í community has organized a planting of thirty trees around Honiara under the supervision of the Minister of Natural Resources and Conservation. A plaque marking the thirty years of the Faith in the Solomon Islands is erected outside the Prime Minister's office. Later, on the fifteenth anniversary of my father's death, a tree will also be planted on the grounds of the National Bahá'í Centre where he lived

At night when Gertrude is alone, she allows her thoughts to go back to the beginning, when we first arrived on the beach. Disparate scenes – some of great hardship, some of joyous triumph – flash through her mind's eye as she scans three decades of living here. Her heart pumps harder with exhilaration, then slows to the tender rhythm of quiet satisfaction.

She gets up to walk across to the bookshelf. She has remembered something. Her eyes squint in the dank light, searching hard for the spine of a book written by Shoghi Effendi called *God Passes By*. She lifts it with two hands and holds it next to her heart as she walks back to her armchair. She opens the book from the back. When she sees the closing paragraph, tears of happiness form in her eyes. It reads:

> Whatever may befall this infant Faith of God in future decades or succeeding centuries . . . we, who have been privileged to apprehend, to the degree our finite minds can fathom, the significance of these marvellous phenomena associated with its rise and establishment, can harbour no doubt that what it has already achieved in the first hundred years of its life provides sufficient guarantee that it will continue to forge ahead, capturing loftier heights, tearing down every obstacle, opening up new horizons and winning still mightier victories until its glorious mission, stretching into the dim ranges of time that lie ahead, is totally fulfilled.

In 1984, Rúḥíyyíh Khánum also visits the Solomon Islands to commemorate the anniversary of our arrival. For Gertrude, her presence is particularly poignant both as her old friend and as the widow of the Guardian, Shoghi Effendi, who first directed her and Alvin to this place, nine degrees from the equator. Rúḥíyyíh Khánum has been on a seven-months tour throughout Asia and the Pacific. Since Shoghi Effendi's passing in 1957, Rúḥíyyíh Khánum has been travelling and speaking throughout the world, received by both dignitaries and the poor.

She is particularly interested in indigenous peoples – travelling by boat through the tributaries of the Amazon for six months and for years through Africa. In the Solomons she is honoured as a Head of State and introduced to the Prime Minister. She also makes radio broadcasts and gives a talk on the world as one country. An elegant and dignified presence, she has a rare gift of being able to capture a child's quiet attention.

Officially, Rúḥíyyíh Khánum is staying at the Mendana Hotel, but at night she often invites herself up for Gertrude's cooking. It is in these moments together that the pair get to reminisce about their early life. Maybe, Gertrude thinks, there is still a glimpse of the feisty young Mary Maxwell inside the Bahá'í Faith's 'first lady'.

There is only a year's difference in age between Rúḥíyyíh Khánum and Gertrude, but time has frayed my mother's beauty more brutally. Since my father died she has become heavier. Years ago she was diagnosed with an underactive thyroid and she now lives on thyroxine to control the sluggishness and poor concentration that plagues her. The island heat swells her feet so that they no longer fit into shoes. She gets around in rubber flip-flops.

Poor circulation has contributed to cellulitis. The slow movement of fluids around her system make it perilous when she gets an insect bite or scratch. Very quickly she becomes delirious and in a matter of hours she could be semi-conscious. Loading my mother up with heavy antibiotics becomes imperative.

It has been a couple of years since we realized that she could no longer live alone, and Marietta, a dear, sweet Bahá'í friend, tiny with a cloud of silver hair, came into Gertrude's life – she is the answer to prayer.

Marietta hails from the Polynesian island of Tikopia and was a Catholic nun until she decided to leave the Church. She took a job as matron of the Teachers' Training College and began studying the Bahá'í Faith. It was after Marietta retired from the College that we asked her to live with Gertrude. Marietta knows how to drive and has become not only Gertrude's companion but also her driver. This has put an end to my mother's years of frustration surrounding driving and waiting on the drivers Bruce has organized through his business.

We have already built her a new house on the Bahá'í Centre property, and soon after Marietta moves in we build another, a smaller version of the first. Both are modest, simple, 'fibro' cottages that match my mother's thrifty sensibility.

I have returned to this side of the world to be closer, but I know I cannot live only in Honiara. Bruce and I moderate the extremes of living on Guadalcanal with a house we have brought in Brisbane. We have developed a base there so that our fortunes are not all tied to a country that is still like a toddler tottering uneasily as it tests out its independence.

Cooking has given me a public life in Brisbane. Through radio and television shows I introduce to people what I have learned in the cordon bleu and cuisine schools in Europe and the kitchens in Asia. After spending two years in English schools, the girls have started high school in Brisbane. They have become weekly boarders and I pick them up on weekends and do pre-recordings and promotions before returning to Guadalcanal. In Honiara I run cooking classes from our house. Like my mother has always done, I adapt my skills to fit the foods available on the island.

For six years I run between my homes in two countries, then one day I receive a call from the Solomon Islands Government in Honiara. I am asked to become the representative for the Solomon Islands at Expo '88 in Brisbane. I have already been looking at doing a Pacific food cooking show as a way to promote the islands, and I accept this offer. The job turns out to be much bigger than expected. What starts off as creating a pavilion grows to creating a South Pacific Village representing Papua New Guinea, Samoa, Tonga, Vanuatu, Fiji and the Cook Islands.

Our budget target to establish the Pacific Pavilion is five million dollars. I have no idea how I am going to raise this money, but I am audacious and I am not working alone – Peter Colton, the Commissioner General working with the Papua New Guinea Pavilion, assists me. I front up to big money business people and give them a spiel about what we're organizing, and the South Pacific Trade Commissioner has a luncheon for me in Sydney inviting all the banks. I end up raising three million dollars, then Australian Aid gives us another two million.

Rick Burge, a prominent architect, designs the village with island huts, a lake and a rock formation as a stage. Our dance programme includes twelve dance performances a day with a different country performing each hour. The Duke and Duchess of Kent from the British Royal family, Middle Eastern Sheiks and the Prime Minister of Canada Brian Mulrowney are among the thousands of guests who visit the South Pacific Village during the six months' Expo.

My mother is here as well. She is a still presence amid the backstage bedlam. Dozens of my young volunteers, dressed in yellow, whom I have assigned to the Pacific Pavilion, weave and dart around her like a lamppost. She listens as I give directions and bring some order to their next actions. 'I can't believe you, Keithie,' she says, slowly shaking her head. 'I can't believe it. You're so much like Alvin.' My thoughts skip a beat. I glance across at her. The sincerity in her eyes touches me. I have always admired my father's ability to get things happening. 'Mum, that's quite a compliment,' I gasp, taken aback.

Tony Hughes, who is now Governor of the Central Bank in the Solomons, reads through my final report on the Solomon Islands participation at Expo. He goes over my detailed outline and suggestions, then he smiles. 'Alvin would have been proud,' he says quietly. 'Alvin would have been proud.' I have no words, so I smile back. Organizing and promoting comes naturally to me, but I haven't yet connected the qualities I have developed, and am developing, to my father. Tony, who originally worked for the Protectorate Government in finance, knew Alvin in his Chamber of Commerce days. And then it comes to me – Alvin the man, the father with whom I share so many qualities, is someone I barely knew.

* * *

Honiara, 1985

She steadies herself, her right hand wrapped firmly around the white stage post. Even with her eyes wide open she can feel Alvin standing by her side. Sir George Lepping, the Governor-General of the Solomon Islands, bends over and places a medal around her neck. She holds the disc in her free hand and thinks of her husband.

My mother is receiving the Member of the British Empire medal for services to the community and the Bahá'í Faith. She has dressed in a pretty, deep blue floral dress and squeezed her swollen feet into shoes for the occasion. Surrounding her is all the white-jacketed formality of the military band, performing the Queen's Birthday Parade.

She was honoured when she found out that Sir Lloyd

Maepeza Gina, Speaker of the National Parliament, had nominated her for the award. Maepeza is the son of Bill Gina, the first Solomon Islander to become a Bahá'í. Taking time to reflect on all that has happened since arriving in the Solomons, she has agreed to accept the award, but only in the names of both her and Alvin.

Just as she felt his presence through all those years when he was away at war, she can feel him now. Alvin has never really left her. Gertrude still speaks of him often, and sometimes, forgetting, in the present tense. Her modesty blocks insight into her own effect on the community.

For her 80th birthday a few years later we hold a party in the gardens of the Bahá'í Centre. The crowd floods over to the edges of the garden where the land falls away steeply with a view of Honiara harbour. Ruhi, her foster daughter, and John are here along with their children, Jalal and Louise, now adults who live in Papua New Guinea. The Royal Solomon Island Police Band announces that it is honoured to be invited to play for her birthday, and have made a large banner saying: 'Happy Birthday Mrs Blum'. The Archbishop of the Catholic Church stops in to wish her well, as do dozens of people from all walks of life.

My mother watches all this from a chair. Her legs have become too sore to stand for too long. People line up by her to say happy birthday. She holds their hand and beams up at them. Gertrude gives a lovely talk recalling the 'one-horse town' that was Honiara when we arrived, saying how proud she is of their involvement in the thriving metropolis it has become today. Sir Mariano Kelesi gives a talk on the Blums' achievements. Charlie Boyle, an architect Bahá'í friend, chuckles and thanks her for their shared cups of coffee at two in the morning.

Despite her age and the state of her health, my mother's door is always open. Marietta, her companion, has become too frail herself to help my mother. Edi Rapasaea, Hamuel's daughter, who came to Honiara to help us when we first came back from the Cook Islands, and her family move into the front cottage, but they too are unable to slow the number of people who come to see Mum Blum.

People arrive at all hours of the day or night. We try to tell my mother that she should put up a sign saying that she is resting between two and five, but she won't hear of it. She sees her home as a haven for all.

One night the sound of knocking at her door cuts through her dreaming. As her eyes open, through the thin slits of light curtained by eyelashes she sees that her clock reads 1 a.m. Her legs are a dead weight. A small moan escapes as she strains to shift them across to get out of bed. When she opens the door she sees the dark face of a young man beneath the porch light.

'I am hungry,' he says.

She doesn't recognize him, but she invites him in anyway. 'Sit down and I'll get you something.' The lounge and kitchen are all one room, but Gertrude's back is turned to the young man as she busies herself with pots and pans. She doesn't hear him as he rifles through her handbag. Already, he is out the door when she turns around with a meal prepared. She sees her open handbag. When she looks inside, she finds all her money is gone.

She takes in a deep breath. When she exhales, her breath is heavy with both sadness and frustration. It is not the first time she has been fleeced, taken for a ride. She cannot work out why some people seem to take kindness as weakness.

Gertrude knows it has become hard for people. The population of Honiara has grown rapidly and development cannot keep up. There is rising unemployment and all the social problems that accompany it. Not enough reinvesting and training has been done, so that more than ten years after Independence there is a marked deterioration in the way the country is running.

She cannot say no to anyone wanting a free meal and the time of day is irrelevant to her. I already know that her commitment to helping people is stronger than any fear for her own well-being. My mother's increasing inability to grasp what I see as the realities of the world is a wedge between us. When I try to talk to her about the practical matters in her life her eyes meet mine, but they are looking past me to something beyond. She intersperses my attempts to bring order to her life with vague placations. 'Really, dear . . . is that so . . . my word,' she says.

I eavesdrop on the conversations she has on her porch with the people who come to see her. When they ask my mother something about her faith, her whole body is transformed. She is no longer floating away. Her spine straightens. Her eyes become shiny. Her answers are immediate and clear.

One time when she is in Brisbane with me, there is a fortune-teller at a café. 'Come on Mum, let's see what she tells us,' I jolly her along. My mother offers her palm to the fortune-teller. The woman stares into the tightly angled trails and crevices that line my mother's palm and pulls back a little. 'I've only seen a palm like this once before and it belonged to a very dedicated nun who had taken strict orders.'

* * *

'Akká, Israel, 1992

The cypress trees that line the paths and edge the gardens point their neat fingers to the sky. I watch my mother's eyes follow them to the sun, squinting, then shut again as she bows her head low, her chin arching inwards towards her heart. A master of ceremonies holds onto a large scroll, reading a list of names out aloud. They are the names of the Knights of Bahá'u'lláh, the two hundred and seventy pioneers who went out into new territories as lone Bahá'ís during the time of the Guardian between 1953 and 1954.

She hears Alvin's name called out, and then her own, but she is no longer sitting here in the gardens outside the Shrine of Bahá'u'lláh. She is back in the room with Alvin and looking over the shoulder of the Guardian, Shoghi Effendi, remembering their visit in 1953. He is pointing out all the countries on a map that are yet to be conquered. Then he is showing them the fine Italian parchment paper on which the names of all the Knights will be written on a scroll. Their names too will be placed on it once they have gone to the Solomon Islands, he is telling them. Once there are Bahá'ís in all parts of the world, he adds, it will be time for the scroll to be buried beneath the threshold of the Shrine.

She breathes in deeply. 'Oh Alvin, it is all happening just as the Guardian said,' she is thinking. Images of all she and her husband have done together are flashing fast through her mind. It is as if everything that has happened in her life has been leading her to this moment and now there is not much left undone.

The illumination of soul that is lighting my mother up from the inside tells us more about what she is feeling than she could say in words. My eldest daughter Natasha is here in Haifa working as a volunteer. My mother listens as her friends praise her granddaughter. She smiles the quiet satisfaction that comes with knowing that what has been such a guiding force in her life is being carried through the generations.

Her friend Mildred Mottahedeh grabs hold of her hand at a special meeting arranged for the pioneers with the nine members of the Universal House of Justice, the international governing body of the Bahá'í Faith. She won't let it go. Rúḥíyyíh Khánum is here with them too. The three reminisce with the ease of content old friends. When Mildred hears a memory that excites her, she reflexively squeezes Gertrude's hand.

Rúḥíyyíh Khánum invites us all to private dinners in 'Abdu'l-Bahá's former home, where she and the Guardian also lived, and the conversations continue on. They are not just about the energetic, bold adventures of their youth; they are also about the achievements of the Faith and the people it has won. Mildred, her confident voice booming, often leads the way. She recalls how she met with Vice-President Nelson Rockefeller to tell him that the Persians were persecuting the Bahá'ís. He got on the phone to the Persian Ambassador in Washington. 'I can't believe your country is being so stupid,' he yelled down the line. 'Stop it!'

Later, when Mildred was helping him with his collection of porcelain they met two or three times a week. 'Mildred, what's going on with the Persian Bahá'ís?' he asked. 'Nelson, they're still killing them,' she replied. He shook his head tightly. 'I don't understand that, because to me Bahá'í is the purest religion on earth.' Three hours later he died.

The current President, George W. Bush, is another of her contacts. 'I gave him the Bahá'í book on "World Order",' Mildred comments. 'He's been using that term in his talks, but I was the one who told him that.'

It is an extraordinary and emotional time for my mother. She stands looking up at the golden-domed glory of the Shrine of the Báb on the slope of Mount Carmel. It is the 100th anniversary of the Ascension of Bahá'u'lláh, and new ground for garden terraces – nine above the Báb's Shrine and nine below – has been broken. The noises of the harbour at the foot of Mount Carmel are becoming softer. The colours on the slope – white, gold and green – fade. A great light comes into her heart and she sees Alvin, 'Abdu'l-Bahá, and Tudor-Pole. She sees them shining and clear against her closed eyelids and she knows. This is the last time she will come here to this hallowed spot.

During our trip my mother's eyes glisten with joy, filled up from silent times of prayer inside the Shrines. Then one day, I look more closely at her. There is a dull milkiness in the whites of her eyes. A grey shadow has formed on her face which is still free from lines. She goes to the toilet often, finding it difficult to control the way fluids flow from her body.

On our way back to Honiara, I get my mother to a doctor in Brisbane. A darkness has been growing inside her womb. She has a hysterectomy to remove the cervical cancer and for a short while we think that's the end of it. Her activities still fill her days. A few months later she is invited to speak at the second World Bahá'í Congress in New York, but the expense of two overseas trips in one year is too much for us. Instead, she travels to Sydney to speak via satellite at the Congress.

One of her proudest moments comes in the next year, in January 1993, when she watches her granddaughter Natasha getting married. Natasha marries Abdul Ramin Jarrah, whose great-great-grandfather was the Colonel in charge of the Prison where Bahá'u'lláh was kept as a prisoner. The Colonel became a Bahá'í after hearing Bahá'u'lláh speak, and the six generations since of this Palestinian family have all become Bahá'ís.

But beneath the surface, in an unexpected corner inside her belly, something that her operation left behind has been steadily transforming itself into a tumour. We bring my mother down to Brisbane to have the tumour removed, and then the doctors want to give her chemotherapy. We all weigh up the side effects for someone eighty-three years of age, and say no. Instead, she receives alternative therapy with vitamin C infusions. A few months later, a Solomon Islands surgeon in Honiara who is a friend does an X-ray of my mother's chest. Black spots show through her lungs.

Back in Brisbane, Rabbani Mihrshahi, a doctor and Bahá'í friend of Natasha's, comes out of the clinic room in tears. She has done some more tests on my mother and the news is not good. My mother doesn't struggle with it. She wants to go back to Honiara. She wants to die, like my father, at the pioneer post the Guardian chose for her, and amongst the people she loves. Bruce and I take her back to her home immediately. Our daughter Monique, who is at university in Brisbane, follows us a few days later. Our other daughter Riswan is already back living in Honiara and Natasha is in Haifa with her new husband Abdul Jarrah.

From her bed, Gertrude calls out to Edi, her companion. 'Will you sit with me and have a prayer?' Edi knows instantly what this means. She knows 'Mum' is preparing to die.

We set up a little camp in her cottage so that we can all be together. In the following days my mother drifts between two worlds. She is barely conscious of our presence as we float in and out of her bedroom with anxious faces.

Rabbani has joined us from Brisbane. She keeps watch over the shunt of morphine she has inserted into my mother's arm to ease her pain. Reciting *Gleanings*, memorized over years from the writings of Bahá'u'lláh, returns some of the colour to my mother's skin. Even in this state, the words bring an alert awakening to her being. From outside her bedroom door we listen as the words form on her lips with her beautiful voice, then disperse into the soft lamplight. Sometimes their gentle rhythm lasts thirty minutes at a time.

We ring Gertrude's sister Rose in New York. She surprises us by saying she wants to fly to the Solomons to say her goodbye. I wish I had called her sooner.

In the smallest hours of morning there is a strange cool that washes through the damp heat of daytime. The air still carries the faintest smell of smoke from yesterday's cooking fires rising up from the village below. Little silvery sounds, of unseen creatures coming through from the bush and the wind playing with palm leaves, filter in from the outside.

At this time, Guadalcanal is held in a calm silence. Gertrude does not feel any of the pain it has caused the islanders and the men from foreign countries who gave up their lives on this little piece of land nine degrees from the equator. Nor the loneliness she saw in her husband's face, or even in mine, her only child. She understands what all that means. She has held the hands of grown military men who, recalling their experiences on Guadalcanal, fought tears to put it into words. 'Guadalcanal is not a name,' said one broken US Admiral, 'but an emotion.'

Gertrude feels its emotion now, but it is one of love. 'How?' she asks as her mind travels back into this world. How could it be that little Gertie, a poor, simple Jewish girl, with nothing to offer but her heart and her will to believe, be called upon to have such a life?

Through closed eyelids, she sees a door opening. She blinks in its brightness. The first person she sees is Alvin; the man who could see beyond her slowness and the things that irritated him and find something he could love in her. Behind him is a parade of people, great leaders in the Faith who have helped her find her own way with it. And then, an immense force rushes through and begins to pull her away from the dying cells of her body. It is what she has been striving to bring into this world all these years. It is the 'Most Great Peace'.

'Edi,' she calls out to that daughter of the Solomon Islands. 'Now will you sit down and have a prayer with me?' she asks sweetly.

Edi pats her hand gently. 'Wait till your sister comes from the States,' she replies.

Gertrude takes hold of Edi's hand and looks up into her face with clear eyes. 'You want me to wait when the door is open and they're all waiting for me?'

Edi comes back through to us with eyes misted in tears. 'Mum is ready to go,' she says quietly to Rabbani.

We pick up our blankets and pillows and shift our small camp into my mother's bedroom. I lie down on her bed beside her. My hands wrap around her, finding comfort in the folds of the fleshier bits of my mother's body. I listen as her breathing becomes shallow and short, the puff of a small bird. The spaces in between grow longer, until, finally, she makes no more sound. I look across at the clock by her bed. For so many years it has indicated the time of people's comings and goings at all hours. The time of her own final leaving is 4 a.m. on 5 June 1993.

* * *

At first, I don't cry for my mother. She has passed calmly and quietly, so ready and sure of where she is going. My mother has spoken of the Abhá Kingdom to me since I was small and I smile inwardly now in her release, knowing she is there.

We call the members of the National Assembly first. They arrive to say prayers over my mother's body. Her face is beautifully peaceful outside the white sheet we have wrapped around her. Word spreads quickly of my mother's death and by eight in the morning the garden is full with hundreds of people who have come to pay their respects to 'Mum'. The Solomon Islanders are open in their grief; their limbs hang loose in their weeping and wailing. I am soon a mess of tears alongside them.

National radio begins announcing my mother's death every two hours. The night before the funeral, a bulletin in both Pidgin and English is broadcast that pays tribute to my mother's life and all that she has done.

She still looks peaceful, lying in her open casket on the day of her funeral. We have draped her in white silk. Her fingers are folded around her prayer beads and a large bouquet of lavender orchids. Over the next three hours more long lines of people line up to pay their respects. The Governor-General and his wife, Sir George and Lady Lepping, arrive half an hour before the service in which groups of children sing songs and read verses. One of the eulogies is given by Sir Maepaeza Gina. He speaks of what my mother meant to the women of the Solomon Islands.

A police escort with flashing lights leads the funeral procession down to my mother's grave. A garlanded truck carries her casket, now smothered in gifts of red, pink and white flowers. Two youth choirs, one costumed in white gowns with pink birds on their chest, the other in green, have paid their own way from Malaita to sing alongside her. The words of 'Queen of Carmel' chorus above the noise of vehicles carrying mourners.

Beautiful Fijian Tapas cloths have been laid across her open grave beside my father. It is a gift from the Fijian community, usually reserved for their greatest leaders. There is sobbing as the casket is lowered. I have grown used to sharing my mother with islanders of all ages who view her as 'Mum'. In Langa Langa Lagoon and throughout the islands in Hau Hui, Gizo and Auki there are gatherings in her honour, spontaneous shows of love. Their voices call her name on through the night and into the morning.

Later, the words to write on her headstone will come to us: 'Loving Prayer Surrounds You Always'. They recall the words from the Guardian's cable that she has held close to her heart since she arrived in the Solomon Islands.

Epilogue

Our home in Honiara is tucked high and deep into the belly of the ridges that terrace steeply around the island's rim. To the north you can see across to the island of Savo where the first battle of the Guadalcanal campaign began. At dusk, the sun throws out its last rays and the graceful arcs of palm fronds form zebra patterns against the flesh-coloured sky. To the east, across Iron Bottom Sound and around to Honiara Harbour, the lights of commercial tankers that queue to offload their goods, sometimes for weeks, shine through the lilac and the silken warmth that the early evening has given up. It is a scene of immense peace and beauty, but I wonder.

I wonder about what went on here all those years ago when Guadalcanal became a name wretched with death and loss of innocence. I wonder whether this island will ever fully recover from all that pain burned so deeply into the land and sea.

I have watched its appetite, voracious in its hunger for human energy, but so unwilling to change. From the beginning I saw how it worked on my parents, wearing them down until they had given to it all they had. And yet, we chose to stay. Not daringly, as the pioneers willing to sacrifice their all, but as the next generation consolidating and bedding down all the many diverse developments my parents built up in this country; in their business, their faith, their community and their friendships.

My husband Bruce picked up where my father left off, seeing the need and the opportunity for new business services that would benefit the community. He created many firsts, opening up areas in the export of Melanesian handicrafts and a packing and forwarding service as well as a tourist information sheet. The creation of a Solomon Islands Trade Directory, I imagine, would have been particularly close to my father's heart – as if it were an outward measure of how its people were developing themselves. So many of Bruce's struggles were a repeat of Alvin's, only the conditions of the era were different as the country claimed its independence, then toddled beyond. But he also never gave up.

These businesses continue today, employing and skilling-up many locals, as part of the BJS Group of companies that has grown to include agencies for insurance, events and recruitment, international courier, the buying of non-ferrous metal as well as a café and catering service. And there is a succession plan. My youngest daughter Monique and her husband Juan Porras are the third generation to be closely involved with developing business and community in this country.

My own career took an unexpected turn in 1996 when the United States Government asked me to take on their first honorary consul style position in the Solomon Islands. Since 1992 there had been no representation here when the focus had shifted to the new countries forming out of the USSR, but the ties with this country were now fifty years old and still tight-held with emotion.

Because of my funny Australian accent, people new to the Solomons were surprised to find out I was an American. I could feel my parents smiling. Two years later the US Government decided that they needed to upgrade the position to Consular Agent. I went to Washington to be trained to act on their behalf as well as to take the oath of office and be given seals.

In the decade since, I have tried to raise the American presence not as a distant donor but as a country that values the Solomon Islanders as a cooperative presence in the Pacific. The 7th of August has become an increasingly important day in commemorating both the involvement of America and the Solomon Islander War Scouts. My father's old friend Vouza has now passed on, but we honour his bravery, surrounding his statue that has been placed outside the Police Station.

And at the top of a high-pitched ridge along Skyline Drive, the United States War Memorial looks over the daily existence of the villagers below and out across the dirt-green ribbon of the Mataniko River and remnants of old Chinatown to the harbour. Amid the marble pillars that are etched with the story of the Guadalcanal campaign, flags are raised and lowered, remembering those who served and those who never returned. It is in the quiet of these moments that I get a strong feeling of my father.

He never talked to me about the war. I knew its history, its brutality, and we didn't need to revisit it. But as

I became more involved with the legacy left behind by a generation of Americans, I began to think about that never-built road around the island. What would it have meant to the future development of the Solomon Islands if the British Government had not rejected the offer of the United States Army all those years ago?

In the years after the deaths of my parents, tensions both old and new surfaced. As Honiara developed many Malaitans, energetic and entrepreneurial, came to the city. Usually they brought families with them, their numbers encroaching on the boundaries. On the storm lashed Weather Coast to the south of Guadalcanal there was increasing aggravation as the people felt forgotten. A notoriously difficult area to access by land, sea or air, there was no road that could allow for trade, movement and tourism around the island.

Between 1999 and 2003 militias arose in a campaign of intimidation and attack. In June 2000 the Malaitan Eagle Force kidnapped Prime Minister Ulufa'alu. They believed he was not providing enough support and protection for Malaitans on Guadalcanal. Later that year a peace agreement was signed by Malaitan Eagle Force, but further attempts at a peace settlement with other militias broke down on 21 February 2001 when Harold Keke, a key Gual leader, refused to sign and the conflict shifted to the Weather Coast.

In 2003 an Australian-led Regional Assistance Mission was brought to the Solomon Islands to restore order. The traditional Wantok system made it difficult. Solomon Islander police had more loyalty to their individual arrangements of kinship than any sense of nationalism or the country as a whole.

The most recent unrest took place through April 2006 when the newly elected Prime Minister was accused of using bribes from Chinese businessmen to buy votes in Parliament. In the days that followed, locals took to the street looting and razing the historic Chinatown that had grown up to the south of the city centre.

Through all these years, the old threat of Ma'asina rule was never far away and each new government kept its watch. What would my father have made of it all? My father, who was himself once watched by the British Government; who had the respect of the great Malaitan chiefs. What would he say to their children now?

And my mother, who was a source of encouragement for women. What would she say to those women on Guadalcanal whose traditional land ownership has been sold off to foreign loggers and miners?

After my mother's death we searched for a way to keep the qualities my parents practised alive in this country. Twenty-five years to the day that my father died, we held the first Blums awards. We put out a call for nominations from right through the Islands of individuals and groups whose actions had been a source of inspiration. Recipients have been both men and women whose contributions are wide-ranging. There is the woman of East Kwaio, a very male-dominated area on Malaita, who began developing women's fellowship and group activities to give them support and confidence. From their small contributions a canteen of store goods and a garden began. And there is the man who trained up unemployed people into a band and dance troupe that has promoted Solomon Islands culture throughout the world. He has also set up a second-hand clothing shop for troupe members to run.

The Blums awards have continued on and off through the years. Sometimes the tensions and corruptions are too rife to stage them. We have received our own awards too. In 2003 Bruce was appointed an Officer of the Most Excellent Order of the British Empire (OBE) for his work with civil society and business development in the Solomons. I have received two medals of the Solomon Islands: the Governor General's personal medal for community work in 1999, and in 2005 the Medal of the Solomon Islands for my work in beautification of the city.

Much of this has come from planting trees. When the main road was widened not a single tree was left. I remembered, as a child, the flame trees that had lined Honiara. I wanted to see them again. This act of planting trees has spread to include all the parks and palm trees on roundabouts. At the airport, that strip of land which brought the battle here, there is now a garden that commemorates soldiers. Relatives can buy trees and plaques in their name. On the other side of the park is a memorial garden for the public. A tree for my parents grows there.

My last major project has been the resuscitation of the botanical gardens that had been laid to waste and filled with rubbish. In all, there are twenty-five gardeners and two office staff who work throughout the city. In 2010, I received my own OBE for long and dedicated services to businesses, charity and the community, and now in 2012, as this book goes to press, we have received the news that Bruce has been appointed a KBE (Knight Commander of the British Empire) from Her Majesty Queen Elizabeth II, for his outstanding services to business, community and the development of Solomon Islands. I view this as a tribute to my parents. They showed us the way and we have been following in their footsteps ever since.

* * *

Almost every day I still hear your names. Often there will be someone who comes up to tell me a memory of an encounter with you. Sometimes they are whimsical stories that run deep and lasting. Father, recently one man told me how as a boy he asked you for an ice cream, even though he didn't have five cents to buy it. You gave him one and said bring the money later. The boy never did and he felt very guilty. Six months later he got his five cents from his mum and dad and came to pay you. You gave him another ice cream free for his honesty. It's through small stories like these that I get closer to knowing your giant self.

Others have wanted to write their stories down. One wrote about how you never tried to push people out of their customary ways. How the men of deep Kwaio would turn up to listen to you, smoking and chewing betel nut and carrying knives. It didn't matter to you, you were just happy to meet them. That meant a lot. And you kept your promises. Mother, you did too.

I want you to know that the spirit of oneness that took you both out into the world and brought you here also runs through your grandchildren. Two of your granddaughters have married men from far-flung countries. The family line of Natasha's husband Abdul Jarrah traces back to his great-great-grandfather who was the commander of the prison in 'Akká. Monique's husband Juan hails from South America. And Riswan's daughter, your eldest great-grandchild Ayesha, has already declared herself a Bahá'í at sixteen.

Amid all the ongoing tensions, the values of equality and unity you wanted to grow in this country continue. There are now around five thousand Bahá'ís spread throughout the islands. But I watch the country selling off its trees and its fish, the corruption that creeps in, and fear all that development you worked and hoped for is going backwards. You never expected change to happen overnight; did you think it would go so slow?

You both spoke so often of unity. Father, I remember it was your favourite prayer. Now, my own view is that the Pacific will have to unite as a group of people and become the United Pacific Islands. In the Solomons, the islands and its five hundred thousand people are so scattered, separated by masses of ocean and different languages. To be a viable country on its own seems a tall task

It is still the hardest place to start a business. The challenges and restrictions of living here suffocate us like a pressure cooker. Around every six weeks we have to get out. We go to Brisbane where we can get away from the heat and indulge in simple pleasures. Often I think about how I don't share your stamina for it. Then I remember that you too knew something of being fed up and frustrated, and it brings you closer.

But you always trusted you had been guided here to play an important role. You loved your faith and your fate. You shone a light on things others did not think of or didn't want to. You showed what was possible.

You never stopped believing.

About the Author

Keithie Saunders (née Blum) was born in Little Rock, Arkansas in 1946, went to New Zealand as a baby with her parents and travelled to Guadalcanal with them in 1954 at the age of seven. She spent most of her early years in Honiara but went to boarding school in Australia at 11 years old.

After training as a nurse, she married Bruce Saunders and lived in the Cook Islands for three years before returning to Guadalcanal after the death of her father Alvin. The couple have three daughters and seven grandchildren.

Keithie continues to live on Guadalcanal, and is one of the longest living expatriates on the island. She is currently the United States Consular Agent to Solomon Islands. Both Bruce and Keithie have received numerous awards for service to the Islands.